A CONCISE
HISTORY OF IRAN

From the early period to the present time

BY
SAEED SHIRAZI

PublishAmerica
Baltimore

DS
272
.S547
2004

First printing

ISBN: 1-4137-6798-2
PUBLISHED BY PUBLISHAMERICA, LLLP
www.publishamerica.com
Baltimore

Printed in the United States of America

List Of Names & Page Numbers

I present this book to my wife, Azar, for her love and support,
and to our children, Bardia and Sara,
and to all Iranian-descent children.
We need to know our roots, while we strive to grow.

PREFACE

Iranians born outside Iran often cannot read Farsi (their native language), though they may speak or understand it. English-speaking readers have not had a chance to study this subject within such a short format, either. This fact is the inspiration for my book, *A Concise History Of Iran* in English. I hope this book will acquaint and interest Iranians outside Iran with their historical past, so that they may do further research on their own.

With this purpose in mind, I have put the information from many sources in Farsi and English in this text rather than in footnotes. The main ideas will be apparent to the reader. However, I must advise my readers that **a lot of contiguous but short information is inserted into every paragraph**. As David Fischer points out in his *Historians' Fallacies*, New York, 1970, p. 64, history is an ocean of facts. This is why historians select information with certain criteria of factual significance as well as relevancy to a purpose. My purpose in this book is to be thorough and brief.

Generally, history is a study about a land and its people. Therefore, it is imperative to start our voyage through time by reflecting on the land (**Pars**) and its people (**Aryans**) in the country of **Persia**. (Persian government requested all foreign countries at the U.N. meeting in 1935 to call the country **Iran** for the sake of consistency).

Unfortunately, the history of the world is filled with horrific pictures of the cruelty of mankind. Yet the survival of our species depends on this evolutionary phase that may take many more centuries. Numerous kingdoms have risen and perished. Naturally, all of them had to be prepared to defend their land and heritage against the invaders, while many weaker kingdoms ceased to exist. It is interesting to note that out of all the empires in the history of man, only a few have withstood the test of time and still exist today such as these: **Iran, China, Italy, India** and **Greece**. It is true that their original glories have faded away, and some of their kings eventually fell ingloriously after achieving a splendid reputation; yet these nations have managed to keep their own land, people, language, and culture. All of which have evolved from their earlier versions.

What enabled Iran to maintain its identity was mostly the survival of its original language—Farsi.

On the other hand, some civilizations, for example Egypt, lost their ancient and original language. This lapse in the continuity of the **Egyptian** heritage was due to political and economical forces beyond its cultural capabilities. **Egyptians** now converse in **Arabic**. Nevertheless, all civilizations and archaic cultures have continuously affected one another through centuries and continue to do so.

Along with the history of Iran, we also need to look at the beliefs, fears, and hopes of its earliest inhabitants. In doing so we must look back into the mythological tales of Iran. By studying mythology we may find some similarities between different cultures. This cannot be coincidental because these civilizations previously lived next to one another for thousands of years. Therefore, they affected each other inevitably.

In mythology, the anthropological term of "convergence" is used to explain that identical appearances of symbols and mythic motifs, scattered among continents and different cultures at separate times, are just pure chance. In Joseph Campbell's *The Mythic Image*, convergence does not bear much scientific value. One fact remains, however; the past is interwoven with Mythology and that is why we need to study it. By studying mythology, we cannot reflect on its literal truthfulness, rather we must look for the messages implied within the images and symbols.

In connection with mythology, history has shown the importance of the role of myths in the cultural development of nations. It is the patriotic insistence of a people to pursue its own trend of thought, based partly on the mythologies, that has resisted the pressure of invaders against the integrity of its culture. In the journal of Iranian studies, called *Iran Shenasi*, the 5th volume printed in 1993 in the U.S., Jalal Matini points out the importance of language and knowledge of our past in his articles. I personally agree with his suggestion that in our Iranian schools Farsi textbooks should be filled with irrefutable facts about our heritage. Thus, our young generation will easily scrutinize false and subtle invasions of others into our history as well as our borders. In his article, Jalal Matini brings on the historical facts about the authenticity of the name of "The Persian Gulf" versus the false claims of some nations to call it "The Arab Gulf"!

Consequently, from these unified myths and beliefs (no matter how archaic) the strong foundation of Iranian heritage and unity as a people is laid implicitly in the realm of Farsi—the language of the Iranians, today. The great literary works of Iranian writers, poets, and scholars, as well as masterpieces left in architecture and music have guaranteed Iran's survival in the history of the world. On top of all, we owe a great deal to the poet, **Abolghasem Ferdowsi**, who wrote *Shah Nameh*. This is an epic-style book of poetry about significant mythological and historical tales of Iranians' ancestors. It is generally agreed by historians that during the turbulent period of **Arab** manipulation of **Persian** language and lifestyle, **Ferdowsi** showed courage and a perseverance (for three decades) to collect and recite these tales in pure Farsi of the time (Dari style). After a thousand years, *Shah Nameh* stands to be a major factor for today's survival of Farsi language and Iranian heritage.

Therefore, **Persian** history and mythology form a fundamental identity of **Iranians**. It is imperative for our younger **Iranian generation** to know about Iran's historic strong points and weaknesses. Our newer generations outside of Iran can hopefully benefit from history books that can give them most of this information. Living among different cultures, children of Iranian descent have the chance to become positively better human beings by first knowing East before appreciating West.

Unfortunately, it may be true to claim that, up to now; there has been no book in English with a concise and yet complete history of Iran. During my continuous search for such material, surprisingly, I was unable to find concise writings that would briefly tell our English-speaking readers about all of Iran's history. As said earlier, this is the purpose of my book.

However, there are a few paragons of such short books about history of Iran. The first one is this: *Chekideh Tarikh-e-Iran* by Hasan

Naraghi published by Akhtaran in Tehran 2000. It is only 173 pages long. This one-of-a-kind book is in Farsi. Although written with skill and enough detail, unfortunately it cannot benefit that segment of new generation who cannot read Farsi. Yet, I am directly benefiting from Naraghi's realistic approach to all of our Iranian history. There are other short history books, but they are also in Farsi. The second paragon of short books is this: *Pictorial History Of Iran* by M.H. Amini Sam published by Eqbal in L.A. 1990. This book is in English and Farsi, but its beauty is lessened by not covering the post-Islam period. Another is *A Glimpse At The History Of Iran* by Farshid Eghbal, printed in 1996 in L.A. This book is in several volumes, but it does not give a tale-like account of the history. Instead, the singled-out and short individual statements take readers through history like an index, without giving knowledge of cause and effects. However, it is conveniently written in both Farsi and English.

In addition to using the above books, I have made references to many related and outstanding sources in Farsi and English (including the masterpiece of Sir Percy Sikes: *History Of Persia)* in two large volumes. Therefore, from all of these I could collate the information into a comparative timetable. My book contains numerous highlights of many historians in a tale-like form and yet stays brief to avoid fatigue.

I wish to thank Ms. Nina Parkhurst for introducing me to the world of her colleague and scholar, Joseph Campbell.

We ought to learn to read history as a living subject. Also, world peace in future may result from each person's awareness of his historical past. We all should know the consequences of known historical mistakes and shortcomings of our heritage. Only then a better path may be selected to establish identity and ensure prosperity for future generations.

Saeed Shirazi
California, 2005

Contents

CHAPTER ONE

Early People

The origin of man is still a mystery. Modern archeological surveys link us as far back as about 40,000 years B.C. This was the age of **Cro-Magnon**; people who looked more like us today. They had mostly gathered around the northern and central lands of Southern Russia. **Cro-Magnon** place of origin was unknown to us until now.

Recently, Dr. Spenser Wells initiated some blood tests from different people in Central Africa, Asia and America. His scientific documentary was aired on PBS in the bay area in California in October 2003. His studies of the DNA patterns conclude that about 50,000 years ago our **Cro-Magnon** fathers separated from an even older generation from Africa. Some of them had eventually traveled north to Central Asia at the edge of the Arctic Circle where Chukchi and Amguerna are now. Later some had continued East through the Bering Sea that was completely covered by ice and gradually scattered through North America. They created many branches and tribes for example, the **Navajos** in Canyon De Chelly in the U.S.

On the other hand, molecular biologists, Alan Wilson and Rebecca Cann, had already tested the DNA of many humans around the globe. These scientists also confirmed the same theory that modern man is offspring of **African Homo Sapiens**. [1]

In addition, *The Encyclopedia Of World History*, confirms the above data that the origin of modern man, traced so far, is known to go back to 150,000 years ago to the time of **African Homo Sapiens**. [2]

Civilizations Around Aryans

Consequently, anthropologists refer to the **Cro-Magnons** of 40,000 B.C., as white **Indo-Europeans**. About 30,000 years later, due to severe cold weather and in search of warmer land, they had divided into two major groups of settlers going different directions: towards West and South. It is this last migration that goes back to about 10,000 B.C.

History shows a clear trace of the westerly branch of **Indo-Europeans** who went through western Asia into Eastern Europe. These people formed **Anglo-Saxons**, **Germans**, **Slavs** and **Greeks** as off shoots of the same race, but their first civilization or urbanism came much later than their southerly cousins.

Our emphasis, however, is on the southerly branch of these **Indo-Europeans**. The records in the world history indicate that they had continued towards the warmer lands around south of Russia or north east of today's Iran. They were known as the **Aryans**, meaning *Nobles*. This segment of **Aryan** race is the foundation to the race of **Iranians** (originally referred to as **Persians**) today.

Early Aryans

Aryans, around 10,000 B.C., lived in a green plateau known as 'Arya Varte'. During thousands of years, this southerly branch (**Aryan**) gradually decentralized into three sub branches. These **Aryan** branches had eventually formed the early **Persians** who consisted of: **Pars** in the South, **Medes** in the West and **Parthia** in the north of today's Iran. History shows that **Aryan** race is also shared with **Hindus** and **Armenians**, as well as **Germans** and **Greeks** who are derivatives of the original **Indo-Europeans**.

Thus, plateau of **Pars** (a part of an area that now is called Iran with 1,680,000 square kilometers or larger than 1/6th of the U.S.) has received its name from the early inhabitants (**Parsians** or **Persians)**. Interestingly, a smaller fertile area was neighboring this plateau of Pars. It laid west of Zagros Mountains, but it had already nestled numerous dwellers of its own. This area is referred to as Fertile Crescent. Its habitants were separated from traveling tribes of **Pars** and **Medes** by the Zagros Mountains. However, the urbanism in Fertile Crescent had formed much earlier than that of the **Aryans**. It is imperative to look at this area in the following paragraphs for its direct effects on its neighboring **Persians**.

To this end, in *The History Of The World* all of the above is confirmed. In addition, it is mentioned that The Fertile Crescent being a vast field to the west of **Pars**—not as high in altitude—was situated between two major rivers of Tigris and Euphrates in the Middle East near today's Iraq. This area is also known as *Bein-ol-Nahrain*, which is the Arabic term meaning "Between two Rivers." The Greek terminology for this area is *Mesopotamia*. This land had witnessed simultaneous flourishing of many tribal and early settlements whose origin is unknown, but managed some astonishing civilizations. [3]

Now, through science, we have more reasons to assume that the earlier people in Fertile Crescent may have been a group of **Homo Sapiens** who were traveling from Africa towards Central Asia. Some of them could have stayed back in Mesopotamia.

Nevertheless, these settlers of the crescent region—their true origin still unknown—had come from many areas including Zagros Mountains, Carcasus Mountains, and Africa. These people were not **Aryans**. Scientific evidence shows that, gradually, land irrigation by means of channels was developed next to the two rivers. Naturally, **Mesopotamians** reached higher stages of urbanism earlier than their **Aryan** neighbors, who were still living in the forms of traveling tribes. But, **Mesopotamians** were constantly fighting between themselves. Naturally, their city-states were engaged in exchange of their goods and cultures as well.

Elam, Sumer and **Akkad** are the most dominant early people who formed individual nations inside Mesopotamia. We have evidence to believe that **Sumerians** were the most advanced settlers in the area; many artifacts found from their earlier ancestors go back to 7000 B.C. **Sumerians** are known to have invented the early alphabets around 3200 B.C. [4]

The oldest form of a letter discovered belongs to ruins of Babylon going back to about 3000 B.C. It was around 2800 B.C. that the government of **Akkad** (a region in North Babylon between today's Syria and Persian Gulf) was established by the insight and bravery of its leader **Sargon** as a dominant force in this area. **Sargon** had ordered collection, translation, and safekeeping of many ancient religious texts. Fifteen hundred years later, these writings were discovered and studied at the time of **Ashur Banipal** of Assyr, thus providing historians with abundant information about the old world. [5]

Of course it was from **Sumerian** language and early alphabets that eventually came the first and the oldest written book of law called *Hammurabi*. This set of archaic laws is attributed to the king of Babylonia in 2081 B.C. (**Babylonians** were later conquered by the **Elamites** in 1190 B.C. and the Semitic **Chaldaeans** from Eastern Arabia in about 800 B.C.). The **Babylonians** had settled in the south of this area. **Assyrians** were their strong neighbors in the north (Assyria had won its independence from Babylonia between 1800 B.C. and 1500 B.C.). The **Medes** tribes later defeated **Assyrians** who had lost their original glory. **Sumerians** also created the big capitol city of "Ur" and developed the division of time into hours and 60-minute increments. [6]

Many historians have come to the same conclusion. J. H. Breasted reflects on this era in his book *Vide Ancient Times*. He believes by moving towards the plateau, the **Semitic** influence (**Arabian** race) is replaced by **Aryans**—as the dominant ruling race, although deeply influenced by the more civilized powers of Babylonia and Assyria. The history of the ancient world is henceforth destined to be a struggle between the battles between the **Semitic** races of the South and the **Aryan** races of the North, which finally ended in the complete victory of the northern races. [7]

Cultural Development of Aryans

Hence, the influence of the **Mesopotamian** civilization on the traveling **Aryans** cannot be denied, yet cultural development of

Aryans was not necessarily under such influence and their religion is a proof of that. **Aryans** developed their unique culture—for thousands of years—as they moved in search of green areas where they could feed their herds and themselves. Consequently, their urbanism occurred later than the early **Mesopotamians,** but not their culture. They had carried their own worldviews and traditions since the last cold age (about 10,000 years ago), but they were without a permanent dwelling or urbanism. So far, the oldest artwork excavated from plateau of Pars goes back to about 7000 years ago. It is the statue of a man in formal standing position with hands locked in front of his waist. This statue is found in hills around a village called *Sialk* near city of Kashan in the south of Iran. It was made about 4800 B.C. and out of a metal that is a conglomeration of copper and lead that forms a type of bronze (mefragh). This statue belongs to the period of **Elam** civilization, in south of today's Iran and guarded by mountains hard to pass. [8] Artifacts of this denomination prove co-existence of cultural ties between early **Aryans** and their neighbors.

Still, new findings reveal further information to archeologists and historians every day. A co-operation project between The Iranian Cultural Heritage Organization and German Archeological Institute since 2000 has revealed new findings in Carcasus Mountains near Kashan. These findings document ancient mining traces through the investigation of prehistoric metal processing in a specialized settlement called **Arisman**. These copper factories were up and running by **Aryans** about 6000 years ago in the central plateau of Persia. Arisman Project has a website address: www.dainst.org/index_558_en.html.

However, the early city building happened about 3800 B.C. when **Babylonians** established their unified kingdom in most of the southern Mesopotamia. **Elam** was thriving in the eastern high lands in the south west of Iran—the word **Elam** meant series of mountains, which borders today's Khuzestan. On the other hand, in northern Mesopotamia, **Assyrians** had simultaneously dominated the land. These neighboring civilizations were constantly in touch with each other for centuries, either in form of deleterious confrontations or beneficial trades. Naturally, they shaped each other's trend of cultural evolution. Nevertheless, the three **Aryan** tribes of **Pars**, **Medes**, and **Parthia** were slowly forming their own early urbanism.

Establishment of a unified kingdom, however, appeared later in **Medes** around 1200 B.C.—their civilization and culture was being formed since their ancestors migration from the north.

In addition to all of the above, Renzo Rossi, in his *Civilization Of Asia*, also confirms the fact that smaller civilization and urbanism was shaping generally around 5000 B.C., but **Mesopotamia** was in advance of other areas in the world. However, **Indo-European** tribes (**Aryans**) had already started their migration. About 10,000 B.C., the southerly tribes of **Aryans** (with their unique nature-loving ideologies) started their migration from the southern lands of today's Russia towards the greener fields of what is now The Middle East. [9] Although, thousands of years geological reformation has turned two third of this green and lush area into an arid and desert-like place.

Further, *The Timetable Of History*, shows that the earliest civilization in the world happened in the Middle East. Its fundamental development was tied in with the city-states and rulers of **Mesopotamia**; however, it flourished into a true **Empire** by the **Aryans** of **Persia**. In order to witness any significant rise of any other major civilization or city-state elsewhere, we have to patiently look at China with the **Shang Dynasty** that did not happen until around 1760 B.C. [10]

In addition, in other parts of the world much slower tribal activities in a scattered form were seen that also prove existence of different worldviews. Travelers of the Bering Sea (**Indo-Europeans**) had settled in North and South America, but more complex forms of society began to emerge later - about 1500 B.C. [11]

It was with this background and influence from neighboring civilizations that **Aryans of Persia** formed a gradual identity of their own.

1.   *History Of Art* , 3rd edition, by H.W. Janson, N.Y 1986, p. 8

2.   *The Encyclopedia Of World History*, edited by Peter N. Stearns, 6th edition, 2001 New York, p. 10

3.   *History of the World*, edited by Jack Zevin, King Fish publisher, 1992, New York, pp. 12-19

4.   *The Visual Dictionary of Ancient Cnivilizatios*, 1994, p. 6

5.   *Tarikh –e- Iran* By Sir Percy Sykes, Translated by Fakhr Daie, Tehran, 1984, pp.78 - 86

6.   *Chekideh Tarikh-e- Iran*, by Hasan Naraghi, 2000, Tehran

7.   *A History Of Persia*, Sir Percy Sykes, Vol. 1, 1921, London, p.95

8.   *Tarikh Iran Zamin*, by Dr. M Javad Mashkur, 3rd edition 1988, Tehran, p. 2

9.   *Civilization of Asia*, by Renzo Rossi, 1996, New York, p. 10

10.   *The Timetable Of History*, by Grun, 3rd Edition, N.Y, 1991, pp. 6 -7

11.   *The Ancient America's*, by Earl H. Swanson, W. Bray, and I. Flemington, printed in N.Y by Peter Bedrick Books, 1989, p. 14

The Plateau of Pars
Ancient Aryans and Their Beliefs

Coming back to the early **Aryans** and their gradual southward migration, one has to look at the elevated Plateau of Pars.

Archeological evidence dating from 5000 to 3000 B.C. indicates massive settling of the regions all around Pars plateau. Early traveling tribes of **Aryans** slowly scattered in this plateau with an area of thousands of square miles (East to west from today's Afghanistan and Pakistan to Iraq and north to south from Russia and north Caspian sea to the south Persian Gulf). Throughout this vast green land, these **Aryans** had carried their language, rituals, crafts, and homes from one area to another in all conditions and terrain. Sometimes they had to find shelter from the elements, and on the other hand, they learned to cherish and respect its beauty and mild climate. Thus, love and respect for nature and its elements became the pivotal foundation for **Aryans**.

But what is noteworthy is that although these **Aryans** were growing fast, they were not the only traveling tribes. Around the same period, village life as well as tribal gatherings—at a slower rate—were also introduced in other areas in the world, such as North America, Africa and the Far East. Ruins of structures made by **Yang Shao** people in China and old city of *Jericho* near today's Jordan are a few substantial evidences of other civilizations. Writing, however, had not appeared in China until around 2800 B.C. (The **Sumerians** had discovered the early alphabets around 3200 B.C.) [1]

As time went by, some tribes of farmers and herders living in the plains of Pars detached from their **Aryan** relatives around 2500 B.C. They began to move towards the Indus Valley that is in today's

Pakistan and West of India. They created a newer civilization called **Harappa** near Ravi River. But around 1500 B.C., **Indus Valley** civilization, as we know it, suddenly disappeared. Historians mostly believe that **Aryans of Pars** conquered the area again and later added it to their future **Persian Empire**. [2]

All these civilizations neighbored one another for thousands of years. Of course there are similarities in beliefs and myths of different cultures in different territories. Naturally, in many shapes, they must have influenced one another. In Joseph Campbell's *The Mythic Image* in pages 118-121, there are references made to the similarities between **T'ao-t'ieh** mask in China around 1300 B.C., and **The Kirttimukha** of India around 800 A.D. It is only logical to wonder about their possible connections. On the other hand, the Mexican **Olmec** culture and the **Chavin** culture of Peru in about 800 – 400 B.C. show similarities about the jaguar-man mythic figure that resembles the **Kirttimukha**. [3]

As mentioned in the next chapters, Persian myths also mention about **Deev** or *Ghoul* as human-beast cannibal. For unknown reasons, Joseph Campbell does not cover the old mythology of **Persians** in his book. Nevertheless, the mythic figures of **Deevs** have an ancient root in the Persian culture going back to the time of creation. Are these images a result of pure chance? Did different people and cultures have a way of affecting one another?

Still, the study of Myths clarifies many archeological mysteries, including the ancient languages. There are many excavated findings and ancient texts, forming a historians' consensus, that tell about these traveling tribes' language and faith. Through artifacts and pictographic objects belonging to **Indus civilization**, one may see similarities in the language, myths and religion of original **Aryan Settlers** in Pars Plateau. As mentioned before, Farsi language that **Iranians** speak today is based on "Mikhi Language" immortalized by cuneiforms and pictographs left on clay and stone. The history of Farsi goes back to over 3000 B.C., and the languages of **Medes**, **Sakkas**, **Sumerians** and **Zarathustra**'s *Avesta* gradually helped to shape this language. [4]

Dr. M.J. Mashkoor explains that the traditions and lifestyles of early **Aryans** were preserved through ancient historical writings. The prophet **Zarathustra (Zartosht** in Farsi) formed the *Book of Vedas* or

Sacred Writings. These writings were commonly used among **Aryans of Indu Valley**. *Book of Vedas* is the oldest source of such historical facts about **Aryans**—It is interesting to know that in rewriting *Vedas* an older root of Farsi writings is used called *Din-Dabireh*. By referring to the facts mentioned in *Vedas*, it is understood that **Aryans**, at some point in time, believed that people were born into a caste and remained in it for life. Thus, people were categorized into three major sectors: **Brahmans** or Priests, **Kshatriyas** or Military caste, and **Vaishiyas**, which consisted of farmers, shepherds and merchants. The *Book of Vedas*, thus, became a gradual and continuous collection of psalms, prayers and hints of all the sectors. Dr. Mashkoor confirms the fact that these writings form an abundant source of cultural history pertaining to the **Aryans** who lived in a plateau called *Aria Varte*. In *Avesta*, the holy book of **Zarathustra**, this name is mentioned as *Aeryana Vaejeh* that means the "Prairies of the **Aryans**." This land was in eastern part of today's Iran—neighboring on the west with today's Pamir in Pakistan and India, also stretching to the west or Mesopotamia. [5]

In addition to the above, the western historic documents reflect the same information. The fact that **Aryans** paid tribute to the elements of nature, Sun, Moon and Stars, has remained intact in the history. This explains why the "Father of History," **Herodotus**, has also mentioned in his ancient Greek notes that **Iranians** never worshipped statues or idols as gods.[6]

Interestingly, **Greeks**, however, made statues of their gods in their own image. Unlike **Egyptians**, whose gods were not made in the human image and sometimes fearsome, the Greek gods were a part of daily activities of the **Greeks**.[7] **Persians** tried to find inner peace through their harmonic existence with the universe, and they did not propitiate or bow to any idols or statues of gods in any shape or form.

Thus, **Aryans** commonly sought spiritual enlightenment in the early light of day. These inner qualities differentiated them from their **Mesopotamian** neighbors. **Aryans** referred to the bright elements in nature as *Davos* meaning *Bright Source*. The early **Aryans** celebrated the forces in nature, particularly the brightness. As per *Tarikh Iran Zamin* by Dr. Mashkoor, **Andra (Indra)** was the symbol of wars and lightning. **Varona** represented skies, **Mithra** or **Mehr** was the agent of the Sun, and **Agni** was the agent of fire. Of course, Dr. Mashkoor found this information in the ancient texts of *Veda*.

As mentioned in *Tarikh Iran Zamin* , *Veda* is originated from the earlier ancestors of **Aryans of Pars** and **Indu Valley**. During thousands of years these aspects of universal harmony on basis of purity of light made the scintillating foundation for **Zorastherianism**. This new ideology from the holy book of *Avesta* has brought forth and introduced the incisive idea of Unity of the Almighty. Historians also believe that "Vandi Dad," which is one of five major parts of *Avesta*, is a revision of ancient texts of *Veda* gathered by the **Prophet Zarathustra**. His birth date is estimated about 2000 to about 1000 B.C. His name originally meant: "The owner of Yellow Camel."[8]

In other words, messages in the texts of *Veda* existed before **Zarathustra**. So did the religion of **Mithra**, common between **Aryans** of Pars and Indu. There are only two references in *Avesta* about **Andra** (only as an agent or angel), however there is a reference to **Andra** in the mythological tale of **Rostam** in *Shah Nameh*. Actually the **Persian** warriors received their strength from this agent of war, which was common in both **Indu** and **Persian** mythology. So were the two **Ashvins**, the two gods, (Khordad and Amordad in *Avesta*) who heal the sick and bring lovers close together.[9] Khordad and Amordad are also the names for two months in spring and summer from the Persian calendar and respectively mean "Perfect in all" and "Immortal."

Therefore, many of these ancient beliefs are based on common history between **Indus** and **Persians**. Yet, **Zarathustra** is uniquely **Persian**. Interestingly, the exact birth date of this great prophet is not set, some historians, such as **Voltaire** and **Plato**, set this date much earlier and to about 6500 B.C.[10] It seems that the ancient beliefs of **Aryans** regarding **Mithra** (going back to over 7000 B.C.) had been the basis for **Plato** and **Voltaire**'s assumption of the birth date of **Zarathustra**. But truly all these ideologies, with variations, actually existed among **Aryans** for thousands of years before **Zarathustra**. There are archeological evidences that prove farmers lived in "Mehrgarh" west of Indus River by 6000 B.C. who believed in **Mehr**.[11] These people could be the early **Aryans** who had continued East from Plateau of Pars. The occupants of Mehrgarh also believed in the divinity of the forces of nature and worshiped **Mehr** the symbol of Sun. Never the less, **Zarathustra** of Persia can be called the pioneer of universal theory of Good versus Evil as well as The Judgment Day in the history of religions.

The extent of the popularity of **Mithraism** does not end at the East. This **Persian** religion had penetrated the West until mid-4th Century A.D.; the remainders of numerous caves or underground shrines are still found in many European countries. Philip K. Hitti believes that these caves were secret places of gathering for earlier believers of **Mithra**. However, the construction of such underground tunnels or wells had to do with the underwater springs in the Plateau of Pars — they still do — as a source of drinking water for peasants in the Middle East. The believers of **Mithra** celebrated "Sol Invictus" or "The immortal Sun" on the 25th day of December. This date was marked as the rising cycle of the Sun in the sky showing the arrival of longer days. Hitti believes that **Europeans** actually borrowed this date from the religion of **Mithra** and used it as the birth date of **Prophet Jesus,** because of the existing popularity of such date among their people.[12]

Also, William Culican testifies to the fact that the history of this period — about 2500 B.C — evolves through the cultural development of this branch of **Indo-Europeans** on the Plateau of Pars who believed in the natural elements as their guardians or gods. But Culican also believes that they gradually divided into two different groups. Some continued southeast to Indu Valley and Panjab and some towards western and southern fields of today's Iran later forming bigger civilizations respectively called **Medes** and **Pars**.[13]

The pivotal myths and ideologies of **Aryans** have affected the worldviews of their descendants up to the present time. The role of the individual in nature as well as in the society was of great importance to these **Aryans**. All members of the tribes believed they could assist the elements in nature to do their jobs. Sacrificing animals or crops did help this. Ancient writings also show how the early **Aryans** respected family and valued its members as the vital units of their society. This basic idea has been kept throughout history up to the present. Man was the head of the family and was named "Pati" which meant *protector* or "Pitri" which meant *feeder*. The name Father is a derivative of these words. The lady of the house was "Matri" or Mother, which meant maker of home. These details can be found in *Veda* texts.[14]

Even in old age, the head of the family , men and women, gained more respect as well as wealth among their tribes. This trend of life in pastoral and horticultural societies is referred to as "Gerontocracy," meaning a form of social organization in which the elderly have the most wealth, power, and prestige.[15] Consequently, Individuals gained values that had roots in their tribes. Each tribe retained its prestige and glory because of the character of the families that formed it.

Out of many families that gathered together, one bigger tribe would immerge. The *book of Veda* refers to this unit as "Jana" or "Big Tribe." These Janas were foundations of bigger civilizations of "Sialk" in Kashan, "Vajhian" in Nahavand, "Marlik" in Gilan, and "Sus" or "Shush" in Khuzestan. [16]

Interestingly, the religious visions of the **Pars** and **Medes Aryans** of 5000 B.C. who believed in and worshipped the elements of nature continued to stay the same on this plateau for thousands of years. Religions of **Mehr** and **Zorastherianism** had grown from this love of nature and its elements. But original ideologies of the **Indus Valley Aryans** must have gradually altered. Since history shows that some of them worshipped idols and some even started to practice the human sacrifice for their Gods. As mentioned before, the invasion of **Persian Aryans** against **Harappa** civilization around 1500 B.C. must have reintroduced newer ideologies into their brutal trends of thought.

It is interesting to know that such sacrificial rites, in India, continued to be practiced up to 1835 A.D., when forbidden by law. **Buddhists**, on the other hand, have nothing to do with either sacrifices of human beings or beasts; for in the **Buddhist** view, what must be sacrificed are fears, desires, and self-interest of the sacrificer himself. [17]

The **Aryans of Persia**, however, did believe in sacrificing animals and crops. This seemed to be a gesture of assisting the major elements in nature, like the Sun, Moon and Stars, in their perpetual struggle to maintain the rhythm of the cosmos. As mentioned earlier, **Aryans** did not worship any idols as gods. But, a ritual of animal sacrifice existed, and still goes on in the Middle East. **Islam** seems to have borrowed this from earlier religions. However, in **Egyptian** and **Indu** civilizations one may easily witness the remaining of the idols and statues that were built to be ostentatiously worshipped and sacrificed to.

As Sir Percy Sykes puts it in his *History of Iran*, it may not be too bold to claim that Iran's **Zarathustra** was the first spiritual leader who pioneered the idea of immortality of souls and the Judgment Day. This ideology has had its fundamental impact on later religions such as **Judaism**. As written down in the Jewish history **Sargon II**, the **Assyrian** king, exiled the **Jews** as slaves or subjects of his empire to the land of **Medes**. These Jewish slaves seemed to have adapted the ideas of immortality of soul from **Persians**. Naturally, the descendants of **Israelites** in **Medes**, many generations later—about 600 years after the death of **Zarathustra**—had started to believe in the Judgment Day. Consequently, upon their freedom—ordered by **Cyrus The Great**—and return to their original lands in Mesopotamia, they still had to face their argumentative and strict priests, referred to as the sect of "Sadducees" or **Sedoughian**, which means "the true believers." The Jewish priests were firm believers of the fact that their holy book, *Torah*, never initially mentioned the existence of Angels, Spirits, or The Judgment Day. Nevertheless these ideologies were adopted from Persia. This shows the strong historical effects of **Zoroastrianism** over **Judaism**.[18]

H.W. Janson explains that **Persian Aryans** were mostly very open to other cultures and new ideas. They welcomed most foreign thoughts and traditions easily. Despite their genius for adaptation, the **Persians** retained their own religious belief drawn from the prophecies of **Zarathustra**. [19]

A.T. Olmstead confessed in his book about the Persian Empire that **Zarathustra's** greatness comes from his doctrines that are native to his soil and his race and show no trace of influence from the more ancient Orient. [20]

1.   *The visual Dictionary of Ancient Civilizations*, 1994

2.   *Ancient Civilizations*, Edited by Arthur Cotterell, 1980, N.Y. p.184

3.   *The Mythic Image*, by Joseph Campbell, 1974 Princeton, N.Jersey. pp. 118-121

4.   *Negahi Be Pishineh-e- Zaban Farsi* , by Kurosh Safavi, 1999 Tehran

5.   *Tarikh Iran Zamin*, by Dr Mohammad Javad Mashkoor, 1988 Tehran. pp. 5-8

6.   *Pictorial History Of Iran*, by M.H. Amini Sam, 1990, California p. 27

7.   *Mythology*, by Edith Hamilton, Boston, 1998, pp. 4 - 11

8   *Tarikh Iran Zamin*, by M. J. Mashkoor, p. 7

9.   Pajhuheshi Dar Asatir Iran , by Mehrdad Bahar, Printed by Agah, 1997, Tehran, pp. 468, 472

10. *Pictorial History of Iran*, p. 23

11. *The Encyclopedia of World history*, Peter N. Stearns, p. 14

12. *The Near East in History* , By Philip K. Hitti, translated by Dr. Ghamar Aryan, 1971, Tehran, p. 234

13. *The Medes and Persians*, by William Culican, 1965, New York, p. 17 - 22

14. *Tarikh Iran Zamin* p. 6

15. *Sociology*, by John J. Macionis, N.J. 1999, p. 384

16. *Tarikh Iran Zamin* pp. 2, 6

17. *The Mythic Image*, by Joseph Campbell, 1974, New Jersey, p. 266

18. *Tarikh-e-Iran*, by Sir Percy Sykes, Vol. 1, translated by M.T Fakhr Daee Gilani, 1984 Tehran, p. 147

19. *History Of Art*, by H.W. Janson, 3rd Edition, N.Y. 1986, p. 82

20. *History of The Persian Empire*, by A.T. Olmstead, 1959, U. of Chicago Press, p.105

CHAPTER TWO

Mythological Kings

It is true to say that the mythic themes and images left by our ancestors reflect their fears and desires in their lives. History of Iran, like any other nation, very much lies on this foundation. Joseph Campbell mentions in his book, *The Mythic Image*, that through dreams a door is opened to mythology, since myths are of the nature of dream, and dreams arise from an inward world unknown to waking consciousness.[1] Heinrich Zimmer is another writer with insights into *Myths and Symbols* in which he talks about these reflections as ways to penetrate into minds of both the people who created them and the people who read them.

For this purpose and for better understanding of the mythological tales about **Iranian kings**, one may refer to one of the best sources, *Shah Nameh* completed in 1010 A.D. by Abolghasem Ferdowsi. This book consists of 50 chronologically arranged episodes in lives of legendary kings. Its voluminous 60,000 rhymed couplets have roots in Iranian people's dreams of universe and its source. Some of its tales take the reader back to the early days to the time of first human. Ferdowsi mastered his rhymes of epic poetry, through awareness of the works of his contemporaries and created a captivating epic in terms of scope and details about 1000 years ago, which has lasted to this date. Ferdowsi is one of the greatest lyrical geniuses in the history of literature. He had an ear for various rhymes to establish subtle differences between moods and attitudes. Today, **Iranians** cherish his Farsi book, which contains almost no Arabic words, and is the result of his tireless effort. *Shah Nameh* has served Iranian culture as a milestone to reflect on both its heritage of about 7000 years of mythology and history, while preserving the Farsi language.

For comparison it is noteworthy that unlike **Persian** Mythology that goes back to the time of creation, the tales of **Greek** mythology do not throw any clear light upon what early mankind was like. The first written record of Greece is the *Iliad*. **Greek** mythology begins with **Homer** only about a thousand years B.C. [2]

Even the **Greeks** would have to read *Shah Nameh* to have a feeling of what early man thought about and feared.

1.   *Tarikh Mardom Iran*, by Dr. Abdolhosain Zarrinkoob, 1985 Tehran, p. 15
2.   *Mythology*, by Edith Hamilton, Boston, 1998, pp. 5-10

PISHDAADIAN Dynasty
(First mythological Kingdom of Aryans)

As mentioned earlier, *Shah Nameh* reflects mythological tales of **Iranian** kings beginning around 7000 B.C. Also, this book reflects a mythological history of early humans going back to the beginning of creation of man. Interestingly, these tales refer to some original traveling tribes of **Aryans**, coming down from Siberia and southern part of Russia who had to struggle against the approaching cold age. The creditability of Ferdowsi is reinforced, because this information matches the meteorological data about the last Ice Age (10,000 B.C.)

These tales of kings show establishment of the first dynasty called "**Pish Dadian**." Some historians interpret this name as *Early Bringers of Justice* as a nickname for **Houshang**, one of the prehistoric kings.

In *Bondahesh*, a mythic book of creation of universe in the language of 'Pahlavi' (old Farsi) **Persian** mythology extends to before time when

48

Ahura Mazda—the name for God in **Zorastherian** faith—had created only light or purity. Later comes the creation of man and then cow. [1]

Many of these mythological figures are given in advance of recorded time as they are not physically traceable. In the **Zorastherian** sources the first King (or first man ever) is referred to as **Giumars**—He may be interpreted as **Adam** in the western mythology. He is believed to be the progenitor of **Persians** (or **Iranians**) who lived in the high mountains near the green fields around the north east of the Plateau of Pars or Iran. He led his people peacefully. A sudden rush of cold weather changed the environment against his people—It's noteworthy that this coldness is usually coincided with the presence of the foes or demons ("**Deev**" in Farsi),[2] These **Deevs,** formidable in appearance, were the enemies of man and were pictured in myths as half beast and half human.

Deevs had apparently killed **Siamak**, the only son to **Giumars**. Therefore, the latter's grandson **Houshang** had to take the control after him. **Houshang** was the triumphant king against the army of **Deevs**. It was this new leader who managed to destroy a great number of **Deevs** (Demons or foes) and arranged for restitutions. He was also the leader who discovered Fire for his fellow men and established the famous **Persian** ritual of "Sadeh," a celebration of nature on the hundredth day after the month of "Aban" or fifty days before "Nowruz." Nowrouz means New Day and is celebrated on the first day of spring marking the **Iranians'** New Year. Some historians believe the nickname for **Houshang** was "**Pishdad**," meaning the first one who brought "Justice" or "Daad." [3]

He was succeeded by his son **Tahmureth**, who taught his people how to domesticate animals and made the captured **Deevs** teach his people the art of reading and writing. We may conclude that **Sumerians** had to do with these mythological foes, or could have been the same, since they were the first to design the early writing.

Interestingly these mythic figures, who introduced the key inventions (fire and cultivation) and institutions of human society, seem to be concurring with other cultures with slight variations. Many historians, like Joseph Campbell, doubt if these similarities can be coincidental.

For example, one may refer to the **Chinese** tales about their first sage ruler, **Fuxi**, who domesticated animals and instituted marriage.

After him came **Huangdi**, the Yellow Emperor. He was credited with the invention of writing and the calendar. Therefore, **Huangdi** most likely learned about it from the **Sumerians**. For **Chinese**, prehistory begins to merge with documented history during the kingdom of **Yu** around 2205 B.C.[4] For **Iranians**, this point of documented history is interestingly around 2450 B.C.

The next king of **Pishdadian Dynasty** is **Jamshid**. He is believed to be the maker of the first wine. During his ruling, it is mentioned, that a great tempest and flood had destroyed his land and livestock. Interestingly, the last three decades of archeological findings by Leonard Wooley pertaining to Mesopotamia's city of Ur confirm the theory of a big flood around this period. The ruins of the ancient city of Ur, which existed around 2450 B.C., confirm the presence of older civilizations buried under the same site. This could have happened due to a gigantic flood. The remainders of this older city still exist in today's Khuzestan in southern Iran and southwestern Iraq. Wooley has explained this in his book called *The Sumerians*. These new findings reveal several civilizations that had been buried under different mud layers, each pertaining to different ages. One of the artifacts found there belongs to early **Indo-Europeans** who had migrated there about 3200 B.C.[5]

Therefore, the myth of the great flood, as mentioned in holy books and ancient writings, coincides with this period.

Jamshid established "Nowrouz" or "New Year" celebration and officially took the throne on that day. **Jamshid** apparently lost his heavenly glory (Far) by indulging in opulence and crime. This marked the end of his reign. **Zahak** (**Azhidehak**), meaning the "dragon of ten vices" as per *Avesta*, who had brain-eating snakes pointing out of his shoulders, killed **Jamshid**. Ferdowsi shows that **Zahak** was from the "Tazi" tribes (Arabic tribes in Syria). After taking the control of the major part of the plateau, **Zahak** started a tyranny. Many **Aryans** revolted against this tyrant. **Kaveh** was one of the patriotic organizers of this resistance. He was a blacksmith by profession, and had already suffered the loss of his sons in continuous fights against the tyrant. **Kaveh** sought help from **Fereidoon**, a descendant of the **Iranian** kings. Ferdowsi refers to **Fereidoon** as the son of "**Abtin**." The latter being one of the members of the noble families of **Aryans**, was also murdered by **Zahak**.

50

Fereidoon's mother was **Faranak**. Finally, **Fereidoon** and **Kaveh** gathered enough followers to start a revolution against the army of **Zahak**, and finally **Aryans** captured him in the Damavand Mountain near Tehran.

Conversely, there have been some arguments recently about this part of **Iranian Mythology**. Through his recent contradictory approach, the renowned and contemporary poet, **Ahmad Shamloo,** presented a controversial approach. In his speech at U.C. Berkeley in April of 1990—a few years before his death—*Shamloo* denounced the blind acceptance of beliefs and legacies and urged all **Iranians** to study history with an open mind. For example, he believed that the legendary act of **Kaveh** could not be an act of heroism as portrayed in the mythology. The real hero was **Zahak** who had—as indirectly mentioned in *Shah Nameh* and *Khoday Namak*—taken the wealth of the elite segment of the society and spread it among the people. Also, **Shamloo** believed that **Bardia** rebelled against his cruel brother, **Cambujia**, and became the kind and true leader of Persia after **Cyrus The Great**. He backs up this opinion with writings of **Herodotus** about the revolutionary changes in the social life of **Persians** during the eight-year ruling of **Bardia**—in the absence of his melancholic brother. According to **Herodotus, Persians** and other nations in the **Persian Empire** really prospered a great deal during this time. **Shamloo** expressed that the tale of **Gaumata** is later on falsified to cover their crime of assassinating **Bardia**. **Shamloo** urged his readers to always explore and scrutinize different views to find the truth.[6]

But, the true lessons and effects of the history will prevail, regardless of any fabrications or alterations. The fact that mythology must be studied for its symbolic imagery leaves the path to further unbiased investigation wide open.

Going back to mythology and in short, **Fereidoon** had 3 sons: **Iraj, Salm** and **Tur**. He divided his vast kingdom, and gave Iran to his youngest son, **Iraj**. Then, **Fereidoon** gave Turan at the East to **Tur**, and Rum—referring to eastern **Roman** territories—at the West to **Salm**.

After a long fight between jealous siblings over the kingdom in Iran, the other two brothers managed to slay **Iraj** who had personally gone to them to make peace. Furious **Fereidoon** was too old to take revenge and left the fighting for **Manochehr**, the son of **Iraj**. Thus,

51

Manochehr annihilated both of his guilty uncles. There were many heroes in the **Iranian** army who helped this new king to fight the enemies. One of the most famous ones is called **Arash**.[7]

On the other hand, **Afrasiab**, the grandson of **Tur**, was the Crown Prince to the king of Turan (ancient eastern lands neighboring Persia). **Afrasiab** was a strong warrior and a young leader who revolted against Persia. He finally managed to kill **Nozar**, **Manochehr**'s son who was the last direct descendant of the kings in **Pishdadian Dynasty**. After **Nozar** came **Zaab** and, not much later, **Garshasep** was elected as the last king of **Pishdadian**, who did not stay in power for more than nine years.

The mythological tales indicate that **Pishdadian Dynasty** ruled for about 2,361 years, and was finally destroyed by the **Sakas** in the northern part of the plateau of Iran—near Azerbaijan.[8]

History, at this period, reflects **Iranian** ancestors' awe and respect for nature. **Aryans** had proven their resilience in finding new ways to live. The **Aryans** of Iranian branch, with whom we are here concerned, were the first to be civilized and to acknowledge one god. They were nature-worshippers in constant search for better lands. Their awareness of their surroundings made them better fighters and stronger people, who relied on nature and cherished the abundance in it. These original worldviews are still present in **Iranians**. Even at the present time, most **Iranians** feel a special respect for wheat and rice that make their basic national rations. They usually try not to waste, throw away, or even step on bread. Water and fire have found special place in the folklore and mythical images of early **Aryans**. Springs and rivers with pure and clean waters were always sought because of its scarcity. **Aryans** always revered fire. The site of fire, springing out of open craters on the ground while steam and sparks covered the snow, has been mysteriously impressive during winters in the northern provinces. The miraculous and purifying characteristics of fire are well-established in the history of Iran even before **Zoroastrianism**.[9]

1. *Tarikh Iran Zamin*, By Dr. Muhammad Javad Mashkur, 1988, Tehran, pp. 9-10

2. *The Mythic Image*, by Joseph Campbell, 1974 Princeton, N.Jersey, p. Xj

3. *Tarikh Iran Zamin*, Dr. MJ Mashkur, Chapter 3, p. 10

4. *A Concise History Of China*, by J.A.G. Roberts, 1999, U.S.A., pp. 2-3

5. *Tarikh-e-Iran*, Sir P. Sykes, Vol. 1, introductory Chapter

6. *Dafter-e-Honar* , Farsi periodical , Vol. 4,, No 8, New Jersey, U.S.A.. 1997, pp. 1047-57

7. *Pictorial History of Iran*, section 3

8. *Tarikh Iran Zamin*, p. 12

9. *A History Of Iran*, Sir Percy Sykes, Vol1, 1921, Macmillan & Co. London, pp. 95-110

KAYANIAN Dynasty
(second mythological kingdom—connecting to written history)

The second mythological era that follows belongs to the period of **Zarathustra**'s *Avesta*. In this ancient book the names of these rulers are usually indicated with a prefix of "**Kay**", which means "**king**" in old Farsi.

After the fall of the **Pishdadian Dynasty**, Persia was searching for a new king. Therefore, **Zal** (the elite governor of Sistan at the southeast of Iran, a strong figure with a different look since he was born with white hair and skin) sent his heroic son, **Rostam**, to find **Ghobad** (a descendant of **Fereidoon** and **Manochehr**) and assist him to gain the throne, as **Kay Ghobad (King Ghobad)**, to lead Persia.

Rostam, the national mythological hero for **Iranians**, possesses extraordinary strength and perseverance. Even his horse is known as an extraordinary charger called **Rakhsh** (lightning). Finally, it is **Rostam** who manages to overcome all odds and become triumphant against the army of **Afrasiab** who occupied Persia for about twelve years. **Rostam** puts on a ghastly fight and kills **Afrasiab** in a one-on-one battle. **Afrasiab**, the almost-invincible king of Turan had overturned **Pishdadian Dynasty** in Persia, but **Rostam** put an end to him.

Ferdowsi has highlighted his patriotic tales of *Shah Nameh* dramatically and with an ironic climax. **Rostam** must finally kill his only son **Sohrab**; in a great combat befitting two heroes. This tale emphasizes the patriotic love over all other loves. The nature of the fight of **Rostam** and **Sohrab** and their heroism have been evaluated by many different approaches all worthy of attention and debate.[1]

After **Ghobad** — referred to as **Kay Ghobad** — his son, **Kay Kavus,** takes the throne. Later, he falls as the prisoner to **Arjhang** (the leader of Mazandaran region in North). Once again **Rostam** rescues the king of Iran. This time by passing through the famous seven hurdles or impediments on his path, he frees **Kay Kavus** from his capturers.

After **Kay Kavus,** within afew years, **Siavash** and subsequently **Kay Khosro** came to throne. As mentioned earlier, with the help of **Rostam, Kay Khosro** managed to defeat the army of **Afrasiab** and asked **Lohrasep,** his cousin, to become the king in his place. **Kay Khosro** did not like to stay a king and left the throne without looking back. After **Lohrasep,** his son, **Gashtasep,** took over. This king is also referred to, as **Vishtasep** in *Avesta* meaning "The Owner of Wild Horse." He married **Katayun** the daughter of the Caesar of **Roman Empire.**[2]

Some names of the kings – in the **Kayanian Dynasty** - have a suffix of "Asep" or "Aseb" meaning "Asb" in Farsi or "Horse" in English. This connotes the importance of fighting spirit and chivalry among the leaders. **Gashtasep** was one of the early leaders who followed the prophet **Zarathustra.** The last king, however, was **Bahman** (**Artaxerxes** or **Ardashir**). He was **Gashtasep**'s grandson. This name is not mentioned in *Avesta*, but history refers to him as "**Ardashir Deraz Dast**", (the **Greeks** called him **Artaxerxes Longimanus**) meaning **Ardashir** with long hands. This nickname was given to this monarch because he had secret police at all corners of his vast **Persian Empire**, so that he could reach for anyone anywhere in his domain.

From this period on we witness more documentary history of Iran based on facts and science. However, it is of importance to know that some historians believe that a lot of these mythological kings are actually variations of their historic counter parts. **Kayanian Dynasty** actually has coincided with the beginning of **Medes Dynasty** – which is discussed in the next chapter. Therefore, the legendary **Kay Kavus** (of **Kayanian Dynasty**) may be the same historical person as **Cyaxares (Huvakhshatra)**, the leader of **Medes.** Also, **Kay Ghobad** may be **Dayauku**, an earlier leader of **Medes.** It is interesting to know that in the mythological tales **Kay Kavus** is said to have fought the white Deevs in north of Persia, but the entire Persian army had become blind, thus incapable of continuing the fight. Historical data indicate when **Cyaxares** of **Medes** fought the Sakas in the north; a sudden darkness due to an eclipse had ended the fight. These similarities, though interesting, are not fully confirmed yet. However, it is important to know that **Iranians** never gave up on their national prehistoric heroes and kings, even after the domination of **Arabs**, which resulted in introduction of new religious figures; therefore it is necessary to learn about them in the field of mythology. [3]

One important mythological data has to do with the realm of the national flag. An indication of **Persians'** insistence in keeping their identity is its official flag. The **Iranian** constitution designates as the official flag of Iran the insignia of a golden lion and sun upon a field of white between a green, and a red stripe. This insignia has a very ancient history. Ferdowsi, in his story of **Rostam** and **Sohrab**, has a description of the banners of famous **Persian** commanders among which was one bearing the figure of a lion, and another bearing a yellow sun. The combination of the lion and sun as a sign of Zodiac appears on objects of **Iranian** art. The earliest form as the heraldic device of Iran is on a silver coin of **Ghyath-u-Din Kay Khosro**, during **Saljugh (Seljuk) Dynasty** minted around 1200 A.D. The **Saffavid** coins of the 16th Century bear the same device. The lion received his sword during the **Ghajar** period in the 20th Century. [4]

1.   *Dar Setiz Rostam Va Sohrab*, by Iraj Tabibniya, Vision Print, San Jose, CA, 2nd edit 2001, pp. 31-40
2.   *Tarikh-e-Iran*, Sir P. Sykes, Translated by F. Daie, Tehran, p. 15
3.   *Tarikh-e-Iran*, pp. 178-181
4.   *Iran Past and Present*, by Donald N. Wilber, 1955, Princeton University Press, p. 253

CHAPTER THREE

Medes
(1200 B.C.- 650 B.C.)

Aryans of Persia were the first to acknowledge one God over all gods. This worldview and extraordinary culture had not yet developed in older civilizations of Babylon or Assyria. The Persian Aryans detested paganism and desired to look for answers in Nature. In this respect, they were truly "noble" as the term "Aryan" implies. But, it is understood that the life style of Aryan travelers was quite limited. Being mostly herders, they could not stay in one place or settle down for long. Thus, as explained before, they did not form any united city-state under one ruler until around 1200 B.C. (the Medes). Nevertheless, they were in constant exploration of newer places and their unique culture had been forming for thousands of years before then.

Sir Percy Sykes finds the early influences of Aryans' culture beyond today's geographical boundaries. History shows some Aryans had invaded Bactria – beyond north east of Iran - before 2500 B.C. and had crossed Hindu Kush and Panjab with their ideologies.[1] The early Hindu and Persian cultural and religious views share many similarities – as mentioned before.

Sir P. Sykes argues that on the other hand, in Mesopotamia and Egypt city building and urbanism were bound to flourish because of accumulation of regional farms and water channels. **Babylonians, Sumerians** and **Assyrians** believed in many gods who were generally very strict and much angrier than **Egyptian** gods. However, each city-state had its own god that would be superior to the ones from other places.[2] Yet, such trends of thought did not travel farther than that area, and did not affect the Persians' future religions.

Aryans lived next to many neighbors with quite a different religious background. **Egyptians** believed in gods who were easier to please, and about this period there were magnificent monuments and colossal statues built to their honor. New reforms and ideas about nature gradually made its way to the minds of **Egyptians**. Around 1385 B.C. **Amniotes IV**, Pharaoh **Ikhnaton**, destroyed the old gods statues and set up **Aton** as the Sun God. He was the pharaoh that built new residence in Amarna and attempted revolutionizing changes in army and priesthood, which was later annulled by **Tutan Khamen**.[3] Paying tribute to the Sun God must have come to Egypt as an extension of **Mithraism** from the plateau of Pars.

It was on this plateau that sizable agglomeration of people and buildings led to need for governing regulations. History shows **Medes** as the early city-state of **Aryans** who managed to form their strong urbanism in the western part of the plateau in today's Iran. After 500 years of continuous battles with neighboring **Assyrians** from the South and **Sakas** from the North, **Medes** had finally finished building a unified city-state around 1200 B.C. Tall walls guarded it just northeast of Mesopotamia on the top of a mountain that is called Alvand (near today's Hamadan).

It is interesting to note that, at this age, small units of families and traveling tribes were not very much in numbers; since the estimated world population was limited to under 90 million around 2000 B.C. [4]

1. *A History Of Persia*, by Sir Percy Sykes, Vol.1, pp.98, 99
2. *A History Of Persia*, pp.63, 64
3. *The Timetable Of History*, Grun, p. 7
4. *A Short History Of The World*, by Geoffrey Blainey, 2002, Chicago, p. 37

Of course, the other branches of **Aryan** tribes like **Parthians**, known as tireless fighters, stayed further north near The Caspian Sea and they shared borders with a savage neighboring tribe named **Khezer** who lived near this sea, which is still named after them. Only the **Pars** continued south to what is Persian Gulf and neighbored the **Elam** civilization. Although separated, these groups of **Aryans** were nature worshipers who shared ethnic culture and language. Therefore, **Medes** (called **Maad** in Farsi) were the first **Aryan** tribes who built towns and citadels with their own garrisons for protection against enemies. But other **Aryan** tribes, although slowly catching up, were still living in less protected and scattered villages on the plateau.

The founder of **Medes** kingdom—not the civilization, but its first official government—was an **Aryan** farmer called **Dayauku (Deiokes)**. He was the first king who was practically elected by his own people, because of his leadership and fairness in judgments. The **Medes** had requested him to rule and, without any bloodshed, voted for him in an election around 708 B.C.[1] This was a decision reached by majority of votes by the citizens of **Medes**. It may very well be one of the earliest signs of civilization in the world, as we know it today.

Subsequently, he chose Ecbatana—now called Hamadan—in the north west of Iran, as his capital. He ruled as a well-respected and wise ruler for about 53 years and tried to stop **Assyrians** from harassing his people by over-taxation. Therefore, the dominant **Assyrian** government finally turned against him and exiled him to Syria.

At this time, his son, **Phraortes** or **Fravartish** took the throne on 655 B.C. He attempted an invasion against the robust army of **Assyrians**, but he was defeated and killed in 633 B.C. by **Ashur Banipal (Assurbanipal)** the powerful and vicious king of **Assyrians**. Then **Huvakhshatra** or **Cyaxares** (**Cyarxes** in some texts and pronounced *ki 'Aksar*) succeeding his father became the greatest king of **Medes**. He ruled between 633 and 585 B.C. [2]

His earlier six-year battle with the **Sakas** of the northern lands neighboring Persia ended with no result for either country because of a sudden eclipse.

On the other hand, **Assyrians** had stayed as a threat to this king. From cuneiforms discovered in the area, **Assyrians** (people of Assyr)

58

are generally portrayed to be very cruel. They were constantly fighting their neighboring **Elam**. Many ancient texts reveal that **Assyrians**, when engaged in wars, destroyed everything on their path even animals. At this time **Cyaxares**, who was worried about his borderlines with **Assyrians**, managed to gather a huge army of **Medes** warriors. These soldiers were better-trained and more skilled for combat. The wars began and **Medes** warriors came close to the walls of Nineveh, the capital city of **Assyrians**. But during the same period, **Sakas** of the North (another **Aryan** descendants, but not **Persian**) started their surprise attack against **Medes** territories. **Cyaxares** had to pull back and confront **Sakas** near northern parts of Lake Rezaieh (Urumia) in northwest of Iran. This war was lost and as a result **Medes** had to tolerate 28 years of severe oppression and harsher taxations by triumphant **Assyrians** as well as **Sakas**.[3]

However, this bitter experience did not stop **Cyaxares** or **Huvakhshatra**. He was still the King of **Medes** and his people believed in him. So, finally, through some traditional protocol he officially invited **Maduyes**, the king of **Sakas**, to a magnificent feast. But **Medes** hosts had poisoned the drinks of **Sakas** and killed all generals and noble men present that night including **Maduyes**. As mentioned earlier, **Sakas** were a descendant of early **Aryans** who had stayed in the northern lands and shared the same line of ancestry with **Parthians**. **Ferdowsi** has referred to these people as **Touranian** in his *Shah Nameh*.

Now that **Sakas** were eliminated, **Cyarxes** maneuvered with political tactics based on the traditions of his time. He gave his grand daughter, **Amethia**, in marriage to the Prince of Babylon called **Nabuchodonsor**. This marriage brought peace and friendship between the two nations. The famous 'Hanging Gardens of Babylon' is a gift from this young prince to his young **Iranian** wife. This is one of "Seven Wonders of the World." Some historians refer to these gardens erroneously and relate them to **Samirames**, the fictional queen of Assyr (Ashur). [4]

In 612 B.C., accompanied by **Babylonian** and **Medes** warriors, **Cyaxares**, attacked Nineveh for the second time. He defeated the **Assyrians** who had deviated from their original glory and led a life of tyranny and bloodshed. Later, he established the greatest **Aryan** kingdom of the time stretching from West (Lydian civilization near

Black Sea) to the East (Indu civilization near Oxos River or Jayhoon or Amu Darya in Pamir of central Asia). [5]

Now, **Medes**, dominating part of Mesopotamia, was directly neighboring and allies with **Babylonians** to the north, but much bigger and stronger. Babylonia bequeathed to mankind law, astronomy, and science. Egypt erected buildings, which still challenge the admiration of the world. Assyria, merely borrowing glories of Babylonia and Egypt shone only as the great predatory power and, after its fall, passed away into utter oblivion. [6]

History has witnessed the fall of many peoples and loss of many empires or lands. After many centuries of cultural and political struggle, **Assyrians** managed to keep their language and heritage alive in spite of their ancient loss of their political independence. They are currently spread out as a race that has citizens living in different countries.

Asthiagus succeeded his father, **Cyaxares**, in 584 B.C. He ruled for 35 years, but he was careless and self-indulged in luxury, and neglected the justice that his fathers had laid in his land. His own people could not tolerate his brutality, and when the right time came his own generals, including **Harpagus**, willfully joined the army of **Pars** under **Cyrus The Great**. The myths in *Shah Nameh* about the **Tazi** leader (**Arab**) named **Azhidehak** or **Zahak**—who was captured and killed by **Fereidoon**—may also be another version of life story of **Asthiagus**. These two names could actually refer to one historic figure, because brutality of **Asthiagus** in torture and manslaughter matches the mythic images of **Zahak** who had man-eating snakes growing out of his shoulders. **Deiokes (Dayauku)** the leader of **Medes** tribes may be the same person as **Kay Ghobad**; and **Cyarxes** may be the same historical figure as **Kay Kavus**.[7]

Thus, the great civilizations of **Mesopotamians** and **Aryans of Medes** mix and create more magnificent masterpieces in the history of art and science. In other parts of the world we may simultaneously witness some slower activities. Just for comparison, we may look at the **Mayan** civilization in Mexico, which was getting a start around 600 B.C. Of course the **Mexican** Sun Pyramid in Teotihuacan was being constructed around 1500 B.C. But this shows very much the extent of mentionable architectural movements elsewhere.[8]

Still, basic supernatural beliefs of **Aryans** were unique to them.

Sumerians and **Babylonians** were pantheistic—believing in a number of gods that looked like humans but had superhuman characteristics, including immortality. The celestial gods of **Shamsh** (the Sun) and **Sin** (the Moon) appear to be of most importance.[9] **Sumerians** erected Ziggurats or shrines with tall ascending stairs to the top, where they could be closer to their gods. As said earlier, these gods seemed to be in connection with the symbol of light that early **Aryans** worshipped and referred to as **Mithra** (Mehr is a variation of this name and is connected to the Sun in old Farsi) Interestingly, **Shamsh** could be a variation of the word **Shams** that also means the Sun in Arabic.

The original written languages are not fully discovered. Sir Percy Sykes refers to Strabo's *Geographica* and argues that the spoken language of **Aryans** of **Medes** closely resembled that of the **Pars**, although no such written texts are discovered yet. Some believe that the written tongue of the **Medes** could be **Assyrian** language.[10]

1.   *Tarikh-e-Mardom-e-Iran*, Dr. A.H Zarrinkub, Tehran 1986, p. 88
2.   *The Medes and Persians*, By Robert Collins, N.Y.
3.   *Tarikh Iran Zamin* , Dr. MJ Mashkur, p. 20
4.   *Tarikh Iran Zamin*, p. 21
5.   *Pictorial History of Iran*, MH Amini Sam, p. 101
6.   *A History Of Persia*, by Sir Percy Sykes, Vol.1, Macmillan Co. 1921, London, p.125
7.   *Tarikh-e-Mardom-e-Iran*, p.103
8.   *The timetables of History*, 3rd edition, Grun, N.Y. 1991, p. 7
9.   *The History of the Ancient & Medieval World*, Marshall Cavendish, 2nd Vol. N.Y 1996, p. 220-250
10.   *A History of Persia*, by Sir Percy Sykes, Vol. 1, published by Macmillan & Co., 1921, London, p. 121

CHAPTER FOUR

Achaemendis Dynasty
(About 750 B.C.- 330 B.C.)

From now on we leave prehistoric era completely behind and only concentrate on real historical figures and move away from mythology.

HACHAEMENESH
(*Hakha' Ma 'Nish*)

Simultaneously with **Medes,** but in another locality in the plateau at a slower pace, other traveling **Aryans** had gathered together to form primary urban areas. Finally, one of these urban centers became **The Achaemendis** early center of power and civilization around 750 B.C.

Its founder was a learned leader of Passargad tribe. He was called **Hachaemenesh**—pronounced *Hakha 'Manesh* in Farsi. He named his capital "Passargad," which was situated near Shiraz. The people of Passargad had more wealth, fame and respect than other towns and villages on the **Pars** plateau. It was **Hachaemenesh** who struggled to persuade the heads of many **Aryan** tribes to unite. His vision was to create a powerful empire that could protect its smaller regions under a broad and central government.

In addition to Persia during this period, some other areas show signs of growing urbanism with smaller kingdoms. For example, that **Mayan** civilization in Mexico goes back to about this period in time— 600 to 500 B.C. In Europe Greece emerges with the first recorded **Olympic games.**[1]

It is interesting to know that the first **Olympic Games** were held in Athens at the Temple of **Zeus** in 776 B.C., during the reign of **King Iphitos** of Elis. The original **Olympics** were superstitiously devised to keep the curse of plague away from the kingdom. These games— including track and field—were played by naked male athletes, but females were not allowed to watch—the punishment for sneaking into audience was death.[2]

It was about this period, in 560 B.C. in India, that **Gautama Buddha** brought forward the rejection of the authority of Brahmanic ritual; he taught that suffering is inseparable from existence, and that one should strive to extinguish the self and the senses in order to achieve a state of illumination called Nirvana.[3]

1.   *The Timetables of History*, 3rd edition, Grun, N.Y, 1991, p. 7
2.   *San Francisco Chronicle*, an article by Meredith May, Thursday, August 19, 2004, p. A14
3.   *A concise History Of India*, Barbara & Thomas Metcalf, Cambridge U.2002, New York, p. xix

CHAESHPESH
(Che' *Esh' Pish*)

After **Hachaemenesh**, his son, **Teispes (Chaeshpesh)** took over and immediately raided neighboring **Elam** because **Ashur Banipal** of Assyria had weakened it with continuous fights. This new area was called Enshan.

Thus, the new central headquarters was chosen and situated in Enshan. This was a prospering area near Karun River in Khuzestan in southeast of Iran around 650 B.C. **Teispes** commanded an army of warriors from many united **Aryan** tribes and conquered **Elam**. This was how **Enshan** formed an even better and stronger army, gradually growing to be a threat to other **Aryans** of **Medes**.

Later on **Teispes** moved to **Pars** and gained its alliance easily and added it to **Enshan** and **Elam** in Khuzestan. He ruled with respect and order over the new and bigger kingdom of Pars and Enshan, which he left respectively to his sons **Arya Ramnae** and **Cyrus I**. Many princes were born into families of these two branches of kings under **Chaeshpesh (Teispes)**. Some of them took the throne before it was time for **Cambyses I**. In comparison with the kings of **Medes**, this leader of **Enshan** was just a calm noble man who did not seem too eager for expansion of his power. For this reason **Asthyagus**, the cruel king of **Medes**, who was cautious about possible **Enshan** threats against his authority, allowed **Cambyses I** to ask his daughter's hand in marriage.[1] This young bride's name was **Mandana**.

CYRUS III (KUROSH) THE GREAT
(*Ku 'Rosh*)

As the result of this marriage, **Mandana** gave birth to **Cyrus III (Kurosh III)**. This **Kurosh** was later referred to as **Cyrus The Great (Kurosh The Great)**, one of the most famous names in the history of the world. Apparently, **Asthyagus** had repetitive and alarming nightmares of losing his nation to this newborn grandson. Being a cruel king, he ordered destruction of baby **Cyrus** to stop this prophecy. But, **Cyrus** managed to escape this fate by the help of a friend of the family. Later, he traveled to Pars, but stayed in touch with the courts and rulers of **Achaemendis**. Later on, while still a young prince, **Cyrus** established an extraordinary fame that went beyond time. He became the king of **Pars** in 559 B.C., succeeding his father. This is the earliest foundation for **The Persian Empire**.[2]

Cyrus finally returns to **Medes**, he fights and captures the cruel and much hated **Asthiagus**—fulfilling the prophecy—and conquers the capitol, Hamadan or Hegmataneh, in 550 B.C. The **Aryans of Medes** were rather content with the replacement of their vicious leader. **Kurosh (Cyrus)**, on the contrary, was the beneficent and popular young ruler who had united all the **Enshan, Pars, Medes,** and **Elam** inhabitants and territories. From this period (around 546 B.C.), he officially called himself the king of Persia referring to the entire land on the plateau of Pars (from the East to the West of today's Iran and far beyond). Although he was firm and just he also knew the ways of war very well. Unlike most of the redoubtable kings after him, he did not lose the faith of his people and did not forget their needs. With insight and courage, he defeated advanced military machines of his insurgent neighbors of Lydia, Babylon, Saard, and Egypt. This is the birth of **The Persian Empire** — the biggest empire in the history of man.[3]

The importance of this era is not because it reflects an important part of Iranian history – although **Iranians** are proud of it. Its importance is not even because this era in history reflects the birth of the biggest empire in the history of man so far. Its real importance, we should realize, is in the fact that this great empire was built on the original human rights declared by a king who is known and praised by the world for being just and humanistic even against his enemies.

This is the era of the king of **The Persian Empire**, known as **Cyrus The Great**.

Although earlier great civilizations and much older kingdoms were built inside Mesopotamia, none of them had grown to become an empire. An empire is a group of different kingdoms, states or territories under sovereign power of an emperor, who is responsible for their prosperity. Thus Persia - or Iran since 1935 - is the birthplace of the very first empire in the world. **Persian Empire** had eventually taken a cluster of nations, tribes, and city-states under one united command, while honoring their diversity in ethnic and cultural standards. Until then, no other kingdom had grown as robust and vast as The **Persian Empire**. This happened around 600 B.C. It was quite unlike the **Mongols** rule, which took place over 1700 years later. **Mongols** were pagans who conquered without mercy and massacred every single civilian without conscience. The source of their actions was greed and hatred not expansion and control. They even burnt the crops after taking what they needed and killed the animals and left behind the cultivated lands that they filled with salt to make the soil barren.

The **Persian Empire,** built by **Cyrus the Great,** conquered many kingdoms and increased its wealth and power by seeking tribute (taxation) and this did not always come without bloodshed. However, his fairness and justice proved to be a blessing for the oppressed. **Kurosh the Great** spread freedom of religion and emancipation of slavery wherever he went.

Cyrus had entered these cities in all the nations as the messenger of peace. He had clearly ordered his troops to conquer and move with respect to laws not with hatred. His great words are depicted on a 45 cm long stone cylinder excavated in where Babylon used to be. He ordered the release of all **Jews** that were kept as slaves in **Medes.** Strategically, he chose his capitol to be Ecbatana between Medes and Passargad. Persia now bordered India from East, Saard near the Mediterranean Sea from West, Black Sea and Armenia in North, and Persian Gulf, and Indian Ocean in the south. This was the biggest nation in the entire world.[4]

In *Tarikh Iran Zamin,* **Dr. Mashkur** also refers to the fall of Babylon by **Cyrus The Great** in 538 B.C., as a well-recorded fact in the history reflecting this great leader's fair and peaceful treatment of all the people of the conquered lands. Through **Cyrus's** peaceful doctrines, kept in the form of Mikhi letters on many cuneiforms, we have the first declaration of Human Rights by the greatest humanitarian leader of all ages. He also conquered Babylon in 538 B.C. and emancipated all the **Jews** who were held for centuries as slaves or laborers; and it was for this reason that they referred to him as the Savior sent by **Yahova**, their God. The information about the religion of **Cyrus,** like the earlier **Achaemendis kings** is not clear—some historians believe him to be a **Zorastherian**, yet he allowed **Jewish immigrants** to keep their temples in Babylon and returned all their wealth and belongings to them, and then he provided for their voluntary and safe return to Jerusalem in 537 B.C.[5] Many historians praised humanitarian rule of this **King of Persia.** The 4th Century B.C. Greek historian **Xenophon** referred to **Cyrus The Great** as a man of wisdom and resilience.

Many historians, such as Sir John Malcolm and Sir Percy Sykes, write about him with great admiration. **Kurosh The Great** was a skilful swordsman who personally encountered his country's enemies face to face like his own soldiers. Along with such qualities, he was noble and humble. During his final battle with "Massagetae" kingdom that attacked Persia from the northeast, **Cyrus The Great** received a fatal injury. His body was escorted to Passargad where he was mummified as per the rituals of the time and buried near today's Shiraz in 529 B.C. One of his famous statements is, "No one is worthy of leadership, unless he possesses the essence of character superior to those he intends to lead." He was faithfully married to a **Hachaemenesh** princess called **Cassandane** and had two sons from her.[6]

Cassandane, the daughter of **pharnasep** of **Achaemenid** dynasty, was raised as a princess and was an influential and outspoken woman in the court. **Persian women** of the late **Achaemendis** reign gradually received greater social status and respect. Some women with elaborate trainings and moral aptitude were even possessing the highest prestigious rank of Judicial **Moghs** or **Magistrates.** This rank was only second to that of the king's family.[7]

CAMBYSES II

Thus, **Kurosh The Great** and **Cassandane** had two sons. **Cambyses II (Cambujia II)** was the eldest son; although he suffered from some emotional depression, he succeeded the great king. But it was the second son who had gained respect and the trust of his parents and all the courts men. This young prince was **Bardia.**[8]

For this matter **Cyrus The Great** who was worried about the far away lands of his empire, had nominated **Bardia** as the viceroy of the East including Kharazm, Parthia, and Karamania (Kerman). Therefore, **Bardia** became more popular among **Persians.** This situation could result in catastrophe and unfortunately it did so.

But, **Cambujia II** had a more severe problem at hand. He led the **Persian** soldiers to withstand the rebellious **Egyptian** and **Greek** armies, although **Persians** were still mourning for the loss of the great king.

Sir Percy Sykes puts it this way: Many years before his death, **Cyrus The Great** had chosen his favorite second son, **Bardia,** as the commander of all Northeastern lands under the reign of **Persian**

Empire. This great humanitarian king trusted **Bardia** who had shown signs of valuable character for leadership. All the **Persians** liked **Bardia** very much and so did the people and officials of other countries under his command- the **Greek** called him **Smerdis** - He was kind and straightforward and treated everyone like his father used to. But **Cambujia II** was more temperamental with a history of hysteric attacks. He was more concerned about reinforcing his future position as the king rather than attending to his people's needs. Now after the death of **Cyrus The Great**, **Cambujia II**, as the King of the **Persian Empire**, inherited the responsibility to deal with Egypt. But, he was too worried to leave the whole nation under his coveted brother. Therefore, in 526 B.C., with the pressure from some high rank advisors, **Cambujia II** committed a great sin and ordered his younger brother **Bardia** to be ambushed and killed in total secrecy.[9]

Cambujia II was quick, he ran several campaigns against all threatening enemies and, later on, he even expanded the vast lands he had inherited under his father's kingdom. It was during **Cambyses II** that the **Persian Empire** extended beyond Egypt into Africa and beyond the Mediterranean Sea into Greece. This growth in territorial coverage called for tighter management and control as well as justice and social reforms that did not, unfortunately, always follow. The act of genocide among the heirs to a throne by the direct order of a leader—repeated in history - was nothing new. Unfortunately, almost all kings from all corners of the world kept this common practice to avoid those who could possibly transgress their authority. Each king contrived his own ways to safeguard what he claimed to be his own right of succession.

As said earlier, **Cambujia II** fought the **Egyptians** and destroyed their statues of their gods in 525 B.C. **Cyrus The Great** would have offered freedom of religion to these people, but **Cambujia II** was different. He was there for about three years and called himself the new **Pharaoh**. His insecurity caused him to betray highest ideals of his father. He lived under mental pressure; had to make sure that the newly acquired land did not revolt against him. But the rumors of someone naming himself **Bardia** and taking the throne in the **Persian Empire** reached him. The intruder was **Gaumata** the Magian—a **Turanian** slave serving as priest. **Cambujia II** was melancholically worried. Knowing this intruder could not be **Bardia**; he was unable to openly contradict this false claim for throne. He did not know whom to blame for this conspiracy, but had to return quickly. On his return, somewhere near Syria and Babylon, while deeply indulged in melancholic thoughts trying to mount his horse, he accidentally injured himself with his own sword and died.[10]

In the Behistun (Bistun) inscription carved into stone — copied and translated by Rawlinson — **Darius** explains the death of **Cambyses II** to have been an act of suicide in epileptic despair.[11]

1.   *Tarikh-e-Iran*, Sir P. Sykes, pp. 182-184
2.   *Tarikh Iran Zamin*, Dr. M.J. Mashkur, p. 25
3.   *Tarikh-e-Iran* , pp. 187-202
4.   *Pictorial History of Iran* , M.H. Amini Sam, p. 118
5.   *Tarikh Iran Zamin*, pp. 26-28
6.   *Tarikh -e-Iran* , pp. 200-202
7.   *Tarikh Iran Zamin*, pp. 50, 51
8.   *History Of The Persian Empire*, by A.T. Olmstead, 1959, U. of Chicago Press, p. 86
9.   *Tarikh-e-Iran*, pp. 203, 204
10.   *Tarikh-e-Mardom Iran*, Dr. A.H. Zarrinkub, pp. 138-139
11.   *A History Of Iran*, by Sir Percy Sykes, Vol.1, 1921, London, pp. 158, 159

DARIUS I (DARIUSH) THE GREAT (Dar 'Yoosh)

Persia (meaning half of Asia, Asia Minor, and North Africa) was in another shock. But in the western hemisphere the troublesome riots were not much less. By looking at the western world around this time, simultaneously in Rome, we see the declaration of first republic state while their last king, **Tarquin,** was expelled in 519 B.C.[1]

But Persia continued its tradition of kingship. After the just fate of **Cambyses II**, it was **Darius** or **Dariush** who led the **Persian Empire** in 521 B.C. He was the grandson of **Arya Ramnae** who was the second son of **Chaeshpesh** (the founder of **Achaemendis** kingdom of **Pars**).

Dariush had realized the need for better communication within the larger territories under his reign; therefore he engineered new channels of decentralized management to run his vast empire.

Before him an **Assyrian** style of management was adopted by kings that ordered relocation of the people within the conquered lands, so that their reunion or possible conspiracy would be stopped, and their reliance upon assistance from the new central government would be guaranteed. But this maneuver would not work any more for such vast territories with large populations.[2]

Thus, **Darius** divided his kingdom to many states and gave his trust-worthy men, called **Satrap**, a specific province to run on his behalf. However, **Darius The Great** maintained random official inspections directly under his supervision. He conquered western borders of China and Greece as well as North Africa into submission and acquired their submission and gained control. He is the first **Iranian** king who ordered the golden coins to be minted and utilized for major trades. His innovative ratios of manufacturing these golden coins were immaculate. His original scales were so precise that they immediately received international admiration and the **Greek** and **Hebrews** commonly referred to them as "Daric" and "Siglo" – the Hebrew word for it was "shekel." This coin was very much valued and was the only one accepted all over the world at the time. Even today's **British** Pound is manufactured to match this Daric and Siglo specifications.[3] Of course the regular coins - conglomerations of copper and other metals - were already in use in Greece, and first **Roman** coins appear in 338 B.C.

Persian tradesmen showed the **Phoenician** sailors, who engaged in commerce, the primary rules and ways of banking and **Phoenicians** gradually took it to their **Greek** neighbors along the Black Sea and The Mediterranean Sea. Then **Romans** learned it from The **Greeks**. The term "Bank" comes from the **Italian** word Banco, which was given to the benches that **Venetians** in **Roman** Empire used, in order to perform their daily monetary services.[4]

Very soon, **Athenians** aided the **Greek** riots against **Persians**. **Darius** finally suppressed this threat which took him about 6 years. Then, he had his eyes on Athens for retaliation. The population in **Persian Empire** was over 15 million and he could gather a large army easily.[5] The total world population then is estimated at 50 million.

In 486 B.C., **Darius The Great** attempted to fight the **Greek Empire**, but his army could not finish this campaign and had to retreat. In 485 B.C., he was thinking of attending to the **Egyptian** riots, but fell sick and passed away. In a cuneiform set on his tomb it is written in Mikhi language:" I pray to **Ahura Mazda** – the **Zarathustra**'s God – to safe keep this great nation from enemies, draught, and lies."[6]

Because of his leadership and his organizing genius, **Darius** was given the nickname of *The Great*. He had begun construction of famous castles and courthouses of "**Persepolis**" "Takht-e-Jamshid" near Shiraz in 518 B.C.—This collection of magnificent palaces and halls were called "**Parsa**" in old Farsi. This magnificent architectural masterpiece was intended to create a centralized quarter accommodating governmental leaders and agents from all corners of his empire. The paid workers and skilled **Persian** craftsmen, invited from all over the kingdom, assisted by foreign master builders from other nations, erected this masterpiece to match the taste of the **Persian** kings. The salaries and wages for these craftsmen are well recorded in tablets excavated on the site.[7] This trend of management was unlike the harsh forced labor that **Egyptians** were imposing on their slaves. Naturally the **Egyptian slaves**, like the **Babylonian Jews**, had dreamed for emancipation that could only happen by an invasion from **The Persian Empire**.

Persians mastered their unique sculpting forms and techniques in Near East in Persepolis castles. Established by the insight of **Cyrus The Great**. They marvelously carved stones to create new forms. One in particular is the entirely unprecedented architecture reflecting connected heads of bulls. **Assyrians** originally introduced this animal's head (griffins), but **Persian** architects redesigned them and connected them back to back as *cradles* on top of 36 columns each 40 feet tall in The Audience Hall of **Darius**. Also innovations were implemented in showing the bulging muscles from underneath the garments of the stone-carved statues of soldiers. These were unique **Persian** innovations over what was already introduced by other nations. Thus, the artistically chiseled human and animal shapes on stonewalls did actually appear three-dimensional. Even the fine and soft texture of the king's clothing was very skillfully reflected and exhibited in these stone carvings.[8]

Farzin Rezaeian produced and directed a 3D documentary under the title of: *"Persepolis Recreated,"* which was played at the campus of Stanford University on November 5, 2004. The book and the CD reflect an unprecedented look at what Persepolis (with gigantic terrace of 125,000 square meters) could be like about 2500 years ago. Xenophon, the 4th Century B.C. Greek historian, had referred to this splendid structure as "the richest city under the sun."[9]

On the other hand, Paul Bahn explains in detail that **Persian** engineers and designers had referred to their predecessors and used many symbols and techniques, but kept the **Persian** style as an omnipresent soul in the architecture of this era. One very impressive result of synthesis of antique **Mesopotamian** themes of power with Classical **Greek** grace, all within the fabric of their own **Iranian** heritage, is the **Achaemendis Persepolis**.[10] Besides, genius attempt of **Darius The Great** can also be seen in his original plan and construction of a canal to connect the Nile to the Red Sea anticipating the construction of the modern Suez Canal.

Unfortunately, regardless of their nationality, kings were always worried about riots and enemies before they had a chance to do what they needed to improve life style of their people. History shows that only a few managed to actually cause improvements. Most were only popular and dominant when there was a fight. **Darius** was a king with vision, he could do a lot more for Persia, but he was heir to a vast land with many enemies.

Darius The Great divided the country into 20 provinces or *Satrapies* for tighter management in order to defeat any invasion to the borders before it get out of hand. He needed uninterrupted communication between these Satrapies. His regular courier service by messengers on horseback was another innovation for fast news release.[11] He was defeated in his battle of "Marathon" in Greece, and a year later while contemplating an invasion against the **Egyptian** territories passed away in 485 B.C., he was over sixty and ruled for thirty-six years.

1. *The Timetables Of History*, Grun, p. 10
2. *A History Of Persia*, Sir Percy Sykes, Vol.1, London, p. 161
3. *Tarikh Iran*, Sir Percy Sykes, pp. 213, 214

4.   *Iran Nameh,* published by The Foundation of Iranian Studies, No 4, 1993, pp. 647-655

5.   *The Encyclopedia of World History,* p. 40

6.   *Tarikh Mardom Iran,* Zarrinkoob, pp. 162, 147

7.   *History Of The Persian Empire,* By A.T. Olmstead, 1959, U. of Chicago Press, pp. 272, 273

8.   *History of Art,* by H.W. Janson, N.Y. 1986, p. 82

9.   *Persepolis Recreated,* Farzin Rezaeian, Tehran, Publisher: Dayereh Sabz, 2004

10.   *Lost Cities,* edited by Paul G. Bahn, 1997, N.Y, p. 110

11.   *The Timetable of History,* p. 11

XERXES (KHASHAYAR)
(Kha Sha 'Yaar)

When **Darius** was old, he chose **Xerxes (Khashayar)** over his other sons to take the throne in 485 B.C. **Khashayar** was born from **Atossa**, one of the wives of **Darius The Great**. She was also the daughter of **Kurosh The Great. Iranians** call this king **Khashayar**. In the *Torah* he is referred to as **Akhshurvash.**[1]

He was the one who finally crushed the rebellion in Egypt in 484 B.C.—more slaves were released. His brother **Achaemenes** was appointed as the Satrap, and Egypt settled down as before, the hereditary princes and the priests being left in full possession of their powers and properties—this act was an extension of the tradition set by **Cyrus The Great.** Then the final revolt in Babylon was suppressed in 483 B.C. Babylon, from this point on, never regained its glory and its power gradually passed away, though the work of this magnificent city was accomplished by its direct part in the civilization on earth.[2]

Herodotus mentions the number of the **Persian warriors** to have been about 2,300,000. They marched through Dardanelle Canal over two rows of anchored ships laying a giant temporary bridge. **Khashayar (Xerxes)** had already suppressed the **Egyptians** completely, though their civilization was not destroyed. But this time, he burned the city of Athens and killed many in rage; this was a change in his character - exact reasons for this hateful act are unknown. Consequently, his marine victory, the battle of Salamis in 480 B.C. over the **Greeks** in Athens, did not hold for long and **Xerxes** retreated with haste after his first defeat at sea. He grew more agitated during later years of his 20 years of stringent ruling. He started a careless life style and put the kingdom in dismay. The incapacity and viciousness of **Xerxes** reached its height until the captain of his own guardsmen, **Artabanus**, finally murdered him in 466 B.C. [3]

The victories of the **Greeks**, which are somewhat exaggerated in their own history notes, at once freed the whole of Hellas and almost all her colonies in Europe and Asia Minor. The **Greeks** who had shown valor played a defensive role since then, being afraid of the return of **Xerxes**. Later on, this brought them the offensive force in the hands of **Alexander**.[4]

The actual number of warriors in this **Persian** army, after deductions of crew and service men, is estimated at 200,000. This figure is still very high – exaggerated by some **Greek** historians - and invasion on such a scale had never before been attempted, although the problem of supplies for such an army had been a negative point.[5]

Our knowledge of the **Persians'** attacks against the West and their grasp over one third of the entire **Greek** civilization is unfortunately limited to that which is given by the **Greek** historians, including **Herodotus**. The invasion of Hellas by the myriads of the **Persian Empire** and their ultimate repulse constitute an event in the history of the world, which is unsurpassed alike in importance and in dramatic grandeur. It was, indeed, the first attempt of the organized East to conquer the less organized West. This bold action opened many attempts in such manner, since **Carthage** made an equally deadly assault on the **Greek** colonies of Sicily.[6]

1. *Tarikh Iran* , Sir P.Sykes, p. 259
2. *A History Of Persia*, Sir Percy Sykes, Vol1, London, pp.195, 196
3. *Chekideh Tarikh Iran*, H. Naraghi, pp. 29,30
4. *A History Of Persia*, Vol. 1, p. 210
5. *A History Of Persia*, Sir Percy Sykes, Vol.1,London, pp.197, 198
6. *A History Of Persia*, p.186

ARTAXERXES I (ARDASHIR I)
(Arda 'Shir)

After **Xerxes**, his assassin named **Artabanus** temporarily takes over the empty throne for seven months until the young king, **Arthaxurces I** (**Artaxerxes I** or **Ardashir I**) takes the throne in 465 B.C. **Ardashir I** entered a plot with the help of **Artabanus**. **Ardashir I** accused his elder brother, **Darius**, for the murder of their father and ordered his execution. Through this sinister plot he took the throne. **Artabanus**, apparently because of a guilty conscience, found the murdering of **Darius** a little too harsh. As a result he revolted against the young **Ardashir I** – greed for power might have been another reason. But, **Megabyzus**, a devoted commander of Persian army stopped **Artabanus** to go further with his attempt and killed him. **Artaxerxes I** is also referred to as **Bahman** in some ancient texts. With the help of **Megabyzus**, his courageous commander of an army of 300,000 men, he defeated **Egyptian** riots. Meanwhile the **Greeks** had come forward to try their hand in battle for one more time with the Persian army far away from its home. But they were utterly pushed back. Had **Artaxerxes I** been a man of character, the Greek colonies in Asia Minor would again have become subject to Persia, and the independence of Hellas would have been seriously hurt. Instead, Persians entered into a peace treaty with the Greeks around 449 B.C.[1] Around this time **Athenians** were engaged in their own fights against **Spartans** for their very existence as a state.

Ardashir I is also referred to as **Deraz Dast** (**Longimanus**). This nickname reflects his tight control all over the land through his spies. He had one riot inside his family by his older brother **Vishtasep** whom he had defeated in 462 B.C. **Artaxerxes I** died in 425 B.C.

XERXES II (KHASHAYAR II)

Xerxes II took the throne after his father, **Ardashir I**. At this time, **Xerxes II** was well known to the **Jewish** people in Babylon where his subjects looked up to him. **Khashayar II** was more in favor of Babylon than Shush that was his official center of command.[2]

Xerxes II had a short rule, since one of his brothers named **Soghdianus** killed him in 358 B.C., while he was drunk. The ex king—**Ardashir I**—had another son named Prince **Okhos (Darius II)**. He was the least capable king of the **Achaemendis Dynasty**. Apparently **Okhos** killed **Soghdianus** in revenge and usurped the throne in 442 B.C. This prince, referred to as **Darius II**, was born out of wedlock. Therefore, he had the epithet of '**Nothus'** (bastard).[3] Once again history is repeated when **Darius II** (or **Okhos**) kills all the other princes and princesses in his court to feel safe from possible assassinations.

Okhos (or Darius II) had two sons who were rivals for the heir. Later on, around 404 B.C., both of his sons **Artaxerxes II** and **Cyrus Jr.** engaged in some fierce rivalry for the throne.

Fear seemed to win the respect and submission of the people; this was not what the foundation of the old empire was set on. Internal scattered rebellions were early signs of civil unrest.

Artaxerxes II *(Ardashir II)* *(Ar 'da 'Shir)*

Artaxerxes II (**Ardashir II**) was born first when, his father, **Darius II (Okhos)** was still a satrap in Hirkania. But **Cyrus Jr.** was born as a prince when **Okhos** had reached his royal rule. **Okhos** died in 404 B.C. Animosity had already started between the brothers. **Artaxerxes II** was very much in love with gold and bought the supports he needed through bribery. **Cyrus the Younger** or (**Jr.**), was a courageous and skilled warrior also experienced in dealing with the affairs of the kingdom. So **Cyrus Jr.** claimed the throne, though he was the second son to the deceased king. He already had arranged for his trained warriors; and to make his position better, he had approached the **Spartans** for assistance. Thus, he opened the way gradually and confronted the extraordinarily huge **Persian** army under his brother. Finally, in 401 B.C., **Cyrus Jr.** was killed in a battle against **Artaxerxes II** over the rule of Persia. **Greeks** learned, through these shameful battles, that their quality of arms and techniques was superior to the quantity of **Persian** soldiers.[4]

On the other hand, the defeat of **Cyrus Jr.** cost Persia dearly in the years that followed. **Cyrus the Younger** had a better character and a greater capacity to take Persia to the glory of **Cyrus The Great**, but he used his insight towards fighting the king rather than supporting him. **Artaxerxes II** did not possess his brother's valor and pride and pushed for a life of luxury and idleness.

Artaxerxes II died at an old age in 358 B.C. after ruling Persia for forty-six years. He had many sons from numerous concubines, but most of them had died before him. He had allowed a direct revival of **Mithraism** during his monarchy, changing the ancient image of peace-loving Mithra to that of the Lord of war.[5]

In his quest to become king himself, **Artaxerxes III (Ardashir III)**, one of many sons of the king, who was also called **Okhos**, destroyed all the possible heirs (princes and even princesses) to ascend the throne in 358 B.C. Persia raided Egypt again. The sad loss of lives was the bitter result for both nations. A politically strong eunuch named **Bagoas** helped **Ardashir III** to achieve many administrative triumphs, but the day came when **Bagoas** became worried about his own execution, and decided to kill **Ardashir III** in 338 B.C in order to save his own life [6]

DARIUS III

In the shock of the grotesque murder of **King Ardashir III**, the next king was chosen to be **Darius III**. However, at the same time a new plot was developing in Asia Minor.

In Macedonia, a vast fertile land beyond Aegean Sea with a growing population, **King Phillip** was gathering forces to invade his neighboring Greece. He did so and defeated the **Greek** army and invaded the whole region about 338 B.C.

On the other hand, the internal conflicts in Persia had made it more vulnerable to outside raids at this time. **Phillip** had plans for Persia, but his death in 336 B.C., caused by his own wife and son, delayed his attack. His son **Alexander,** charged with parricide, assumed power and followed his father's brilliant plans for sudden expansion. In spring of 334 B.C., he led his army in an eleven-year march into Asia from which he did not return.

Thus, **Alexander**'s army wins battlefields one after the other all over Asia Minor and into the **Persian** territories. The brave **Persian** warrior **Arya Barzan** ameliorates the numerous defeats of **Persians** and does achieve some victories against this invading army, but the **Greek** army comes to assist **Alexander**'s men and **Persians** finally submit to defeat.[7]

The last **Achaemendis** king of Persia, **Darius III**, made many historical mistakes in facing **Alexander**. A trained commander in the Persian Army was **Charidemus** who was born in **Athens**. He was knowledgeable about the famous **Phalanx** military formation of **Macedonian** army. **Darius III** ignorantly chose not to adhere to his good advices on the battlefield and paid dearly for this mistake.[8]

Alexander moved triumphantly to Saard in 334 B.C. and around 330 B.C. he invaded Persia. Persepolis, Passargad and Echbatana fell, but he did not stop at this and burned everything down. Some historians believe this could be in retaliation against **Khashayar** or **Xerxes,** who had, about hundred fifty years earlier, defeated the **Greeks** and burned the city of Athens. But, history has shown that **Alexander** did burn and destroy the conquered lands while invading other countries.

After continuous and shameless retreats and hidings, the entourage to **Darius III** lost hope in this king and killed him in 330 B.C. In the eyes of his people , **Darius III** possessed a weak character that parted him from his own people. His greed for luxury had blinded him. At this time **Alexander** shows the good character expected from a great soldier and orders his body to be taken with respect and arranges its proper burial. **Alexander** takes on the throne of Persia and his followers call him **Alexander The Great**. He could truly be great and receive more approbation, if he had not slaughtered women and children on his path during ten years of constant battles. This was how a 200-year great **Aryan** empire of The **Hachaemenesh** came to a halt.

Nevertheless, **Aryans** upheld a high standard of ethics amongst themselves that kept them separate from their neighbors in surrounding lands. **Herodotus** had witnessed and praised the way **Persians** treated wounded **Greek** soldiers who had fought well. Even the valiant enemy soldiers were treated like heroes; their wounds were healed and they were set free. **Persian women** raised their youngsters at home and taught them to always tell the truth.

Polygamy was a trend among men of more wealth. Although women were usually kept covered, they possessed a great deal of influence over their men and the affairs of the family. Even the women of harem—and sometimes eunuchs - maintained direct influence upon **kings**. The interest in luxury was noticeable among the **Aryans**, yet they were very hospitable to the needy or traveling strangers. Breaking the law was severely punished—which is justified by the traditions and the universal history of man at that time. Stealing was punishable by death. Interestingly, such severe punishments were popular among all the ancient nations. Even during the **Queen Victoria** of England the punishment for stealing a sheep was death. In Persia, drinking wine at ceremonies and during formal councils of civic matters was customary—however, the final decisions were reviewed the next day for the approval of majority. Many facts about lifestyle of this period came from stone carvings in Behistun (Beestoon meaning of twenty columns) mountains. These were deciphered by the tireless efforts of the great archeologist Sir Henry Rawlinson. The high quality of character in **Persians** was far superior to their few weaknesses. It is no wonder that the **Persians** managed to create an empire sovereign to the **Sumerians** and the **Turanian** from whom they had received some of their earlier civilization.[9]

With the fall of such empire, **Alexander** of Macedonia takes over a large area in the world that once was dominated by many kings before him. Alexander was fond of sciences and his vision in politics and administration was supreme. Unlike predictions of his teacher, **Aristotle**, he witnessed a great culture in the East and Middle East to which he had shown some proclivity. East was where, he was told, the **Barbarians** would live. His successors after him had more chance to learn about the greatness of the Eastern cultures. Byzantium culture of Asia Minor and east Europe unfortunately preserved this prejudice, which confused the idea of **Barbarians** with that of peoples who did not speak **Greek**.[10]

Alexander is said to have been moved by reading the epitaph on the tomb stone of **Cyrus The Great** that said:" Do not covet this piece of earth and grudge me not this monument, whoever you may be, since I brought to Persia all of this glory."[11]

Alexander had ordered thousands of marriages between his soldiers and **Persian princesses** to expiate the agonies he had caused.

This was an old recipe to make peace between conqueror and the conquered. Many of these political marriages dissolved after his own death. He died in 322 B.C., under fatigue and mental pressure. He had been grieving for the loss of a close friend and had indulged himself in excess drinking. **Alexander** was only 32 years old.

1. *A History Of Persia*, Vol. 1, London, p. 214, 215
2. *Tarikh Mardom Iran* , A. Zarrinkoob, p. 176
3. *Tarikh-e-Iran*, P. Sykes, p. 290
4. *A History of Persia*, Vol.1, pp. 222-230
5. *Chekideh Tarikh Iran*, H. Naraghi, p. 30
6. *A History Of Persia*, Vol.1, p. 233
7. *Pictorial History Of Iran* , Amini Sam, p. 147, 151
8. *The Ifs of Iran's History*, By Dr. M. Javanbakht, Isfahan, Iran, 2002, p. 47
9. *Tarikh-e-Iran*, Vol.1, translated by Fakhr Daie, Tehran, pp. 222-232
10. *A History Of Europe*, by J.M. Roberts, 1997, U.S.A., p. 93
11. *Tarikh Mardom Iran*, p. 225

CHAPTER FIVE

The Seleucian (Seleucidan)
(Se 'Lushan)
(330 B.C. – 250 B.C.)

Towards the end of the 4th Century B.C. Asia Minor, Middle East, and the area near Indus River were facing a new era. The **Seleucian Dynasty** (pronounced *Solu 'Kieh* in Farsi) dominated Persia for about 80 years (their domination over other lands varied). Following the unexpected death of the tireless warrior, **Alexander**, three of his army generals divided his conquered lands between them. He had not contemplated about running these new territories and had a lot to learn about the science of running large nations. His sudden death did not help the successors who cared even less about restoration of peace or commerce on their path. Thus, The **Seleucian Dynasty** became the heirs to the lands taken by **Alexander The Great**.

However, at this period in western hemisphere, very little political turmoil was happening. Other parts of the world were not so involved in chaos. Especially where New Mexico and Arizona are today, signs of early village life had just begun to appear. First signs of irrigation and water canals in this part of the world are just being implemented around 300 B.C.

In the Eastern hemisphere, **Greeks** had dominated an immense ill-defined area between Mediterranean and the Indian Ocean. But, **Alexander**'s invasions did not have much justification except fame and greed, since all the conquered lands were treated as colonies and their inhabitants as subjects with lesser human values. Ironically, the **Greek** philosophers who were banished by their own kings had to take refuge in the colonies of Mesopotamia, Persia, and finally the Far East.[1] It seems that for the humanitarian treatment of newly dominated lands, only **Cyrus The Great** stands to be the righteous conqueror of all time. (This admirable king set such high standards in rightful treatment of people that are still hard to follow for many rulers.)

At this period, one of the three generals of **Alexander**, called **Seleucus**, puts up a ghastly fight and receives the kingdom of Persia after many years of rivalry between relatives and other claimants. Even the other two generals were toppled. This is how **Seleucus** takes the control of entire Asia Minor, Persia, and Egypt in 301 B.C.

He married **Apamea**, the daughter of a **Persian** army general. These types of marriages were very common all over the world and reduced tensions and benefited both nations for selecting the future heirs.[2]

Seleucus attempted another invasion of India, to copy **Alexander**. But, this time the **Greeks** were repulsed by **Chandragupta** the wise king of India. **Seleucus** had to forfeit most territories that **Alexander** had secured and retreat fast.[3]

After him his son **Antiochus** takes over. His seditious wife later poisons him in 264 B.C. It is true to say that major influent cultures in the world around this time belong to Persia, Greece, Egypt, and Rome. In other parts of the world smaller civilizations were still in process of forming urbanism, but there were not much signs of any rising empires before this period. The first East Asia's united empire was **Qin** in China around 221B.C..This coincides with the rise of **Buddhism** in India around 200 B.C. It is interesting to know that **Hinduism** was the dominant world-view in India around 500 B.C.[4]

But, it was **Mithraism** and **Zoroastrianism** that were popularly growing from Middle East to Asia Minor and Europe and, later on, into **Roman** and **Greek** civilizations. The **Romans** took the religion of **Mithraism** from **Aryans of Persia** and continued its practice for centuries. **Mithraism** spread to Europe through wars with Persia. It grew Initially between the ordinary people and soldiers in Rome and gradually expanded into the elite and noble layers of **Roman** and **Greek** societies. The **Roman kings** did not resist this eastern ideology, because through its emphasis on the divine position of kings in the universe, **Roman** rulers would be representing the power of God on earth. For about four centuries after the death of **Christ**, the religion of **Mithraism** was dominant in Europe. Until **Theodosius**, the **Roman Emperor**, ordered this religion to be abandoned and **Christianity** to replace it in 394 C.E. There are many older temples belonging to **Mehr** worshipers that still exist in Europe, although most of them are revamped still some greater statues and monuments are left such as the statue of **Mehr** sacrificing a cow for the enrichment of Earth, which is now kept in Vatican.[5]

Seleucian kings ruled about 248 years, out of which about eighty years was spent in Persia and the rest in Syria and Asia Minor. Finally, the **Romans** and **Aryans of Parthia** started pushing them out of their lands.

1.   *A History Of Civilizations*, by Fernard Braudel, Translated by Richard Mayne, 1993, Paris, p. 43

2.   *Chekideh Tarikh Iran*, pp. 32, 33

3.   *Tarikh-e-Iran Zamin*, by Dr. M.J. Mashkur, Eshraghi Prints, 1987, Tehran, p. 58

4.   *The Encyclopedia of World History*, Peter N. Stearns, p. 49

5.   *Tarikh Iran*, P. Sykes, Tehran, pp. 528, 529

CHAPTER SIX

Parthian Dynasty (Ashkanian)
(249 B.C. – 220 A.D.)

Parthians lived in the northeastern region of the Plateau of Pars (Persia) – Khorasan and Mazandaran. As mentioned earlier, these were the same group of **Aryans** who had chosen to remain in the northern areas of the plateau close to the Caspian Sea and today's Khorasan.

In 249 B.C., some united tribes in this area stood up against the harsh rulings of a new **Seleucian** ruler called **Pherecles**. This particular uprise, led by **Arashk I**, (**Arsaces I**) resulted in establishment of The **Ashkanian (Arsacid)** or **Parthian Dynasty**. During the zenith of this dynasty, over 400 years, the lands and power that were lost since **Darius The Great** were recaptured and added into Persia. **Ashkanian** or **Parthian Dynasty** was in direct contact with the **Hellenic** culture of the ancient Greece, that is why the names of **Persian kings** have equivalents in **Greek**.

It is interesting to know that history of Persia and China also connects together around this age. The nomadic peril of the savage hordes of **Scythians** or nomads of China (under the name of **Yue-Chi**) is not only felt by **Persians**, but is evenly felt by other nations in the history of the world. At first these nomadic and savage tribes were defeated by the **Huns** of China (**Hiung-Nu** in Chinese term) in 250 B.C. under a great ruler called **Tsin**, who restored the central power and ordered the construction of the great wall of China to protect his kingdom against the nomadic enemies. **Scythians**, were pagans who held their women in common and devoured their aged relatives. After being subdued by **Tsin**, **Scythians** ran away from China and penetrated into Afghanistan and Sistan area (they were called **Sakas** in Farsi) and kept raiding northeastern borders of Persia. They were also called **Turanian** - this name is commonly used by historians of east and west, and in some texts is shown in the form of **Tartars** (or **Tatars**) as well.[1]

1. *A History Of Persia*, by Sir Percy Sykes, Vol.1, Macmillan & Co, 1921, London, p. 333

Arsaces I (Arashk I) (Ar 'Ashk)

The first king of **Ashkanian (Parthian) Dynasty** is **Arashk I**. The courageous **Arashk I** (or **Arsaces I** as the **Greeks** called him) is the founder of **Ashkanian Dynasty** (or **Arsacid Dynasty**). He called himself a direct descendant of **Artaxerxes II** of **Achaemendis Dynasty**. Apparently, this desire to be connected to a royal blood is known in **Persian** history to provide a social legitimacy for new rulers.[1]

Arashk I was killed in a battle in 247 B.C. and **Arsaces II** (or **Tir Dad**) and then **Arsaces III** (or **Ardavan I**) succeeded him in 209 B.C. Persia under these rulers was getting back more territories from the **Seleucian** rulers. **Roman Empire** also started its hostility with **Macedonians (Greeks)** around 205 B.C. **Phraates I** or **Farhad I** succeeded **Arsaces III** in 181 B.C. However, it was only during **Mehrdad I** or **Mithridates I**, in 170 B.C., that **Ashkanian** grew to be strong enough to put an end to **Greek** and **Roman** domination for centuries in this part of the world. **Mithridates I** regained many lost territories. Armenia, which was a province of **Persian Empire** as per the Behistun inscriptions of **Xerxes**, was taken back during this period. Finally **Mehrdad I** (**Mithradates I**) died of old age in 138 B.C. after years of service with honor – a phenomenon not very much seen in the history of this era.

It was around this period and particularly in 140 B.C. that China received its first knowledge of the West. Under **Han dynasty** new missions were dispatched in every direction. Some reached as far as **Parthia**, which was termed **An-Sih** (the Chinese version of **Arsaces**).[2]

After the gradual fall of the **Seleucian Dynasty**, the **Romans** were getting stronger. **Demetrius** the emperor of Rome, having the false percept that he is always victorious and being boastful of his earlier victories in the area, invaded the **Parthian** borders in Asia Minor during the reign of **Mithradates I** - the sixth king of this dynasty. This area seemed to be growing very fast around 141 B.C. To the surprise of Rome, although **Demetrius** lost this battle and was captured by **Parthian** soldiers, he was treated fairly. **Demetrius** stayed in the new land. After changing his nationality, he was allowed to marry a **Persian** princess.

Phraates II (Farhad II) (Far 'Haad)

Farhad II took the throne in 138 B.C. **Antiochus**, the new **Roman** king, attacked Persia in 129 B.C. about nine years into the ruling of **Farhad II**. This was supposed to be in retaliation of **Demetrius**'s failures, but **Antiochus** was also defeated. Thus, humiliated **Antiochus** threw himself from a cliff to avoid capture. At this time the remnants of **Seleucian** kingdom in Macedonia was also suppressed and vanished forever.

When **Farhad II** died, his successor **Mithridates II** (**Mehrdad II**) ruled Persia until 88 B.C. E. H. Parker writes about him and the Far East in his book: *Chinese Knowledge of Early Persia*. **Mithridates II** was the first **Iranian king** that officially allowed presence of the first foreign ambassador in his court – a **Chinese** ambassador.[3]

Mithradates II crushed the rebellions of Nomads – believed to be of **Sakas** (**Scythians**) around Afghanistan – and then rushed to the west and put an end to the revolting army of **Himerus** the viceroy of Babylon. **Parthian Empire** had grown again to be recognized by the East and West as a major force in the world. Consequently, the first friendly confrontations with proposals for alliance were made between **Parthians**, **Romans**, and **Chinese** ambassadors between 100 – 88 B.C. (These empires were the only superpowers of the world at that time.

Persia, an expanding superpower, regained territories lost since the **Achaemenid** dynasty. From some artifacts and coins discovered in the Himalayan Mountains, new evidence exists that proves the **Parthian (Ashkanian)** influence in that area as well.[4]

The fact about the recovery of **Parthian** artifacts in remote places reflects the advancement in technology and means of travel that had caused farther expansion of cultures and people. The world population, then, growing at a larger rate since the early migration of **Aryans**, is estimated at 300 million.[5]

Persia, then, was neighboring western borders of Mongolian China. **Pan Chao**, a **Chinese** emperor, sent some of his trusted politicians to Persia and Rome. **Kan Ying** was a traveling ambassador who knew the **Romans** were eager for future trades. Also, **Parthian Empire** had shown a willingness to enhance trade - beginning of the **Silk Road** legacy. For this reason better roads were built with Caravan-Saras (rest areas) for travelers and their animals. Persia itself was strategically located – and still is – as a bridge between the Orient and Europe.[6]

1.   *Chekideh Tarikh Iran*, H Naraghi, p. 34
2.   *A History of Persia*, by Sir Percy Sykes, Vol.1, Macmillan & Co., 1921,London, p. 339
3.   *A History Of Persia*, Vol. 1, p. 339
4.   *Tarikh-e-Iran*, Vol.1, P. Sykes, Translated by F. Daie, Tehran, p.450
5.   *A Short History Of The World*, By Geoffrey Blainey, 2002, Chicago, p. 37
6.   *Tarikh-e-Iran*, Vol.1,Tehran, Translated by F. Daie pp. 525-527

Phraates III (Farhad III)

The fame of The Silk Road expanded into reign of Phraates III. But, at the time **Farhad III** took over the Persian throne, there was already a great uproar in Europe against the **Roman** emperor by some slaves under the influence of **Spartacus**. Unfortunately, courage and leadership of a **Roman** general called **Pompey** about 74 B.C. suppressed this revolt against the tyrant emperor. But later on in Persia, about 50 B.C., two of his sons killed **Farhad III**. After a short period of ruling by his first son, the second one took over. He was **Orodes.**

Orodes

Orodes, who had killed his own father to reach power, finds out about an imminent danger of invasion by **Romans** into the western borders of Persia. **Crassus** who was the commander of Syria under the **Roman Empire** had planned this sudden attack. He was a professional soldier with a strong army that had already defeated the **Parthian (Persian)** viceroys in some of the border provinces in Euphrates. He was delegated by the **Romans** to command the Euphrates area bordering Syria. The news came to **Orodes** and he selected the famous Persian commander **Surena** to stop **Crassus**.

On the other hand, around the same date, an embassy was sent from **Orodes** to deliver a proposal for retreat to the **Romans**. **Crassus** sarcastically replied that his answer would be given at Seleucia (a major commanding post of **Ashkanian** dynasty), whereupon the leader of the embassy laughed and said, "Hair will grow on the palm of my hand before you will see Seleucia."[1]

Crassus started his great undertaking, but **Surena** won this battle and destroyed the **Roman** army. Even the enemy had praised the outstanding valor and combat tactics of **Surena**. But, **Orodes** had become cowardly intimidated and fearful of the rapidly growing fame of this gallant general, who had become a national hero. Therefore, shortly upon his return, **Surena** gets unjustly executed. At this time **Caesar** of the **Roman Empire** is furiously gathering his consultants to start a serious campaign against Persia (Parthia). But his own trusted men, **Octavius** and **Cassius**, assassinate him in 44 B.C. and this plan comes to a halt.[2]

Many historians or sociologists, like Hasan Naraghi, point out that one of the causes of the fall of **Persian Empire** has been the unjust removal of the popular heroes and leaders who posed a threat to the monarchs. Consequently, this country or sometimes the whole world have continuously been deprived of their outstanding services.[3]

Phraates IV (Farhad IV)

Orodes selects his elder son **Farhad IV** to replace him on the throne. The old king had to resign because of the stress, since his courageous son, **Pacorus**, was killed in 83 B.C. in a combat against the **Romans**. But, **Phraates IV (Farhad IV)** viciously orders all his brothers even his own father, **Orodes**, to be killed. Thus, the old **Orodes** finally shares the same fate that he had caused for his own father. Now **Farhad IV (Phraates IV)** could take control without fear of similar family jealousy in his land.

Phraates IV instituted a reign of terror in the country, which drove many important nobles away from his court. The rule of this tyrant had made many officials to defect. **Monaeses** was a known general under **Pacorus** who fled to **Marcus Anthony,** the **Roman** commander, and suggested to him that conditions were favorable for an invasion of **Parthia**.

In the years that followed, **Phraates IV** fought against many **Roman** invasions, around Azerbaijan (west of Caspian Sea in Persia), which were led by **Marcus Anthony.** Although the latter was pushed back to his love **Cleopatra** in Rome, **Farhad IV** did not gain much trust and respect of **Persians**. Ironically, **Farhad IV** once had to flee a coup against him, but he finally returned to power after 3 years of seclusion in mountains. In 23 B.C., he entered a peace agreement with **Augustus** who was the **Roman** emperor. Thus, a long period of truce started between these two empires bordering each other in Asia and Europe.[4]

Farhad IV had a **Roman** mistress called **Muse**, who had born him a son many years ago, but the mother and the son eventually poisoned this king. In 2 C.E, this son takes the throne and is referred to as **Farhad V**. The most important historical fact about his reign is that it coincided with the birth of **Jesus Christ** in Bethlehem. Initially refusing, **Augustus** agreed to recognize the monarchy of **Farhad V**, if the latter agreed to refrain from the total affairs of Armenia. This historical debate was conducted in 1 C.E. Armenia, as history reveals, was to be constantly invaded by East and West as a prize for ambitious rulers.

Farhad V (Phraates V) also referred to as **Farhad Jr.**, was hated by his subjects. This was partly because of his foreign Roman habits and partly because he had forced official honors being paid to his **Roman** mother, whose image and effigy was placed on the coinage. He was killed.

Parthians were, as the term "Philhellen" appearing on their coins, very much familiar with the western **Greek** and **Roman** ideology. A freedom of religion and trade had been given to all the city-states and provinces under Parthian domain. **Jewish** communities, though in a lesser degree, were granted municipal independence. Traditions strictly ruled so that no one without a royal blood in his veins stood a chance of the throne. The Senate, composed of spiritual and temporal lords, would check on the **Parthian** kings.[5]

The world history is filled with bloodshed and fearless revenges. Beside the outbreak of tribal fights, another reason for bloodshed among the royal families was the greed for absolute power of the heirs or princes, who committed these crimes. The fact that most of the times such acts would go unpunished, did provoke their reoccurrence.

Vonones II, residing outside Persia, was one of the **Persian** princes and a possible heir to the throne. Being called upon by the power of the Senate and **Persian** courts to take the empty throne, **Vonones II** came to Parthia. He was also raised differently in the **Roman** and **Greek** courts and his Roman manners did not fit his position among the **Persian** priests and elite social figures in his **Parthian** nation. Therefore, **Ardavan (Artabanus)** from the **Medes** families who was the ruler of Azerbaijan, a province in north of Persia, was chosen to replace him in 16 C.E by the support and direct invitation of the heads of the states and the **Magis** in Persia.

Ardavan (Artabanus) (Ar 'davan)

He also claimed to be a direct descendant of **Parthian** or **Ashkanian** **kings**. In 36 C.E **Ardavan** personally invaded Armenia – a buffer state between Europe and Middle East. This had come after loosing his both sons in the battles connected with this area. At the same time **Vitellius** of Roman territories raided the borders of Euphrates and **Ardavan** had to immediately retreat from Armenia. Through some deceitful arrangements between Rome and his own men (including **Tirdad** or **Tiridates** - a prince in his own court), he ended up powerless in Hirkania, today's Mazandaran near Caspian Sea. **Tirdad** took the control that did not last much. **Ardavan** managed to gather his faithful guards and planned a counter attack to restore his kingdom again. Some massacres against the **Jews** happened during his reign. **Persians** were not generally content during 24 years of **Ardavan**'s kingdom. **Ardavan** ruled Persia until his death in 40 C.E.[6]

History of the world repeatedly shows deceit from trusted men. Sadly enough, it still can happen through our negligence or indifference that is even more dreadful. A Russian writer once said: "One should not worry about his friends, since they may only betray him. Further, he may not fear his enemies, since they can only kill him once. Instead, one must be afraid of the indifferent companions who shamelessly close their eyes to everyday mischief". The fact of the matter is that no patriot can stay indifferent to things happening to his people and his land. For those who live outside their native countries, the distance should never be used as an excuse for their indifference to their homeland.[7]

May be this continuous apathy towards human rights has permitted many conflicts. Universal declaration of human rights, conceived in 1948 by **The United Nations**, upholds the human dignity and expects all governments to recognize the most basic elements of humanity like freedom of speech. Yet there is a constant breach of these sacred and primal rights in all the countries, including those that blame others for not upholding them.

1. *A History Of Persia*, by Sir Percy Sykes, Vol.1, Macmillan,1921, p. 347
2. *Chekideh Tarikh Iran*, pp. 35, 36
3. *Jame Shenasi Khodemani*, Hasan Naraghi, 3rd edition, 2003, Tehran, Akhtaran, pp. 79, 119
4. *Tarikh-e-Iran*, pp. 488-490
5. *A History Of Persia*, Vol.1. London, p. 365
6. *Chekideh Tarikh Iran* , p. 38
7. *Negah Az Biroun*, By Dariush Homayoon, 1984, U.S.A., p. 38

Volgases I (Blash I)

Ashkanian period is filled with agitated quarrels and bloodshed between those claiming power. About this time, Persia seems to be caught in a civil war. Until **Blash I (Vologases I)** put an end to it. He was the eldest son to **Vonones II** from a **Greek** concubine, who reigned for a few months. Diverting the public attention to the affairs abroad the country, the first thing **Blash I** thought to accomplish was to set out for Armenia again. By this invasion, he quickly united all scattered tribes and provinces inside Persia into one unified force. But new troubles started when he conquered Armenia in 51C.E. and chose **Tirdad**, another prince in **Ashkanian** dynasty, to rule this land. Fortunately, through a political agreement between Rome and Persia, this new king of Armenia was to receive his crown from the hands of **Nero,** the **Caesar** of Rome. This friendly gesture in 66CE between the nations actually created another peaceful period that lasted for 50 years and enhanced cultural ties.[1]

However, **Parthians** or **Ashkanian** were not getting any stronger on the social or cultural grounds. The true heritage of **Persian** identity was somewhat covered underneath the **Hellenism** of the **Greek**. The **Persian** language (Old Farsi) did not evolve or spread much, and the kings were too involved in their internal and external struggles. The religion of **Parthians** was not fully set. Some even had accepted **Christianity**. The emphasis was laid on reviving and reciting of Avesta by the order of **Volagases I**, which helped to shape the language and heritage of Persia. The **Parthian** culture and civilization of this era is assorted with that of the **Greek** and **Romans**. There was also a profound belief in magic, and innovations, which recalls the ancient faith of Babylon. The fact mentioned by **Plutarch** that **Greek** was widely taught and **Greek** plays were enjoyed may be true, because a substantial native literature is not available from this era—these **Greek** plays were probably enjoyed mostly by the elite royal families in Persia; however, such entertainment could not necessarily prove the broad usage of the **Greek** tongue instead of **Old Farsi.** There is no substantial **Greek** literature found in Iran either to prove its popular use in this era.[2]

On the other hand, Rome was growing in armed forces while Persia (Parthia) was becoming weaker due to internal conflicts. After **Blash I,** who died in 77 A.D., **Pacorus** sat on the throne and the country faced another range of chaos and internal wars. When

Pacorus received the kingdom of Persia the country was torn among several leaders who claimed to be the king. He delegated one of his sons, **Exedares**, to become the new **Armenian** king and did this without asking the traditional approval of the **Caesar** of Rome.

Osroes (Khosro)

When **Pacorus** died in 105 A.D., among several prospective heirs **Khosro (Osroes)** finally got the control. It was during him that the long peace period with Rome came to an end. The **Caesar** of Rome, then, was **Trajan**. He was an opportunistic commander and was selfishly burning to imitate the career of a great conqueror like **Alexander**. Naturally, he was not content with the recent replacement of the **Armenian** king by the unilateral order of **Pacorus**. Therefore, **Khosro**, who knew about this and strived to improve relations between powers, replaced the **Armenian** king again with a **Persian** noble man called **Partha Masiris**. Then he sought **Trajan's** approval by sending him many gifts and asking him to crown this noble man according to the previous agreements or traditions. For **Trajan** who was waiting for a chance to try his luck at the battlefields against **Persians**, this came as an excuse to break the peace. He did not accept the gifts and had **Partha Masiris** and his delegates ambushed and killed. This portended war. His own people scolded **Trajan** for dishonoring peace and did not approve his brutality. Never the less he invaded Armenia, Babylonia, and Ctesiphon—west of Mesopotamia, while **Khosro** remained silent but was patiently following his moves.

Trajan army continued triumphantly south bond to the shores of Persian Gulf. Meanwhile, **Khosro** sent his special attaché to meet with the leaders of occupied territories along the path and arranged a series of uprises against this traveling **Roman** army. Then Emperor **Trajan** saw the danger of being surrounded by the **Parthian** army. Especially when he was too far away from his homeland and decided to retreat fast. **Khosro** got Ctesiphon back; this city was **Parthians** winter capitol. About this time, **Trajan** died in 117A.D. and **Augustus** took the throne as the new **Caesar**. Soon he had to face his own problems with the surrounding nations attacking his state. **Trajan** reluctantly abandoned all the **Mesopotamian** and **Armenian** lands and withdrew from Persia. This saved both nations from further bloodshed.[3]

Volagases II (Blash II) and then **Volagases III (Blash III)** took the throne. It was **Blash III** who decided to break the peace this time. He invaded Armenia for more tribute. This nation had played the role of a political prize for **Roman** and **Persian** kings during this period of history. These series of combats did not really bring any satisfying results for either side. **Blash III** died in 191 A.D., **Blash IV (Volagases IV)** took over after his father's death and reigned until 209 A.D. After him his two sons **Blash V** and **Arbatanus V (Ardavan V)** took over by dividing the nation into East and West. The great empire of Parthia or Persia, now weakened by this partition, was gradually approaching its last days around 220 A.D. **Caracalla**, the **Emperor of Rome** in 211 A.D., congratulated his senate members for witnessing a divided Persia caught in civil war. **Caracalla** had planned to ambush **Ardavan V** in an official ceremony. **Caracalla** was insisting to be married to a **Parthian** princess for a lasting peace between the countries. **Ardavan V** finds out about this vicious plan and flees the scene of the ceremony. **Caracalla,** who had indulged himself in continuous raids against the towns and villages—especially in the short absence of **Ardavan V**—received an early death while still on Persian lands. **Ardavan V** who had returned with his army of warriors found about the death of **Caracalla** and offered peace and demanded heavy retribution. His offer was rejected by **Romans** and war broke out which ended with absolute victory of **Parthian** army, consequently heavier retribution was agreed by the **Romans**. The end for the **Parthian** or **Ashkanian** dynasty came around 220 A.D. by the hands of a ruler named **Artaxerxes** or **Ardashir** from Pars. He finally invaded and conquered all the **Parthian** territories under **Ardavan V** and killed him in the last battle east of Ahwaz in South of Iran. This was the completion of the downfall of Parthia.[4]

Parthians or **Ashkanian** ruled Persia and Asia Minor as well as lands in East close to the Himalayan mountains for about 500 years. Their leaders were great soldiers, but when it came to building the country from within, they were mostly idle. We do not see much industrial achievements or artistic renovations from this period.[5] Also, women's civic rights and prestige were withdrawn by social changes.

Zorastherianism as well as **Mithraism** of this period did affect the worldviews of **Persians** as nature worshippers who used these natural elements in their art and culture, however during this dynasty not much change occurred over this basic foundation. There was also a profound belief in magic and invocations, which recalls the ancient faith of **Babylonians**. The literature and arts seemed to have not flourished due to continuous battles, though Persia familiarized itself with the **Hellenic** ideologies. The coins in circulation were not of gold, but silver or copper. They mostly had both **Old Pahlavi** and **Greek** language used on them. Personal character of **Parthians** was high. They treated prisoners kindly and generally observed their pledged word, and kept treaties when concluded. Their clothing was a robe like the **Medes** with baggy trousers. For head-dress they used a ribbon terminating in two long ends or else a rounded tiara. Their music included the flute, the pipe, and the drum, and their feasts frequently closed with dancing. Their bread was leavened , light , and porous, and was known and esteemed in Rome. They drank wine made from dates. The position of women, as usual in the polygamous East, was subordinate. The monarch, like the **Achaemendis kings**, had a chief wife, who was recognized as the **Queen**, and a multitude of **concubines** (many of whom were **Greeks**). The Harem system generally prevailed. Eunuchs of **Ashkanian (Parthian)** Dynasty never obtained the influence that existed under the **Achaemenians (Achaemendis)** Dynasty.[6]

1.   *A History Of Persia*, Sir Percy Sykes, Vol.1. 1921, MacMillan, London, pp. 376-379
2.   *A History Of Persia*, Vol. 1, MacMilan Publishers, p. 369
3.   *Tarikh-e-Iran*, Vol.1, Tehran, Sir P. Sykes, pp. 514-520
4.   *Tarikh-e-Iran*, Vol 1, Tehran, pp. 522-525
5.   *Chekideh Tarikh Iran*, H. Naraghi, pp. 38-40
6.   *A History of Persia*, Sir Percy Sykes, Vol.1, London, pp. 364-372

CHAPTER SEVEN

The Sassanid (Sassanian) Dynasty
(Saasa 'Niaan)
(220 A.D. - 652 A.D.)

This era reflects overflow of a new principal; a gradual introduction of divinity and its fundamental doctrines in the courts of Persia.

Sassan was a learned man in the temple of **Anahita** or **Nahid** (ancient nature-goddess who conveyed fertility) in Estakhr near Shiraz in the province of Pars. **Sassan** had priesthood interests in the temples of **Zarathustra**. He had a son called **Baabak** or **Paapak** who ruled the area with moderate popularity and after his death, his son **Artaxerxes** or **Ardashir** gathered his troops against the falling **Ashkanian King (Ardavan V)** and in 224 A.D. suppressed all the internal resistance and called himself the new king of entire Persia. Because of his ancestor this dynasty is referred to as **Sassanid** or **Sassanian**.

Contrary to the earlier dynasties of **Achaemendis** and **Parthian** who practiced a more secular system of government, **Sassanid** kings believed a great deal in the power of religion and laid the lasting foundation for mixing religion and politics together in order to run the nation. **Ardashir** or **Artaxerxes** is the first king in **Persian** history that practically allows religion—**Zorastherianism** in particular—to mix with the political doctrines. He practically restored to the **Magi** or **Mogh (Zorastherian** elite **Clergy)** their privileges as the council of the nation.[1]

ARTAXERXES (ARDASHIR)
(Arda Sheer)

The mythical tales of **Ferdowsi**—as discussed earlier—fundamentally connect the spiritual power of **Bahman** or **Ardashir** to the heavens, thus insinuating the philosophical changes in the **Persian** state of mind by placing grace in the existence of their kings.[2]

Through **Ferdowsi's** *Shahnameh*, the mythical **Persian** hero, **Rostam**, stays immortal. He managed to destroy the old enemy of Iran called **Isfandiar**. The latter apparently had a son called **Bahman** who was referred to as **Ardashir Deraz Dast (Longimanus)**. This mythological figure finds his historical place right in this era, emphasizing a change in the **Persian** kingdom. He is known to be the same **Ardashir** who founded the **Sassanid Dynasty**.[3]

Ardashir—also called **Artaxerxes** or **Bahman**—claimed to be a descendant of **Achaemendis Dynasty**. This is another occasion where **Iranians** find dignity for the new king through the chain of blood within the royal family.

Shortly afterward, **Ardashir** triumphantly takes **Medes** territories and Armenia back from the **Roman** Cesar called **Severus Alexander** in 232 A.D. and then enters a peace treaty with that country.

Later, he chose a group of the elite **Zorastherian** high priests, referred to as **Mogh,** to consult with his governors in running the nation and he advised his own crown prince, **Shapur I,** to treat religion and politics as inseparable. **Christianity** was not much tolerable in his states, especially after **Constantine** had declared **Christianity** as the official religion of the **Roman** Empire.[4]

Interestingly, many historians find this particular mixture of religion and politics to be one of the fundamental elements of corruption in the social fabric of the **Sassanid** society. History shows that these counselors (**Moghs** or **Mobeds**) mostly affected the fluid boundaries of the spheres of authority of rival heirs to the throne. The results were mostly bloody. At the same time, in Europe, a different trend may be seen while the senatorial aristocracy of Rome was the pivotal point of power and reluctant to give in to the domination of **Christianity**.

However, this superpower in the western hemisphere had its own flaws. One may see that **Roman Empire** was also deteriorating from within, although it produced men in abundance that were administrators, generals, and supervisors of building and engineering works, advocates and judges. The government they ran, however, was often harsh and brutal. Slavery was a part of **Roman** institutional violence, which accelerated its decay from within. Between 226 A.D. and 379, there were thirty-five **Roman emperors**, while only nine **Sassanid** kings ruled in Persia.[5]

In *Farhang Irani Pish Az Islam*, M. Muhammadi explains how the clusters of Religion and Politics grew closer in **Sassanid** Persia. **Ardeshir** had advised his son, **Shapur**, not to forget that Divinity and Kingdom are like two brothers watching over and needing each other.[6]

Interestingly, this point of view, to some extent, has held its grip on the social and political movements that followed in the history of Iran.

Shapur I

He succeeded his father in 240 A.D.—it is mentioned in the historical texts that this king possessed a striking beauty in appearance and character, but this is not confirmed.

Soon the news about **Ardashir**'s death started a revolt in Armenia and surrounding areas, which **Shapur I** successfully ended. The next rebellion was from Hatra in Mesopotamia, which had been under **Persian** territories for centuries. **Shapur I** knew about the strong walls surrounding the city that had stopped **Roman emperors** before; so he sent a messenger to the daughter of the rebel king. She was ready to betray her father's castle for the promise of marriage with the great King. Hatra was duly captured by this act of treachery, but

Shapur I broke his pledge and handed over the traitress to the executioner. Then, he found himself ready to push the **Romans** back into their European borders.[7]

Persia was, once again, in a position to be of threat to the Roman Empire, its neighbor in the Western Europe. Around this time in medieval Europe **Valerian** was the **Emperor** of Rome. He had come closer to **Persian** border and took residence in Antioch in 256 A.D. He initially favored the **Christians** to a degree they themselves found surprising, but soon his attitude at this new location changed. The growth of **Christianity**, particularly amongst the most influential sectors of society, was disturbing to imperial regimes of a conservative cast.[8] Thus **Valerian**'s popularity amongst these **Christians** seemed more sparse and contradictory. Valerian did finally attack the Persian garrisons inside the Persian borders. His information about the strength of Persian military muscle proved to be underestimated.

In 260 A.D., **Shapur I** ended his long battles of twenty years and victoriously captured **Valerian** as his prisoner. **Shapur I** did not show him the mercy and fair treatment that was expected from a great **Persian** king - the trend that **Cyrus The Great** had started seemed to be forgotten after all these years. Although, **Mehrdad I** of **Ashkanian** dynasty had shown **Demetrius**, the **Roman Emperor**, such mercy about 400 years before. **Shapur I** apparently climbed his horse using **Valerian** as his mounting platform. This mean act is recorded in history in the form of stone carvings and paintings in Passargad.

At this time **Adineh** or **Odenathus** the ruler of Tedmer, a famous Arab city in Mesopotamia—referred to as Palmyra by western historians—found himself in a great eminent danger. Therefore, as a common gesture of friendship and diplomacy, he sent many gifts and treaties to **Shapur I** who arrogantly rejected them. He wanted **Adineh** to come and kneel at his feet in person. This pretentious gesture caused **Shapur I** a great deal later when his troops were coming back from their battles passing through Euphrates River. It was then that he suddenly was confronted by Tedmer's army and sustained embarrassing losses; and he barely made it back to Persia.

In 263 A.D., **Adineh** (**Odenathus**) invaded the **Persian** major city of Madayen (west of Persia) and after his death his beautiful wife **Zenobia** took over Palmyra. This land that was newly expanded and was bordering Persia from east became allies with Rome against Persia—mostly because of the past demeaning attitudes of **Shapur I** and his officials. **Zenobia** had a political mind and managed to bring the neighboring Egypt to her submission and ruled for a short period. But her semi-independent kingdom of Palmyra did not last when she refused advices from her counselors—regarding her strong neighboring Persia—and finally lost her hastily prepared battle and her kingdom to **Persians**.[9]

Shapur I died in 272 A.D. He had wisely dedicated his last years in construction rather than fighting. Shushtar Dam was built under his supervision and by the assistance of **Roman** engineers and workers in his capture. He also built famous cities such as Bei Shapur near Kazerun—between Bushehr and Shiraz—and Nei Shapur in Khorasan that was a center for science and education for centuries. It is fair to view building of dams and irrigation canals and maintaining safe trade routes a great endeavor, considering the limited degree of technological achievements of man at that age. These acts by the **Persian Kings** were quite unlike the **Egyptian Pharos**, who built most of their monuments by forced labor and for their own glory and purpose. One of the major historical points during the reign of **Shapur I** is the birth of **Mani** in 215 A.D. **Mani** is the great ideologue that introduced new visions based on **Mithraism**, which later influenced many nations in The Middle East as well as Europe. However, **Shapur I** who was not very much in support of this new religion had exiled **Mani** to Tibet and Indu valley.[10]

Hormisdas (Hormuzd I)

Unlike the two previous kings of **Sassanid Dynasty**, who had restored **Persian** supremacy in much of Near East and Asia Minor, the following heirs were not capable of running the nation against the surrounding enemies. They were mostly indolent and lacked the individual motivation for growth of their nation.

Contrary to the declining **Sassanid** in the Middle East and Asia Minor, a new power in the Far East was emerging. **Yamato** was the earliest state in Japan in 265 A.D. that goes back to this period, but its

100

exact location is still not very clear.[11] China was also standing with several scattered regional kingdoms.

However, around same time in Persia, **Hormuzd I** the ruler of Khorasan took over the empire after **Shapur I**, but his kingdom did not last due to his sudden death in 275 A.D. A series of future rulers, like **Bahram I**, took over the throne, but unfortunately none had the mind and insight of running this huge country. When **Bahram I** succeeded **Hormuzd I**, being a man of small capacity, instead of leading all forces to protect **Zenobia** when attacked by **Romans** under **Aurelian**, he adopted a fatal policy of half measures, and sent only an insignificant force to her assistance. The result was fall of the state of Palmyra, which could be a valuable buffer for Persia against Rome. Fortunately **Aurelian** was assassinated by his own court men; otherwise his immediate plan was a huge invasion against Persia.[12]

Bahram I seemed to have problem for achieving popularity and establishing authority, so he did the only thing he could think of; he ordered **Mani** and many of **Manichaeans** (followers of **Mani**) to be incarcerated and killed later with torture and humiliation. This hateful ordeal did not stop **Manichaeans**; instead they grew stronger and spread this new religion even farther in the world. **Saint Augustine** had been one of the followers of **Mani** before he converted to **Christianity**. The believers of **Mani** were also in Tibet and Central Asia. Some in Europe had grown into areas in southern France even up to the 13th Century.[13]

Mani based his philosophy on **Zorastherian** beliefs, emphasizing the ultimate combat between power of light or righteousness against that of darkness or evil. His viewpoint called on man as a weak source of earthly desires, much like the **Christianity**, that would only be spiritually saved or purified by the mercy of the creator. He despised the earthly matters, including marriage and birth of children, because it would put more souls under the pressure of worldly demise. His interpretation of **Jesus** was that he was nothing but pure soul; therefore the crucified body belonged to another person not him. It is interesting to know that the **prophet of Islam** would also use this idea concerning the disappearance of the real **Jesus** about four centuries later.

Simultaneously, in the same year that **Aurelian** was assassinated, **Bahram I** passed away, and his son **Bahram II** took control of the country under sizable social issues. His people detested his cruelty, and he managed to avoid a deadly attack against his life by the help of the high priest or **Mogh** in his court. About eight years into the ruling of **Bahram II**, the **Roman** emperor **Orlius Carus** who knew Persia was caught in some internal conflicts between the **Moghs** and **Mani** followers found the chance to start a riot at the Ctesiphon area. **Orlius**, who was an old king, but lived in simplicity, managed to pass Bein-ol Nahrain or Mesopotamian land with considerable ease and get close to the central Persia. However, his sudden death - apparently caused by lightning - in 282 A.D., saved Persia from a serious attack, since he had refused any peace talks.[14]

Surprisingly, **Bahram II** died in the same year, 282 A.D. His successor was **Bahram III** who lasted for only four months. There was rivalry between brothers, **Narsee** (**Narses**) and **Hormuzd II**. Their political fight over the empty throne ended with victory for **Narsee** who invaded Armenia in 296 A.D. **Narsee** made **Tirdad** the **Ashkanian** prince who was the ruler of Armenia to run for his life. **Narsee** spent the rest of his time in fights with **Romans**, which ended in an embarrassing peace agreement signing five important provinces in south and west to **Romans**. Thus, Armenia was completely passed outside the orbit of Persia. **Narsee** spent his last years in grief because his nation was never shrunk to this size under any dynasty. In 301 A.D. after his death, **Hormuzd II** (his brother) took the throne per traditions. This kingdom lasted only eight years. Meanwhile this monarch established a new court of justice specifically for the poor in case the rich oppressed them. **Hormuzd II** was killed in a battle against **Arabs** in 309 A.D.[15]

1. *Tarikh Mardom Iran*, Dr. A. Zarrinkoob, pp. 407, 408
2. *Tarikh –e- Iran*, Sir P. Sykes, pp. 532-535
3. *Chekideh Tarikh Iran*, H. Naraghi, p. 41
4. *Chekideh Tarikh Iran*, pp. 42, 43
5. *A History Of Europe*, by J.M. Roberts, 1996, U.S.A., pp. 62, 65
6. *Farhang Irani Pish Az Islam*, by Muhammad Muhammadi, 3rd print, 1996, Tehran, p.70
7. *A History of Persia*, Sir Percy Sykes , printed in London, Vol. 1, pp. 399,400
8. *Early Medieval Europe*, by Roger Collins, 1999, N.Y, pp. 14, 15

9. *Tarikh-e-Iran,* pp. 549, 550

10. *Chekideh Tarikh Iran,* p. 45

11. *A History Of Japan,* by R.H.P. Mason and J.G. Caiger, 5th edition, 2003,Boston, pp. 25-27

12. *A History Of Persia,* Sir Percy Sykes, Vol.1, 1921, Macmillan, London, p. 406, 407

13. *Tarikh -e-Iran,* p. 553

14. *Tarikh Mardom Iran,* pp. 442-444

15. *Chekideh Tarikh Iran,* p. 46

SHAPUR II (THE GREAT)

At this period transformed lifestyle of the **Sassanid Bishop** (clergy) under the influence of **Moghs** was greatly felt in the high courts in the form of direct interference with civic laws.

Shapur II was chosen by **Mogh** (or **Mobed**) advisors to succeed his deceased father, **Hormuzd II**. This arrangement had come while **Shapur II** was not born yet. The **Zarathustrian** clergies (**Moghs**) were not ready to give the kingdom to other heirs who were not worthy of their trust. Therefore **Shapur II,** who was a posthumous son, was elected the king before he was born. Other sons of **Hormuzd II** were set aside by the noble classes accused of having inclinations towards the Hellenic culture. After his birth in 309 A.D., **Shapur II** was diligently trained in the royal court of **Sassanid**. He was king for seventy years—all of his life!—while, during this period, in Rome ten **Caesars** had been replaced one after the other.

He grew to become a very experienced politician and leader who made the acquisition of control over the whole **Empire** look very easy. Under the influence of his special tutors, **Shapur II** victoriously led his early battles at a younger age. These wars were not much important in size, yet a way to put his knowledge to test.

Shapur II's first serious battle was against the **Arab** invaders who had already taken over Ctesiphon. This happened when he was thirteen. It was a tactful marine invasion in the **Persian Gulf** against the **Arabian** neighbors of Mesopotamia. He successfully suppressed all his **Arab** rebels in the region and ordered a long rope to be pulled through the pierced shoulders of some captured enemy soldiers. Due to this harsh punishment towards his prisoners of war he was called **Shapur Zol Aktaf**; an **Arabic** nickname referring to him as the 'Lord of the Shoulders' for the rest of his life.[1]

This era, about 320 A.D., coincides with the realm of the **Roman** Caesar, **Constantine**, who is famous for the city he built in today's Turkey (now called Istanbul). He was also the first **Caesar** who converted to **Christianity** and declared it the official religion of **The Romans**. **Zorastherianism** and even the older religion of **Mithraism** were dominant in Europe up to this period. This was naturally a political move for the Roman emperor, and he was cynically self-interested in his conversion to this new faith (**Christianity**) that was breaking ground among his people fast. But, he died in 337 A.D. while **Shapur II** was getting ready to start a new campaign against him. Unfortunately believers of **Christianity** and **Zorastherianism** in both countries became targets for hate crimes for centuries.

Shapur II had subjected all **Christians** inside Persia and its other subordinate territories, who refrained from fighting against **Romans**, to a double taxation instead. In 339 A.D. he captured the head of the Church in Shush along with hundred more priests who had refused to collect these taxes and brutally executed all of them as traitors. Nevertheless, their natural inclination towards a **Christian** state may not be denied. During the last forty years of his ruling, **Persians** and **Romans** were continuously engaged in several battles that finally ended in favor of Persia with return of all lost territories including all five major provinces back to the **Sassanid Empire,** including Armenia. This victory had come after **Julian** the **Caesar** of Rome at the time, had attacked Persia and advanced all the way to Ctesiphon. But after witnessing the fortification of **Sassanian** war machine and for some other unknown reasons, he had decided to retreat before getting tangled with heavier **Persian** armies. **Julian** was surrounded and killed with most of his men on his retreat pass along Samarra in 363 A.D. Persia became dominant in the East once more; this victory came through expertise of **Shapur II** in foreign affairs as well as his attention to the internal development of Persia.[2] He was called **Shapur The Great** for his achievements – some of which were not achieved peacefully. **Shapur The Great** died of natural causes in 379 A.D.[3]

He was taught to care for the future agriculture and industrial renovations in the country. He actually ordered many dams for better irrigations to be built. Further advancement of cities of Nei Shapur and Bei Shapur are attributed to him.

Persia was getting stronger , while Rome was caught in some religious and social dilemmas. It is logical to assume that the common problem of the early **Christians** of **Byzantine** (the eastern half of the **Roman** Empire including Alexandria and Antioch) was the uncompromising nature of the ideology of **Christianity** that instigated the persecution of **Christians**. After all **Christians** required no act of hostility or revenge towards enemies.

Rome was struggling with its own social predicament. **Christians of Rome** had several problems with their own government. The numerical rise of the **Christian** communities and the fact that their religious practices prevented them from participating in the public festivals of their pagan neighbors was bound to be a cause of mounting tension anytime, but especially in periods of economic hardship.[4]

1. *Tarikh-e-Iran* , Sir P. Sykes, Vol. 1, Tehran, pp. 561,562
2. *A History of Persia,* Sir Percy Sykes, Vol. 1, printed in London, pp. 418-423
3. *Chekideh Tarikh Iran,* H. Naraghi, pp. 47, 48
4. *Early Medieval Europe,* by Roger Collins, 1999, N.Y., p. 14

Artaxerxes II (Ardashir II)

After **Shapur The Great,** Persia fell again into the hands of numerous successors with limited visions. For example, **Ardashir II** took over immediately in 379 A.D.; there is not much in the history about him except that he stepped forward and actually abolished a lot of taxation for the benefit of the people regardless of their faith. Thus, he is remembered as **Ardashir the Benevolent.** But the stronghold of opposition to his beliefs were the **Moghs** (or **Mobeds**) who suddenly contemplated an end to his short rule resulting in his abdication so his nephew **Shapur III** was chosen as his successor in 379 A.D. **Shapur III** started a peace talk with Rome and was more lenient towards **Christians.** Once more, being worried about loss of their power in the court, the **Moghs** announced this new monarch unsuitable and not assertive enough. Subsequently, they arranged for **Shapur III's** mysterious death in 388 A.D.

Bahram IV in 388 A.D. succeeded **Shapur III**. He was the viceroy of Kerman, before his succession. After a few years, in 399 A.D., **Bahram IV** was also killed in a mutiny by his own soldiers.[1]

Yazdigird I (Yazdi 'Gird)

Living condition for **Christians** in Armenia and other **Persian** territories improved rapidly during **Yazdigird I**. The **Roman Empire** was experiencing invasions by the **Barbarians** at this period, but **Yazdigird I** was not a war-making king. At this time **Arcadius** was the king of Eastern Rome—**Byzantium**. Before his death, **Arcadius** had requested **Yazdigird I** to look after his young prince. The king of Persia accepted his request and a long peace period began. Western **Roman Empire** had delegated **Maruta,** the high priest of Mesopotamia along with representatives of the empire to seek blessings and friendship from the **Persian** emperor. **Yazdigird I** openly accepted them in his court and this priest managed to cure an old illness of the king. Therefore, strong ties were established that continued until the death of this **Persian** monarch. **Yazdigird I** even ordered all **Christian** rituals to continue in his land without any obstacles or harassments in 409 A.D.[2]

The circle of politically active **Moghs** (elite **Zorastherian clergies**), with their concomitant intolerance of other faiths, did not seem very thrilled about all the sudden freedom of religion. Consequently, they tightened their influence on **Yazdigird I** and scolded him by calling him **The Sinner**. **Yazdigird I** tried to retrieve his lost popularity among the powerful clergies. Therefore, he ordered his generals to reinforce the older restrictions gradually. Consequently, a new persecution of believers of other faiths raged for 5 years, until **Yazdigird I** was eliminated mysteriously. **Ferdowsi** reflects on the sudden death of the king, in his mythical *Shah Nameh*. Apparently, **Yazdigird I** chases a wild white horse (symbol of eternal glory) into the woods. **Yazdigird I** receives a fatal kick from this white horse that suddenly disappears in a lake in the misty Nei Shapur Mountains.

One of the cities constructed by **Yazdigird I** is Yazd, which is a city in the south central part of today's Iran and still a center for **Zorastherian** ideologies.

BAHRAM GOOR

After the puzzling death of **Yazdigird I** in 420 A.D., according to some mythic tales, **Bahram V** or **Bahram Goor** managed to receive the throne as a prize for a race between numerous royal contestants. The royal crown was laid in a cage filled with wild lions. **Bahram Goor**, who was a brave hunter, managed to grab the crown and walk out safely. However, as a totalitarian ruler, he continued the hardship that his father had ordained for the **Christian** minorities. Because of this hardship, some **Christians** attempted migration from Persia to **Roman** territories. Soon, **Bahram V** officially requested their return to him. But, **Emperor Diocletian** did not accept this request. The antagonistic confrontations led to more serious battles between **Persian** and **Roman** empires. This ended with a peace agreement mostly against **Persians** in 422 A.D. This agreement actually resulted in some freedom for all minorities in both nations, while it also diverted public attention from the bitter results of the recent wars. In 425 A.D. the nomadic **Hepthalite** (or **White Huns**) army from the northeast crossed the Oxus River and rushed into **Persian** borders. **Bahram V** played weak on one side of his army to pull these yellow skinned warriors inside his land where he launched a severe counter attack and destroyed every one of them. He was a skilful hunter and the nickname of **Goor** (Wild Ass) suggests his taste for prey.[3]

Bahram Goor had a sense of adventure and unlike other **Bahrams** preceding him; he promoted arts and literature along with cultivation and farming. He died in 440 A.D. after being trapped in a quicksand while dashing after a goor.

Yazdigird II

The elite circle of **Moghs** appointed **Yazdigird II** in 440 A.D. to succeed his father (**Bahram Goor**). By overtaking the throne,

Yazdigird II succumbed to the pressure from **Moghs**. The result was not pleasant to minorities in Persia. He attempted to urge **Armenians** again to convert to **Zorastherianism** without success. His secondary approach was enforcement of his will against these people. That resulted in death of their Christian leader named **Joseph** or **Yusef**: and the hostilities lasted till **Yazdigird II**'s own death in 457 A.D.

Consequently, **Yazdigird II**'s elder son **Pirooz**, finally defeated his younger brother and rival in the empire, **Hormuzd III**, and took the throne in 459 A.D. This coincided with a severe drought that took over parts of Middle East, but **Pirooz** managed to ration food and water saving a great number of lives. One of his hasty battles with **Hepthalites** (the **White Huns**) – who had regained number and strength - resulted in his defeat. As a negotiated condition to peace, **Pirooz** was to bow to the **Hepthalite** conqueror. In order to maintain his dignity, he did this bow as a ritual towards the East at sunrise, as his **Moghs** had advised him.

Pirooz's brutal tactics to suppress the resisting **Armenians** to convert to **Zorastherianism**, in spite of some minor victories, was interrupted by his sudden death in 483 A.D. unsuccessful in his zest to convert **Armenians**. His brother **Blash** (**Volagases**, **Val gash**, or **Balash** are all **Greek** and **Roman** variations for this name) succeeded him, and entered a new treaty with the **Hepthalites**. In addition, **Blash** entered into another agreement with the **Armenians** and ordered demolition of the **Zorastherian** temples built by force in Armenia; leaving the **Armenians** free to practice the religion of their choice – **Christianity**. Thus some peace finally came back to these people. **Blash** (**Volagases**) died four years later in 487 A.D.

Ghobad (Kuvad)
(Gho 'Baad)

This age (487 A.D.) is the time of **Ghobad** (or **Kuvad** as pronounced by the **Greek**), the son of **Pirooz** of **Sassanid Dynasty**. His most important maneuver against the **Hepthalite** or **Khezer** tribes (a nomadic wild **Turkish** tribe near Caspian Sea) brought him the prize of absolute victory. The other significant historic milestone

108

during the reign of **Ghobad** was the uprising of **Mazdak**. He was a priest from Nei Shapur who believed in revolutionary social ideas—for which he lost his life. **Mazdak** insisted that there was no divine superiority in any group in society. Further, he argued that because the wealth of the earth belonged to everyone therefore, it should be distributed equally.[4]

Mazdak's ideas in the 20th Century have been targets of many argumentative comparisons with the principals of communism. However, the essence of his doctrines urges his followers to high measures of fairness and piety. The believers of **Mazdak** were growing in number even in Armenia, but the communities within the reach of distrustful **Moghs** (**Zorastherian** elite **clergy**) were harshly resisting.

The argument against **Mazdak** by the elite aristocracy was based on the knowledge that equal distribution of wealth abolished their divine cycle of power over all other classes in Persia. On the other hand, the socialistic laws of **Mazdak** gave **Ghobad** the benefit of a more comprehensive control over a secular monarchy. This would keep the monarchy away from these greedy **Moghs** (sometimes referred to as **Mobeds**) who constantly pressed him with their own special demands.[5]

Consequently, even **Kay Ghobad (king Ghobad)**, himself, who had shown sympathetic inclinations towards **Mazdak**, was abolished by **Moghs** and even imprisoned in 498 A.D. Therefore, **Jamasep**, his own brother, was appointed by **Moghs** (elite clergy) to replace him. **Jamasep** did so reluctantly, but refused to harm his brother. **Jamasep** must have believed in **Ghobad**'s righteousness as his king. **Ghobad**, with the help of his wife, came back in 501 A.D. and **Jamasep** gave him the throne without any complications. **Ghobad** still adhered to the doctrines of **Mazdak**, but privately.

Again the buffer states in Armenia and Asia Minor became a temptation for this self-confident warrior. **Kay Ghobad** ended the sixty-year-old peace between the countries and invaded Rome. As mentioned earlier, these series of wars were without real justifications and only resulted in drastic reductions of wealth and human resources of **Persians** and **Greeks**. These losses, in turn, paved the way for the future **Arab** domination against both **Romans** and **Persians**.

It is true that **Ghobad** had shown superior ability in commanding the **Persian** army against the savage **Hepthalites** (the **White Huns**) and the well-trained **Romans**. Also, **Ghobad** left behind a robust army equipped with heavy arms and extensive experience on the battlefields. Further, M.J.Tabari - in his book *Tabari History*—states the intensive desire of **Ghobad** to build new cities. Kazerun is one example between the cities of Shiraz and Bushehr. The other famous city is Ganjeh in Ghafghaz area (today's Russia) now referred to as Elizabetpol.[6]

King Ghobad (Kay Ghobad) stimulated the **Chinese**, after two centuries of mediocre commercial ties, to resume their direct exchange of treaties and trade consultants with the **Sassanid Dynasty** in **Persia**. In fact, the **Emperor** of the **Tobawei Dynasty** from North China sent his political representatives to **Ghobad (Kuvad)**. The reports of the **Chinese** embassies pertaining to this age reveal that their representatives had found handicrafts, jewelry and rugs in Persia to be of outstanding quality. Specific **Persian** cultural behaviors and moral beliefs such as abomination of incest marriages were highlighted in the embassy reports.[7]

1. *A History of Persia*, Vol. 1, London, p. 428
2. *Tarikh-e-Iran*, Sir P Sykes, Vol.1, Tehran, pp. 585-588
3. *Chekideh Tarikh Iran*, H. Naraghi, pp. 50, 51
4. *Chekideh Tarikh Iran*, p. 52-54
5. *Tarikh Mardom Iran*, Dr. A. Zarrinkoob, pp. 482-485
6. *A History Of Persia*, Vol.1, p. 446
7. *Tarikh-e-Iran*, Vol.1, Tehran, p. 614-617

Khosro (Anushirwan) (Khos Row) (Anu' Sheer One)

The name **Khosro**, however, is told to have various connotations implied within it. The title **Nu Shirwan** was given to him meaning "New King". Another interpretation, more likely to be the real reasoning behind the nickname, is **Anoshak Ravan** reflecting the idea of "Immortal Spirit."[1] **Arabs** called him **Kasra**.

In 531 A.D., **Khosro** took the control of his father's empire. **Khosro** was selected over his other brothers by **Ghobad**'s order. Because he was the third son to the king, **Khosro** still had fears of adversaries' competition against his reign. As a common brutal practice, **Khosro** decided to kill all his brothers and their sons.

In addition, his persecution of **Mazdak**'s believers that approached a hundred thousand put an end to the expanding boundaries of this faith.

In 523 A.D., **Khosro Anushirwan** entered a much-needed peace agreement with the **Romans**. Afterward, he concentrated on the remainder of **Hepthalite (White Huns)** tribes in northeast—these were the descendants of those previously annihilated by **Ghobad**. By this triumph, politically, **Persian** borders expanded once again beyond Oxus River and Jaxartes River closer to the **Chinese** territories. Following this show down of logistic supremacy, his sudden attack against **Roman** colonies in Syria in 540 A.D. brought him astonishing success. His cruel treatment of his prisoners sent a vivid message to Rome. Next city was the rich Antioch, which fell in the hands of **Persian Empire**. In 572 A.D., after a decade of peace, **Justin** the emperor of Rome broke the silence and started a campaign against **King Anushirwan** who was then about seventy years old. To the Roman warriors' surprise, this old **Persian king** led his own strong army in this fight and not only pushed the **Romans** back, but also conquered several of their strategic castles that were regarded as untouchable.

Battlefields were not the only place that brought this king his fame. Astonishingly, **Khosro Anushirwan** dedicated quite a large amount of time taking special care of agriculture. He supported farmers through abundant supply of domesticated animals as well as improved seeds. Also, he eliminated the harsh land taxations. These incentives improved the life of farmers. **Anushirwan** established the appropriate degree of law and order for national security. Also, this allowed him to concentrate on civil reforms. For example, he repaired older commercial routes and constructed many roads to improve international trades. His interest in higher education (science, medicine, arts, and literature) led to foundation of Jondi Shapur University, which became an academic haven for all Western and Middle Eastern scholars. During the 6th and 7th Century A.D. this center was world famous for its highly knowledgeable graduates in all medical fields of that time. During his ruling by his order scientific and literary scripts from all corners of the world were translated into Pahlavi (older version of Farsi)—this magnificent trend continued for centuries after him. For example, Sanskrit literary tales of *Kelileh and Demeneh*, about imaginary kingdom of animals, and the game of "Chess" were originally imported from India under the ordinance of **Khosro Anushirwan**. As a counter part of the philosophy behind Chess, **Persians** created "Backgammon." Chess implies that man makes his choices and moves, and these moves will determine his possible victory or failure in life. Backgammon, however, implies that although man makes his own decisions in life, but he has no choice but to play the hand that he is dealt by his fate (determined by the roll of dice in Backgammon). In other words, **Persians** believed that man makes choices, but under the force (Gebra) of his fate (predestination). Algebra also devised by the Persian scientist, **Abu Ali Sina (Avi Cenna)**, is a derivative of the same theory.

Through the systematic political connections and scientific and social reforms in Persia, these works and many ideologies of the East were poured into the western world. On the other hand, scientific viewpoints of western thinkers such as **Aristotle** and **Plato** were translated, critically studied, and made available to the eastern world.

Because of **Anushirwan's** accomplishments, **The Sassanid Dynasty** (224 A.D.-652 A.D.) had achieved extraordinary tactics and innovations in military, very much superior to their predecessors **The Ashkanian Dynasty**. Their meticulous modernization of the military, by adding elephants and camels to the regiments, enabled them to overthrow the most fortified enemies and castles on their path. In addition they had heavier metals for swords and catapults. However, it is true to claim that the genuine creativity in construction techniques of this period were mostly utilized in wars rather than civil reforms. (This problem still exists in the world.)

The famous primary advisor or "**Vazir**" of this period was **Bozorg Mehr**, a scholar to whom many of these social progressive reforms of this dynasty may be attributed.

Also, many castles and royal courthouses were built in this period. Surprisingly, women had gained a social prestige equal to men and this freedom was not very much available before. It is recorded in

Masoudi Diary that when Roman **Diocletian** attaché visited the elegant Kasra Palace, he inquired about a conspicuous dissymmetry in the design of a corner wall. He was told that this end of the wall was shared with a neighbor, an old lady, who had refused to sell and move. Therefore, engineers had to design the king's palace around her property, resulting in an inevitable flaw. **2** The voice of an old widowed woman could easily reach the courts of **Anushirwan**, and this shows the incredible degree of justice for any age—especially about 1500 years ago. **Anushirwan** died of old age in 578 A.D. His other nickname was "**Adel**", meaning "**The Righteous**" in Farsi. However, he was everything but kind to his enemies and to those who opposed him.

The fabulous ruins of Kasra Palace still intrigue viewers. **Khaghani**, a great poet of Iran, has artistically referred to the ruins of Kasra Palace. Connoting the mortality awaiting all living things, his poem calls the viewers to pay tribute to this mighty structure (called Madayen by **Arabs**), which once stood so tall and yet could not outlive time (destiny).

Sir Percy Sykes, being a General in the British army and a learned historian focusing on The Middle East, puts it this way; both mendacity and idleness were punishable offences under this strenuous monarch. **Khosro Anushirwan**'s policy of free seeds for farmers fostered the agriculture. **Anushirwan** ordered *Khoday – Namak* (or *Book of the Kings*) to be written that gives all the history and legends of Persia, and it was mainly on this work that the famous epic of **Ferdowsi** (*Shah Nameh*) was based.[3]

1. *Tarikh-e-Iran*, Sir P. Sykes, p. 619
2. Tarikh-e-Iran, pp. 628-649
3. A History Of Persia, Vol.1, London, pp. 458-460

Hormuzdus IV (Hormuzd IV) (Hoor 'Mazdis) (Hor 'Moz)

Upon the death of **Anoshiravan The Righteous**, his son, **Hormuzd IV**, took the control. **The Romans**, under **Maurice** and **Heraclius** (610-641 A.D.), not to be confused with **Heraclitus** the **Greek** philosopher - were tired of paying monetary tributes as per earlier agreements with Persia, consequently they initiated peace and negotiations, which were denied, and thus the wars started again between Persia and Rome circa 580 A.D.

The yellow-skinned Turks in the Northeast (**Turkman** tribes with oriental ancestry also referred to as **Huns**) took advantage of the tension between Rome and Persia and crossed the Oxus River and attacked the bordering towns inside Persian lands. **Hormuzd IV** delegated his general called **Bahram Chubin** to lead this defiance. In 589 A.D., this warrior was very successful, but **Hormuzdus IV** scolded him in a degrading manner for his defeat against the **Roman** invaders in a previous battle. This psychologically tormented general started a rebel around Ctesiphon with his close men in the army at his side, and finally ambushed **Hormuzd IV** who was immediately located and killed at his own castle. In 590 A.D., **Khosro II**, son of **Hormuzd IV**, succeeded him.

History refers to **Khosro II** as **Khosro Parviz** who attempted an amicable relation with **Bahram Chubin**, but failed because of the latter's feeling of indignation. The army, split between the two, Persia found itself in midst of a coup against this king. **Bahram Chubin** took over the throne against the traditions of his own people. **Khosro Parviz** had to take refuge with the **Roman** court of **Maurice**, where he was aided with support for a triumphant return to power that resulted in **Bahram Chubin**'s capture and execution in 591 A.D.

In 602, when **Maurice** himself was betrayed and killed by some of his trusted men in the Roman court, **Khosro II** (**Parviz**) found the excuse to take revenge for his death. **Khosro Parviz** attacked **Phocas**, the newly appointed but weak **Roman** emperor. **The Romans**, then, appointed **Heraclius** as the new **Caesar**, but wars continued between the two nations.[1]

In 611, **Khosro Parviz** took over Syria and Jerusalem and indulging in his egotistic pride, he sent a disgraceful letter to **Heraclius** and called him a shameful slave while degrading **Christianity**. In addition, **Khosro Parviz** had led successful campaigns against some **Christian** territories beyond the captured city of Antioch and Jerusalem. Many lands that were taken away from Persia since the final period of **Achaemendis Dynasty** were retrieved again. These strong campaigns had heightened the fear in

The Roman Empire. Concurrently, **Heraclius** used this letter in the religious factions all over Europe and induced their monetary and emotional support to assist his army in this holy war against Persia as enemy of **Christianity**. This was the start of the **Crusaders**.

It was around this time in Arabia, a new religion and a new prophet immerged. **Khosro Parviz**, unlike **Heraclius**, had not welcomed the representatives and introductory letters of this new prophet who was called **Muhammad**.[2] This harsh and non-political reaction from **Khosro Parviz**, as history unfolds, cost his empire a great deal. For years Arabia was caught in its own internal and tribal conflicts over the new ideology, and as a result, Arabia did not seem a threat to either of the giant empires in Middle East and Asia Minor.

Therefore, from 622 to 627 A.D., both **Byzantines** and **Persians** were caught in many bloody and scattered wars that ended with series of defeats for the **Persians**. The aftermath of these failures was too much for **Khosro Parviz** who lost his mind to the point that commanded execution of his close men in spite of their heroic services for the country. His lack of understanding of the **Christian** ideology of the West and its direct impact on the **Byzantine** social layers had caused his outrage against **Christianity**. **Khosro Parviz** showed an immediate nervous reaction and started blaming his generals for his own miscalculated maneuvers. He started preparations for a shelter to save his own life against possible enemy threats. In 628 A.D., his own close courts men imprisoned and finally killed **Khosro Parviz**.[3]

Khosro Parviz had helped the literary scholars, musicians, and industrial craftsmen of his time to achieve immense freedom in their trades and workmanship. However, his superficial love of luxury surpassed his inner desire for art and science. Therefore, newly acquired blend of many cultures from Greece, India, China and Iran did not find a chance to grow.[4] In spite of numerous concubines, his special love for his **Christian** wife called **Shirin** is recorded in many historic and literary works. His initial triumphs and territorial seizures enabled **Persian Empire** to regain all the old glory, but his temperament and lack of administrative skills towards the end left him without adequate support against relentless warriors like **Heraclius**. The cruelty and the stringency in personality of **Khosro Parviz** during his last years of kingdom did not exempt Persia from dismay and defeat.

Ghobad II (Shiruyeh)

Ghobad II succeeded his father, **Khosro Parviz**, in 628 A.D. His affable conciliations with those imprisoned or prosecuted by his father brought the country into a more stabilized estate. Naturally these strategic achievements came with massacre of his own brothers who could threaten his throne. However, the plague ended his life quickly.

In the mid 7th Century, and during 14 years that followed, many **Sassanid** princes — 12 precisely — and even two princesses such as **Poran Dokht** and **Azar Midokht** as the first lady kings, took over the throne of **Persian** Empire — the social prestige and freedom of women during The **Sassanid Dynasty** did not last beyond this period. Also, **Khosro III**, **Pirooz Farokh-Zad**, and **Hormuzdus V** were among these 12 princes, who had tried their luck at the kingdom. But it was finally **Yazdigird III** who was destined to bear the blame of history for the infamous invasion of **Arabs** and the fall of **Persian Empire**.[5]

Now the **Persians** had entered a chaotic state of political dismay, much like the **Romans**. Rapid abdications of those in power in Persia cost the nation a diversion from its solidarity that was being closely observed by its surrounding enemies- mostly **Arabs**.

1. *Tarikh-e-Iran* , pp. 660-667
2. *Tarikh Iran Zamin*, p.120
3. *Chekideh Tarikh Iran* , p.56-59
4. *Tarikh Mardom Iran*, Dr. A. H. Zarrinkub, p. 521
5. *Pictorial History Of Iran* , by M.H. Amini Sam p. 199

YAZDIGIRD III

His nomination as the new **Sassanid** king came from the **Moghs** or **Clergies** of the Anahita Temple of **Zarathustra** in 632 A.D. They had sent for him who had chosen a life of seclusion in Estakhr (near Shiraz) away from the rest of his family. He was grandson of **Khosro Parviz** but his mother was a colored slave, therefore he was not regarded as a serious threat to **Ghobad II** and thus spared.

Yazdigird III inherited a disordered kingdom that is marked by the earliest invasions of **Muslim Arabs** after passing of the **Prophet Muhammad.** This attack was deemed politically sound under the **Arabs** new leader who was called **Abu Bakr.** The suffix of "Abu" in Arabic means "Father" and was commonly used as a way to mark kinship. This successor to the **prophet** had taken the control of a new and strong theocracy in the East. His mission as **Imam** or **Religious Leader** called for missionary maneuvers, and his much needed economic reforms dictated the invasion of the rich and populated soil under **the Sassanid kings.** Naturally, the survival of **Abu Bakr** and **Islam** depended on the scattered confrontations along the borderlines with **Persians** who were at their weakest due to their internal conflicts. The wealth of the **Sassanid Persia** was the true prize for the suffering **Arabs.** This new Arab ruler or **Imam** knew invasion of Persia was essential for domination of his faith and survival of his rule. These were the same **Arabs** who once, before **Islam**, were polytheists, believing in nature gods, demons and spirits. The new faith of **Islam** had revolutionized the lifestyle of these tribes, broadened their outlook, and united them as a nation.

In Ghadessieh, near city of Kufeh in 637 A.D.—now in Iraq—following numerous trivial victories for **Arabs**, their first biggest victory ever against the highly sophisticated war machine of the **Persians** occurred. The inexperienced **Yazdigird III,** who had underestimated his empty-handed opponents had to leave Ctesiphon and flee.

The next decisive battle in Nahavand, northwest of Iran, ended in defeat , because the **Persians'** resistance was scattered . Suddenly the occupation of Iran was not as unachievable as it seemed for centuries; and all of this appeared more miraculous than anything else. The inhabitants of these towns had lost their will to defend their corrupt **Persian kings** and their courts, especially against a new doctrine that promised equality for all. The success of **Arab** was actually the triumph of simplicity and sacrifice of **Muslim** ideology against the luxury and corruption of the golden kingdom of **Sassanid.**[1]

Finally, in 652 A.D., **Yazdigird III** was stabbed in a remote farm by the hands of a greedy miller who had noted his valuable clothing, but had not recognized him. This miserable ending was a tragic incident in the history, but it was not the only one. **Darius III** had shared the same fate while running away from **Alexander The Great**. His own men, who also had lost hope in their king, had assassinated **Darius III**. The stories of the deaths of the last emperors of **Achaemenid** and **Sassanid** are sadly alike, although they happened about 1000 years apart.[2]

Arab soldiers, although untrained and lacking the heavy artillery, believed in their new faith that had guaranteed their well being either as victors in this world or as rewarded martyrs in the next.

How deep some historians have summed up the causing factors of the fall of **Persian Empire** is unsettling. However, most of them commonly look at the following major points:

• Abundant and antagonistic sources of authority among **Moghs (clergies)** and **statesmen** in the hierarchy of social power created mediocrity, which in turn caused bigger gaps between people and their government. (*Cultural Factor*)

• The heavy taxations imposed on the lower class brought economic hardship for majority. (*Administrative Factor*)

• Continued raging wars with other nations increased the inflation and created poor families who had lost their bread earner. (*Economical Factor*)

• Neglecting the agricultural lands, lack of maintenance of existing dams and watering channels increased famine and poverty. (*Physical Factor*)

• The tragic and customary elimination of popular leaders who would show promise, but were treated as a danger to the popularity of the king, deprived the nation of its essential seers and leaders. (*Moral Factor*)

• **Kings** and their **Moghs** were absolute monarchs and they could intervene personally at any level of government and administration. (*Political Factors*)

• A new trend of thought overcame the society during this period. It was based on the orthodox doctrine of predestination, referred to as 'Gebra' or 'Force' in the East; persuading the concept that man in nature has no choice of his own, but can only surrender to a predetermined fate. This worldview, in turn, promoted individual's indifference and mendacity that started the decay of democracy and justice. (*Psychological Factor*)

• Finally, the diminishing attention to basic human rights, once upheld dearly during the early period of **Achaemendis Dynasty,** especially by **Cyrus The Great,** caused unlawful persecutions of innocent people because of their faiths. (*Social Factor*)

Naturally, **Roman** and **Sassanid Empires** had many common flaws that resulted in their fall. Most of these shortcomings are shared with contemporary superpowers at any given time.

As an example, economically, the reasons for the fall of Rome can be summed up as too much dependency on conquest, tribute, and slavery. Actually, the reasons can be as numerous as the ways we may approach this issue. There can be social, political, moral, physical and even pathological approaches to this historic fall.[3] The reasons for the fall of **The Sassanid** interestingly seem very identical with that of **The Romans,** except for the latter's dependency on slavery.

In spite of the shortcomings of the **Sassanid** period, the kings of this dynasty served **Iranian** culture by collecting and reintroducing of **Zorastherian** doctrines and rituals. This attempt was purely pro **Persian** and an improvement over the Greek - oriented civilization of **Ashkanian.** The science of book keeping and statistics reached its climax during this period and was completely controlled by **Persian** writers and scholars even after domination of **Arabs** in the centuries that followed.[4]

The newer **Persian** or **Farsi** language most popular after the **Sassanid** (by 900 A.D.) was using the Arabic alphabet and script. It was called *Dari* or *of the court* in the eastern plateau of Persia – this was because of the universal use of Dari in judicial courts in all the eastern territories throughout today's India, Pakistan, and Afghanistan.[5] Arabic letters and even the grammar received fundamental facelift and academic revision in the hands of Persian scribes and scholars.

1.   *Two Centuries of Silence,* by Dr. Abdul Hussein Zarinkoob, 2000, Tehran, pp. 82-84
2.   *Tarikh Mardom Iran* , pp. 530-539
3.   *The Middle Ages* , by Morris Bishop, published by Harrington Mifflin, 1987, N.Y. pp. 8-10
4.   *Farhang Iran Pish Az Islam,* by M. Muhammadi, 1996, Tehran, pp. 30, 69-84
5.   *Iran, Past and Present,* by Donald N. Wilber, 9th edition. Princeton, 1981, N. Jersey, p. 86

CHAPTER EIGHT

ISLAM

Islam is the dominant religion in Iran today. The history of a large part of the world at this time, including Persia, ties directly with Islam, although its origin was Arabia.

In 614 A.D., (about six hundred years after the introduction of **Christianity**), a new theology was born in the Arab segment of the Middle East. This ideology grew very rapidly. The rising **Arab Empire** was founded on this new worldview that promised the economically suppressed inner peace on this world and salvation after death. This message, combined with the idea that God is one, was the pivotal point of the new faith called **Islam**. This new religion shook part of the world and called for a change in all ancient beliefs at a speed that had not been seen before.

While It took **Christianity** about a thousand years to extend from Middle East to as far as **Scandinavian** lands in Europe, it took **Islam** much less time to cover that much land. **Islam** surprisingly transformed the entire Middle East and many parts of paganish Asia and Africa into Islamic territories in no time. Such rate of success was not seen in any other religion before. It took **Christianity** ten centuries to reach same level of expansion. (The year 1016, when the **Danish** prince **Cnut** ascended the throne of England and Denmark, can be seen in retrospect to mark the beginning of the transformation of **Viking** Scandinavia into an outpost of the **Christendom**) Although **Islam** was born at the same area on the planet, it had a faster pace; **Islam** had covered more areas than **Christianity** in a period of three centuries.[1]

One reason for this astonishing record of Arab success in the region was that **Byzantium** and **Sassanid Persia** were focusing all their energy and time on fighting one another and dealing with their other commitments. It seems that this made them incapable of seeing the rapid birth and growth of a strong ideology next door. The motivation that drove **Arabs** through combat was different from that of the **Persians** or **Romans**. It is generally true to believe that **Arabs** did not have much to lose; their soldiers already suffered from poverty. This was actually one of the major reasons why they, themselves, had willingly submitted to the new ways that **Islam** introduced. The term **Islam** literally means surrender—to the will of the only God. **Prophet Muhammad** saw himself, as the mouthpiece through which God made known his will to men.[2]

Islam, very soon, became the fastest growing ideology in the world in terms of the number of its new followers. In today's world, **Christians** and **Muslims** make up almost one-half of the world's population. The Abrahamic religions of **Judaism, Christianity**, and **Islam** share the view of one omnipotent and omnipresent God. The region of Middle East, including Mesopotamia, has continuously been caught in its escalating violence between these believers since the start of civilization. Unfortunately, controversial disagreements regarding religious beliefs (still in the year 2005) continue to stimulate wars around the world. The idea of religion continues to be under scrutiny.

However, the record of history shows that noble acts of love, self-sacrifice, and service to others are frequently rooted in deeply held religious worldviews. At the same time, history clearly shows that religion has often been linked directly to the worst examples of human behavior. But where, actually, does the root of the problem of violence reside?[3]

It is hard to pinpoint the source of these troubles in the world's religious orders. Each of the Abrahamic religions circles around one divinity. However, in the practice when theory and reality meet, problems happen. (For example: Requiring tithing—10%—for the

Christian Clergy and requiring no birth control for the poor.) However, in 2003 and 2004 some **Catholic priests** have been found to be involved in moral crimes.

Persia has had its share of pedophilia between its **Muslim** and **non-Muslim clergies, priests,** and **rabbis.** All over the world religious arguments arise everyday that may take the appearance of irreconcilable differences. Emotional distress and physical violence (religious wars) are not usually caused by religious differences, but very well fed by it.

Another controversial issue is that of "politics." In the Middle East the idea of leadership assumes a relationship between earthly power and divine authority. Therefore, the word "politics" implies divine authenticity or approval.

However, the western and **American** concept, in particular, of "Politics" is limited to those people choosing to run for a government office. This choice has nothing to do with divine approval or disapproval. So, the history of Middle East has a different connotation for "Politics" and "Politician." Even at the present time, in the Middle East as well as many other areas in Asia and Africa, politicians usually possess a higher level of respect and dignity within their own people. For example, Alexander's teacher (**Aristotle**), or **Heraclius** of Rome (who started the **Crusades**), or even **Cyrus The Great** of Persia (Who is praised for his humanitarian doctrines and practices) are all referred to as 'Politicians' who once enjoyed a divine approval. Knowing that, it is easy to believe that, during the history, Politics has had many misleading effects on the minds of ordinary people. Politicians were not always what they claimed to be. For example, the proclamation of the state of Israel on May 14th of 1948 by **Ben Gurion** had followed the massacre of **Palestinians** in Deir Yassin. This cruel act of the military, by the order of the politicians, had made many **Israelis** and **Palestinians** furious. But the military machine was not adhering to any opposing voice. The new nation was finally built on blood of innocent civilians and under leadership of **Menachin Begin**, who was on the top ten terrorist list most wanted by the **British**. Unfortunately, the U.S. immediately recognized the new nation of Israel under **Zionist** rule of Irgun without much thought. Alfred Lilienthal has put it this way, "One man's dream has become another man's nightmare."[4]

It is because of these types of misleading political maneuvers that some, caught in the problem of definitions limited by their perspectives, look for and find all sorts of contradictory arguments about the three most popular religions in the world. Politics and religious ideologies mix bitterly. But unbiased research, founded on historic documentations is still missing. The fact is that man has very little factual proof of his religious historical documents past or present. Yet people still make critical judgments based on their perception of the truth; and political rhetoric has this assumption that all these maneuvers are for the good of the people.

These problems have been going on in the history and biased theological arguments have not made it any less painful. However, one fact remains that out of all these Abrahamic religions, **Islam** is the newest and the most accurately recorded (established about 1400 years ago).

Stewart Schwartz believes that the history of the **Prophets** and their initial purpose vary a lot. **Judaism** is based on the lives of honored Prophets separated from modern **Jews** by thousands of years. Thus, these Prophets' historical existence cannot be verified. By contrast, the existence of **Muhammad** is undeniably recorded, and his down-to-earth life is very much closer to the lives of ordinary men living at any time and place. On the other hand, **Christianity** centers on the life and works of a gentle rabbi, **Jesus**, who was incapable of deceit or violence. But no substantial document proves whether or not there was a historical **Jesus**.[5] What we have at hand from this great prophet is the words of twelve apostles spreading His words after His death.

When **Muhammad** introduced the religion of **Islam** in 614 A.D., the world was to be witnessing a revolutionary ideological approach to the universe. Meanwhile, the West, mostly with the struggles between **Christianity** and **Paganism,** was experiencing its own internal conflicts. Europe was deeply involved with challenging a new invasion against its own territory—the **Barbarians**.

It was around 500 A.D.—following the decline of the ancient **Roman Empire**—that **Barbarian tribes** (all the invaders were labeled **Barbarians**) plundered the Western Europe, occupying and looting towns. The first invaders were the **Germans**, who occupied central Europe. East of them were the savage **Slavs**, and farther east, the still more savage **Huns** (a people of **Mongol** origin). But the **Romans**, the **Visigoths**, and other **German** tribes united against **Huns** and their leader, **Attila**, and pushed them back in decisive battles. About 571 A.D., one of the early leaders of Briton, a legendary **King Arthur**, who was a **British** chieftain fought against these **Saxon** invaders from Germany and Denmark. He ruled as a noble chivalric monarch with his **Knights of the Round Table**, though his myth is not historically proven. However, by the end of the 6th Century **Saxons** were firmly established and **Britons** who refused foreign domination retreated to the west, to Wales and Cornwall, and Brittany across the Channel.[6]

But, in the Middle East, it was around this period that many nations were about to face the new worldview of **Islam**.

Muhammad the Prophet

As historic documents reveal, the prophet of **Islam** is **Muhammad ibn Abdullah ibn Abd-al-Muttalib**. The suffix of *ibn* means *the son of.* He was born on Monday 17th of Rabi Al Aval (month of May) in the year 570 A.D. The place was the city of Mecca in southwestern Arabia. His mother was named **Amineh**. His father, **Abdullah**, had died not long after **Muhammad**'s birth.[7]

Muhammad was a popular trusted young man among many tribes around Mecca. He had earned the nickname of "Amin" meaning "Honest" through his honest handling of the wealth and goods of different traders. He lacked a formal education, but was very keen to learn about history and theology of the world. He was also a very skilful business negotiator trusted with money. He married **Khadijeh**, a wealthy widow. Through business ties with **Muhammad**, she had witnessed a series of complex and mystical qualities in his character. **Khadijeh** gave birth to two sons for him, but both died as infants. However, **Fatimah**, who was their only daughter, managed to survive. **Muhammad** declared his prophecy in 614 A.D. when he was 44 years old. He claimed to be the last messenger of God. It was then that he miraculously opened his mouth and uttered words in statements that by the style of diction and rules of Arabic grammar were impeccable and certainly unprecedented among the ordinary dwellers of the Arab tribes. **Muslims** believe that this was his miracle and he was, through occasional state of transcendence, the mouthpiece of God, and his words – originating from God or Allah - are well kept in the holy book of **Islam** called the *Koran.*

Like **Prophet Mazdak** before him, **Prophet Muhammad** concluded that the entire world was to be finally shared by the lower class and the needy, and no royal blood among different tribes can claim sovereignty over people or the riches of the land. Consequently, a lot of antagonism followed. Finally, on the 20th of June 622 A.D., when 52 years old, and still not very successful at his mission, **Muhammad** was forced by violent non-believers to migrate to the city of Medina, where he might spread his message in peace. **Khadijeh** had already passed away, and he started this historical migration (Hejrat), with a number of his close believers. **Muhammad** became much more successful in Medina and the new faith's popularity grew stronger everyday. After several years, he finally found the chance to return to Mecca with a great number of followers without much resistance from skeptics and enemies.

Due to the importance of this historical migration in global spread of **Islam, Persians** chose its date as the base of their lunar and solar calendars. Finally by the eleventh year since his migration, in 632 A.D., this last great prophet passed away amid hundreds of thousands of believers at the age of 63.[8]

Muslims believe that **Muhammad** was the last of the God's Messengers. This belief is noteworthy because after **Muhammad**, no other person in the world has claimed to be a messenger of God.

1.   *A History of Scandinavia,* by T.K. Derry, Minnesota University Press, 3rd edition, 1983, pp.34, 35

2.   *A History Of Europe,* by J.M. Roberts, 1997, U.S.A., pp. 96, 97

3.   *When Religion Becomes Evil,* by Charles Kimball, Harper Collins Publishers, 2003, N.Y, pp. 1- 41

4.   *A Time For Peace, Between Muslims and the West.,* by Judith I. Shadzi, 1994, R&E Publisher, Saratoga, CA , pp. 137- 139

5.   *The Two Faces of Islam,* by Stephen Schwartz, 2002, New York, P 1- 3

6.   *The Middle Ages ,* By Morris Bishop, P.13- 15

7.   *Tarikh Iran Zamin*, Dr. M.J. Mashkur, P.117
8.   *Tarikh-e-Iran*, Sir Percy Sykes, Translated by F.D. Gilani, Volume 1, Tehran, 1983, p. 698

These rapid changes were happening in Mesopotamia.

By contrast the **Sassanid Dynasty** in Persia still believed in **Zorastherianism**—with its constant struggle between God and the Devil (God was known as Ahura-Mazda).

The Omayyad (Omavian) Caliphate (Oma 'Yeh) (Oma Vian) (632 in Arabia and since 650 A.D.-749 A.D. in Persia.)

The word "**Caliph**" comes from the Arabic word "**Khalifa**." The title of "**Omavian**" is the Farsi equivalent for the Arabic "**Bani Omaieh**" referring to the dynasty of kings after **Prophet Muhammad**. Therefore, the word *Caliphate* derived from the Arabic *Khalafat* refers to the word "Empire."

The word "**King**" refers to a person ruling only one nation; whereas, the title of "**Emperor**" refers to one person who rules two or more unified nations. This "**Emperor**" normally chooses a successor from his own family. Also, to control a large empire, the **Emperor** may appoint several trusted generals or **Viceroys** to keep control or govern extensive areas in his empire. In **The Islamic Empire, "The Emperor"** was referred to as The "**Caliph**."

Thus with Islam, what was once a tribe starts a generation of **Caliphs** (descendants of **Arabs**). This is the rise of **Omavian Dynasty (Bani Omaieh)** in Arabia that is interwoven with the history of Persia at this period. Simultaneously with the growth of **The Islamic Empire** in Arabia, comes the **First Imam** or successor of The **Prophet Muhammad** in 632 A.D. This period also ties in with the history of many other countries in the world.

The founder of the **Omavian Dynasty** in Arabia was **Abu Bakr**. He was a learned man and one of the very early followers of

Muhammad. He was appointed by the elite members of tribes to succeed **Prophet Muhammad**. Eventually, gaining the trust of numerous Arab clans, **Abu Bakr** gathered his troops of many **Muslim** tribesmen and sent them towards **Romans** and **Persians** as messengers and soldiers. Because the earlier attempts of **Arabs** demanding recognition of **Islam** by **Persians** and payment of tribute had been ignored, **Abu Bakr** initiated the preparation for wars. This was more a monetary influx much needed by a poverty-stricken Arabic army.

Thus, **Khalid ibn Valid**, a famous Arab warrior, received orders to lead his army of mostly unskilled **Muslim Arabs** towards the heavily armed **Zorastherian Persians** from the West near today's Kuwait. This was the first serious fight. It finally raged between the two nations in which the **Persian** general, **Hormozan**, was killed and subsequently, **Khalid** pushed victoriously towards the North in 633 A.D.

Iranians, although clumsily preparing for an unfamiliar and underestimated enemy, showed much more resistance in the North and brought heavy casualties upon **Arabs**. This last blow of the **Persian** army caused furious **Khalid** to swear to God that he would run a mill just by the blood flow of his enemy and grind wheat for his bread. He had to repudiate this statement. Instead, **Khalid** was forced to modify his extravagant oath by merely adding some **Persian** blood to the creek water in a running mill. Not much later, he reluctantly had to transfer his power to a newly appointed successor, **Mossana**, and leave **Persia** in 634 A.D.[1]

Abu Bakr had also sent a formidable westerly army to a fight at Wakusa near **Byzantine** borders. This war also ended in a surprising defeat for **Heraclius** army.[2] Not only the **Persian** army, but also the **Roman** army was defeated.

Probably not suspecting this invasion from his **Arab** neighbor, **Heraclius** had his eyes mostly on **Zorastherian Persia**. Therefore, he did not anticipate the ultimate defeat that was coming his way.

About this time, some areas inside Persia were successfully resisting **Arabs**. Victory for **Iranians** was at hand in one decisive battle. **Meitam**, the **Iranian general**, had courageously surrounded the vulnerable **Arab** invaders inside the **Persian** territories, but **Mossana** (the **Arab general** under **Abu Bakr**) had anticipated this maneuver and rushed to their aid in time.

The domination of **Arab Muslims** inside Iran expanded farther after **Abu Bakr** in 635 A.D. **Abu Bakr**, near his death, had personally selected **Omar** to be the **Second Imam**. Some **Arabs** did not look at this succession amicably. Contrary to **Prophet Muhammad**'s specific orders that his successors were to be elected by the vote of the citizens rather than appointment, **Omar**'s appointment caused a great concern among many protesting **Arabs**.

This unilateral nomination seemed to be biased and against the original tradition set by the **Prophet Muhammad**. All and every **Imam** needed to be chosen by the vote of the majority of **Muslims**.[3]

Omar, however, was a faithful believer and possessed the respect of all tribal heads. In the fall of the following year, by his direct order the second most brutal fight occurred between **Persians** and **Arabs** in a place called Ghadessieh- the western border of Persia with Arabian territories. Relying on their heavily armed troops, **Yazdigird III** and his generals, boastfully underestimated the morale of **Muslim soldiers**. The wise commander of Persian army, **Rostam**, had given warnings to king **Yazdigird III** of the strong morale and reasoning of these Arab mediators and convoys. The king had not given it much thought. To the surprise of the **Persians**, this fight lasted only a few days. Finally a sudden arrival of a sand storm against the faces of **Persian soldiers** turned the table against them. The **Arabs** took this as a sign of their divine sovereignty against the enemy. **Rostam** was finally killed and the news of the retreat of **Persians** made troubled **Yazdigird III** run for shelter and leave Ctesiphon for the **Arab** conquerors in 636 A.D.[4]

Omar was approached by his generals in Persia about the fate of an extraordinarily abundant source of scientific and philosophical texts in **Old Farsi, Pahlavi, Sanskrit, Greek, Hebrew**, and **Hindu** languages. **Omar** ordered all to be collected from the **Persian** libraries and burned. He had reasoned that **Islam** would provide them with all the worldly knowledge they needed, and contradictory ideas in any other books would be false and could only cause harm to the faith of followers.

Thus, **Arabs** initiated the unprecedented destruction of minds in one of the most advanced centers of science in that time. The burning of books by Arab conquerors truly must have brought a severe wound to the body of the world civilization.

The third detrimental confrontation between the two nations happened in 640 A.D. at a place called Nahavand in northwest of Iran.

In spite of the last heroic resistance of the famous Iranian general, **Firoozan**, many strategically significant cities were conquered and destroyed. In 642 A.D. the cities of Zanjan, Ghazvin, Ray, and Ghumes (today's Semnan), which were mostly in the northwest and central part of Iran surrendered to the **Arabs**. Following this, more populated areas fell. The bigger cities of Hamadan, Ghom, Kashan, and Isfahan shared the same fate. Those towns that did not resist the **Arab invaders** had to pay tribute. Eventually, **Yazdigird III** had to run away farther to Khorasan (northeastern province bordering with Afghanistan and Russia). This must have been a tremendous shock that **Yazdigird III** could not cope with.

In heyday of Arab invasions of Persia, some areas had resisted heavily, but with no result. In the Persian city of Estakhr in the southern province of Fars, due to an unsuccessful coup against **Arabs**, over forty thousand Persian men were captured and killed and their women and children were taken as prisoners. It was around this time, as mentioned before, that a farmer in a remote field near the town of Marv killed the last **Sassanid** king, **Yazdigird III,** in 652 A.D. out of greed for his jewels.[5]

In the western world, **Heraclius**, the **Byzantine Emperor**, had to run, too. He left the biggest cities in Byzantium to **Arab conquerors**; the major cities of Antiochus and Jerusalem were taken and added to the Islamic terrain in 636 A.D. **Heraclius** died shortly after. His life was filled with wars. His empire and the rest of Europe had long been an open field for the **German** invaders from the North. Now **Muslims** of Arabia and surrounding lands were the new invaders.

1. *Chekideh Tarikh Iran*, Hasan Naraghi, pp. 60-61
2. *Tarikh-e-Iran*, Sir Percy Sykes, p. 735
3. *Dar Piramoon-e-Tarikh*, by Ahmad Kasravi, 1999,Tehran, p. 40
4. *Do Gharn Sokut*, By Abdul Hussein Zarrinkub, 9th edition, 1998, Tehran, pp. 63-66
5. *Chekideh Tarikh Iran*, p. 62

World affairs, however, seemed a little different in the Middle East. **Arab Muslims** were raiding and occupying more lands every year without having to share it with any other power. But they were not ready to meet the administrative challenges that it required to run these large occupied lands. Resistance against many social rules of **Arabs** existed within the occupied lands, although some of the **Arabs'** civic traditions were accepted easier among foreign lands.

For example, one tradition that was readily accepted was the **Muslims'** call for prayer called "Azan." The Azan tradition and its strong words came from the *Koran.* Azan was always recited at noon with a loud and harmonic voice, which announced the arrival of a new faith to all the lands in the Middle East, Africa and East Europe. Azan contained—and it still does—the message of "La Elaha Ella Allah", meaning "there is no god but Allah." This message rejected polytheism; God is one and alone (no matter where or what name is used). This was truly a radical monotheism against any cosmic dualism or trinity. Now the Islamic call to faith was carried to all corners of Persia. The message was deeply felt by many in the land, but the harsh way the message was delivered into their lives was equally detested.

Although Azan sounded captivating in the alleys and streets of Persia, **Arabic** language sounded rough and its harsh resonance did not stand equal to the flow of Farsi especially in music. **Arab rulers**, on the other hand, were specifically against those who spoke Farsi or even other dialects in this occupied land. **Arabs** feared these languages could be used against them in future. Islamic laws looked down on music and poetry in general. Many rulers such as **Ghatibat ibn Muslim** (in Kharazm in north east of Iran) and **Hadjaj** (in Iraq) ordered all **Farsi** and **Sanskrit** books and documents, in any subject, to be burned.[1]

Resolute **Arab** rulers could not abolish Farsi completely. Farsi was still the language that all official and judicial texts and records in **Iranian** courts were being kept in. Even the first coins, which were minted during the eighth year of **Omar**'s rule, had the insignia of **Zarathustra**'s holy fire and the face of one of the **Sassanid** kings with Pahlavi letters. This trend continued for about two centuries. Nomadic **Arabs** could not keep official records of written accounts, and reluctantly used **Persian** scholars and book keepers. Except for these important purposes, Farsi was strongly discouraged by the Arab occupiers.

Logically, many reluctant Persian scholars and artists were bound to create their writings in **Arabic**, simply for economic reasons, if not for any other. Some **Persians**, however, through adulation, chose to use Arabic terms and expressions to show off or to gain economical and social advantages from their **Arab rulers**. The **Sassanid** government was forced to sluggishly pass through this transitional phase of the change of power. This was exactly how the **Persian** mathematicians, physicians, engineers and bookkeepers in the courts of **Arab** masters regained their respect and high status, since **Arabs** could not execute any of these vital services by themselves.

Nevertheless, the **Arab rulers** in Persia did not easily accept this fact. It was fundamentally against their racial prejudices. **Arabs** believed that **non-Arabs** are inferior to them. Soon the ugly truth about the internal problems of Arab social fabric surfaced. Their bigotry against *non-Arabs* (referred to as *Ajam*), contrary to the teachings of Islam, revealed its loathsome face in the new land. The promised brotherhood and equality and justice for all had turned into a racial suppression of **Arabs** in all layers of the society. **Georgi Zeidan**, the famous Arab historian, confessed in his *The History of Islamic Civilization* that for the **Arab conquerors** a touch by a dog as well as a touch by "Mavali", meaning (non-Arab **Muslims**) could nullify their ablution thus rendering them unholy and dirty.

Thus, many villagers and farmers in Persia chose to retain their earlier beliefs in Ahura-Mazda. Even into the 4th Century after the invasion of **Arabs**, the farmers and herders of provinces of Gilan and Mazandaran in North held **Zorastherianism** as the dominant faith in these areas. In Kerman and Yazd, there were many **Zoroastrians** who held their rituals secretly. Any resistance against the political regime of the **Arab Caliph** meant an equal resentment or resistance towards God.

As a matter of fact, the **Arabs** did not hold on to their initial missionary intentions in Persia. Everywhere, **Persians** were forced to submit to the faith or bear the consequences. Many Persian **Zorastherians** or **Christians**, who did not want to convert, were allowed to keep their faith by paying a poll tax or tribute instead. On the other hand, many **Persians** actually started to believe in the new ideology of Islam and freely chose to follow the doctrines laid by **Prophet Muhammad**. Ironically, some **Persians** even found their way to the top of the social hierarchy of **Arabs'** monarchy and became popular and respectful members of their community. Among most of the **Muslim** scientists and scholars of Persia, the name of **Salman** from Fars is well known in Arab history. During the life of **Prophet Muhammad, Salman Farsi** was the mastermind behind the successful construction of moats defending the city of Medina against the threats of other Arab tribes. **Georgi Zeidan** expressly refers to the fact that **Persians** were unanimously managing the entire official books of legislature and finance for their **Arab rulers.**[2]

Yahya Balazary the Arab historian wrote in his *Fotuh-ul-Baladan*, (*Conquering of Lands*) that many **Caliphs** had been sending huge numbers of **Arabs** into the Persian states to live among **Persians**. The **Arab Caliph, Moavieh,** had ordered migration of 50 thousand Arab soldiers along with their families into Persian towns of Neishabour, Balkh, Marv, and Khorasan. These assimilated Arab families would serve as "the eyes and ears of the **Caliph**."[3] Nevertheless, some **Persians** - proud of their own heritage - showed continuous resistance against the way this Islamic ideology was being enforced upon them. But, this resistance caused more harsh treatments and higher tributes for these **Persians**.

In *A Literary History of Arabs*, Raynold Nicholson writes that **Arabs** soon found themselves mesmerized by the profound culture of **Persians**. Their important ministers as well as scholars were chosen among **Persians** who easily proved their cultural supremacy in Persia and Arabia, especially after **Bani Omaieh** and during the **Abbasid Dynasty** after 749 A.D.[4]

Omar ruled for about ten years. A **Persian** slave killed him in 644A.D. The slave had not found **Omar**'s indifference towards the exorbitant taxes imposed on him tolerable. Following this, **Osman** took over as the **Third Imam** or **Caliph** of **Islamic** nations centered at Medina. Due to his weaker personality **Osman** could not withstand the internal tribal arguments considering his leadership. However, the remarkably positive step he took was to order professional scribes and **Muslim** scholars to gather all scattered hand-written copies and transcripts of the *Koran* and keep them in an orderly fashion in one complete book. But, the next twelve years of turmoil and unsatisfied claims of different parties and sections inside the government ended his terror at his own house in Medina.

Ali ibn Abitalib, Prophet Muhammad's son in law, was chosen by some of the people to replace **Osman** in 656 A.D. as the **Fourth Imam** or **Caliph** of the **Muslims**. He was actually the first person who had accepted the faith of **Islam** directly from the **Prophet** and became the first **Muslim** man when he was very young. He had chosen to stay silent during all the other **Imams'** leadership in Medina. Most people liked **Ali ibn Abitalib** very much because of his virtues, and yet he had many enemies who looked for a way to blind his followers who respected him and his family. He was a man of law and justice and his simple life style was the proof of it. But **Ali** knew that he had to overcome a lot of deceitful claims for power from **Moavieh**, the viceroy of the city of Sham and a descendant of **Bani Omaieh Dynasty**. On top of this **Ali** had to face hypocritical dissensions within the **Muslim** community by a group of unhappy radical **Muslims** called **Khavarej**. **Moavieh's** money and political promises had already toppled other **Imams** and had caused **Muslims** fighting **Muslims** in Arabia. Thus more uprises led to radical and hostile reactions. **Ali** was also assassinated in 661 A.D. while praying in a mosque. He had a legendary and pious life style. One of his famous statements is: "A man's treasure is his wisdom."[5] **Ali** was deeply respected among other **Muslim** nations because of his virtues as a modest and rightful viceroy. He was a brave soldier and a firm judge who possessed versatile and magnificent characteristics. His munificent gifts to the needy were well known, and his fame superceded him in all the Islamic lands. **Ali ibn Abitalib** was to all **Muslims** like **Cyrus The Great** was to all peoples within his empire.

At this time, the faith of Islam had grown to two major sub-divisions: **Shiite (Shia)** and **Sunni**. The social resistance of **Persians**, mostly the **Shiite**, against the Arab conquerors grew stronger. The **Shiite** doctrine flourished inside Persia as a way of patriotic protest against **Arab Caliphs**, although this resistance was relatively dispersed. In the absence of **Ali**, after much anticipation **Moavieh** found the chance to foist his rule over the entire Islamic Empire, and shape this regime into a hereditary rule. It was about the same time that the newly formed group of protesters, called **Khavarej**, segregated their path from the rest of Muslim communities. They believed that the **Imams** or **Caliphs** had misused the Islamic laws and had allowed their personal judgments to overshadow the way they treated different tribes. This group had already caused a lot of trouble and internal conflicts for the previous **Imams**.

Hassan who had his own followers was the older son of **Ali ibn Abitalib**. His reluctant acceptance of a politically influenced peace agreement with **Moavieh**, avoided an imminent bloodshed. But **Bani Omaieh Dynasty** used this new chance to expand its political control. Contrary to the clear democratic ways laid by **Prophet Muhammad** for choosing the rightful **Imam** to lead the **Muslims**, **Moavieh** personally appointed his own son to be the next king. His name was **Yazid**, and he took the throne amidst a wave of protesting tribes. Many were against this outrageously unilateral succession in leadership, and found it specious, but all criticism was dealt with viciously.

This new ruler, **Yazid**, had only one salient opponent who was not giving up easily. This opponent was **Hussein**, the second son of **Ali** and the **Third Imam** of **Shiite Muslims**. **Hussein** did not count the other earlier **Imams** before **Ali** as legitimate. So the **Shiite** sect believed in **Ali** as the First **Imam** succeeding **Muhammad** the prophet, and **Hasan** and **Hussein** as the **Second** and **Third Imams**. Worried about his position, **Yazid** sent his troops to stop **Hussein** who was outnumbered because only a few of his family members and close friends and followers had chosen to stand by him. These truly devoted friends and relatives had knowingly chosen to stand by **Hussein**, in spite of the odds. They chose to fight against the tyranny of **Yazid**. Hence, in an unfair ambush in the desert of Karbala in today's Iraq, **Hussein** and almost all of his family members were brutally massacred in 680 A.D. This appeared contrary to what **Moavieh** had advised **Yazid**. **Moavieh** had advised his son to be lenient with **Hussein** upon his capture; after all, he was the grandson of the **Prophet Muhammad**.[6]

Thus the followers of the two sects of **Shiite** and **Sunni** divided the nation of **Islam** and caused many conflicts that followed. **Yazid** immediately sent **Muslim ibn Ziad** to rule Khorasan in northeast Persia where a great number of followers of the **Shiite** had gathered. At this time, many rebellious confrontations with **Arabs** surfaced, but none were strong enough to bring about important changes. After **Yazid**'s death, however, the **Omavian Dynasty** came to its gradual fall.

Hadjaj ibn Yusef (also referred to as **Abdul Malek**) was a ruthless warrior that **Persians** hated with passion—he had insisted that all libraries in Persia to be burned to ashes. To insert his tyrannical rule further in Persia, after taking over **Yazid**'s position, **Hadjaj** minted the first **Arabic** coins. Later, he annulled the tradition of maintenance of governmental transactions by Farsi—speaking writers. All the books were to be written in **Arabic** only. After his death, his son **Valid** took the throne. During his kingdom (between 704 and 714 A.D.) **Islam** expanded further towards the eastern lands of Sind and India. Also, the famous **Muslims'** invasion of Spain occurred during this king's reign. The world of **Islam** had by now accumulated the civilization and the scientific knowledge of many nations. **Persians, Turks, Indus, Egyptians**, and **Arabs** were all a part of this Islamic world.

This expansion was not limited to Middle East but other people of Asia, Africa, and Europe. The Islamization of southern Europe, especially Portugal and Iberia occurred between 710 and 732 A.D. With the help of all subdued nations, the power of **Arab** armies persuaded conversion of a large proportion of the population of Portugal to **Islam**. Old **Roman** temples were adapted or rebuilt to make new mosques. Science and learning were among the most profound contributions, which **Muslim** scholars brought to this part of Europe—If **Arabs** had not burned thousands of original and hand written scientific texts in **Persian** libraries, this contribution would be greater—Nevertheless, the old Greek philosophers and mathematicians were rediscovered through the medium of Arabic translations of the classics—which happened centuries after the religious wars. Even better engineering in building stronger ships was borrowed from the **Arabs**.[7]

Following **Valid**, the Arab heirs **Solomon** and then **Omar ibn Abdul Aziz** took over, and after the latter **Yazid II (Abdul Aziz's son)** took the control. But, the **Omaieh** kingdom was caught in the internal up rises against the central power. Finally, **Hesham** was the next **Caliph**, he ordered the daring invasion against France in 732 A.D.

It was during this period that **Persians** maneuvered their first successful rebellion against the **Omavian** rulers. **Hesham** (the latest **Caliph**) was aggressively threatening Europe. **Iranian Muslims** under **Abu Muslim Khorasani**, a **Persian** general, gathered some two hundred thousand soldiers and started a serious war with **Nasr** ibn **Sayar** the **Omavian (Omaieh)** viceroy of Khorasan. **Abu Muslim**'s victories in Khorasan continued to worry even the new **Caliph, Marvan.** Soon, **Abu Muslim** managed to urge and pull this worrying **Caliph** personally into the combat zone. Persian warriors circled and killed **Marvan** along with his soldiers and put an end to **Bani Omaieh (Omavian) Dynasty** in 749 A.D.[8] Europe was relieved. **Abu Muslim** had shown perseverance to follow and defeat **Bani Omaieh** rulers who had been acting more like raiders than missionaries. Surprisingly, **Abu Muslim** mostly favored the **Arabic Abbasid** family rather than a descendant of his own **Persian kings.** One reason for the lack of interest in ruling **Persia** himself could be that his military was formed with thousands of **Abbasid** followers, anyway. Therefore, a new era of domination over the plateau of Persia (or Iran) had just started. This is the beginning of the rule of Arabic **Abbasid Dynasty** over the entire **Islamic lands**—with heroism and direct assistance of Persian commander **Abu Muslim.**

It was around this time in Europe that **Christianity** was also being expanded with military power. At the same time **Scandinavians,** mostly **Danes** and **Norwegians,** figure prominently in the history of Western Europe as raiders. The English called them **Danes.** The Irish called them **Pagans.** The **Slavs** of Eastern Europe called these invaders **Rus,** meaning Oarsmen. In **Arabic** and **Byzantine Greek** texts, **Rus** is ultimately used to refer to Russia.[9]

In Asia Minor and Middle East the newest era of theocratic supremacy and missionary domination had immerged. All **Iranians-** Muslim or non- generally looked at **Muslim Arabs** as raiders. Later on, **Asceticism** and **Sufism** that were born into **Islam** diverted some of the potential resistance of **Persians,** which was needed against these invaders. **Sufism** was a mystic approach about the role of man in nature. It was in turn based on the older religions of **Christianity** and **Judaism.** Severe meditative life style of **Dervish** and **Sufi** emphasized the lack of will for man to choose his own path in the universe. To many, these doctrines seem to be a blow against the patriotic resistance of **Persians** against the **Arab raiders.** Thus, some historians and scholars have criticized these worldviews as damaging and depressingly negative.[10]

On the other hand, some historians believe that the followers of major sects **(Christians, Muslims,** and **Jews)** lack understanding about the implied meaning in these three divine messages. Further, this lack of understanding is the root of the conflicts in the Middle East, Europe, and The United States..

In *When Religion Becomes Evil*, Kimball states that one must note that the narrow understanding of mission - expansion and carrying of faith to others – has unfortunately combined with cultural imperialism and military power in ways that result in nothing but sin and crime against all humanity.[11]

1. *Two Centuries Of Silence*, Dr. A. Zarinkoob, pp. 113-126

2. *Chekideh Tarikh Iran*, pp. 64-65

3. *Notes and Observations on The History Of Iran*, Ali Mirfetros, Farhang Publications, 2001, p. 86

4. *Farhang-e-Irani Pish Az Islam*, Muhammad Muhammadi, 3rd edition, Tehran, 1996, p. 90

5. *Tarikh-e-Iran*, pp. 737-745

6. *Tarikh-e-Iran*, pp. 749-770

7. *A Concise History Of Portugal*, by David Birmingham, Cambridge UK, 1993, p. 15

8. *Chekideh Tarikh Iran*, pp. 66-67

9. *The Oxford Illustrated History Of The Vikings*, edited by Peter Sawyer, 1997, N.Y, p. 3

10. *Dar Piramoon-e-Tarikh*, by Ahmad Kasravi, 1999,Tehran, pp. 40-44

11. When Religion Becomes Evil, by Charles Kimball, Harper Collins Publishers, 2003, N.Y. p. 62

CHAPTER NINE

The Abbasid Dynasty (749-809 A.D.)
(A'bba See)

As mentioned earlier, this new kingdom actually grew on the basis of heroism of **Abu Muslim** and his army in Khorasan. Actually, the fame of **The Islamic Empire** had grown more during the dominion of The **Omavian Dynasty**. The following **Abbasid Dynasty** was not as dominant as **Omavian**, especially in Africa and Asia Minor. However, the **Abbasid Dynasty** found a safer and more intimate shelter among **Persians** in Khorasan. Naturally, the **Abbasid** had various ethnic rivals in their homeland, Arabia, and mostly among **Bani Omaieh (Omavian)** tribes, who continued residual bloody confrontations to regain power. But this effort was in vain, because **Persians** seemed more inclined to the **Abbasid** than the racist **Omavian**, although both were **Arabs**.

Arabs inside Persia (as well as Afghanistan, part of India and Pakistan) still had to rely on **Persians** for their administrative needs in judicial and legislative processes. For this reason, many patriotic **Persians** came to realize that they were culturally superior to the **Arab** conquerors. **Persians**, under **Abu Muslim**, leader of the **Black Standard (Siah Jamegan)**, who had toppled the **Omavian Dynasty**, gave up their lives to fight **Omavian** rulers who had long lost their original missionary purpose.

Ironically, this resistance had brought another **Arab** tribe to power—**the Abbasid**. Gradually, the military machine of the declining **Omavian** inside Arabia was deteriorating, because its leaders chose a luxurious lifestyle, which had deviated from the Islamic pious standards. The **Caliph** as **Imam** (a religious leader and emperor) was supposed to be the bridge between God (Allah) and the **Muslims** (Ummat).

It was during this period that **Abol Abbas**, with the nickname of **Sabbah**, which means "Ruthless killer", took over and went after the last of **Omaieh** rulers until his own death in 754 A.D. His brother, **Abraham**, hated **Arabs** so much that he had ordered **Abu Muslim** to kill anyone who spoke **Arabic** in Khorasan. Ironically, **Abraham** was an **Arab** himself and from the Ghuraish tribe near Mecca.[1]

Abol Abbas had massacred all who rejected his kingdom in Iraq and Sham. He had even assassinated his own loyal bishops, like **Abu Salmeh**. When he died of measles, **Mansoor** took over and had **Abu Muslim** killed in spite of all his past heroic actions for bringing this dynasty to power. History has witnessed many Iranian heroes like **Sinbad** from Neishabour, and **Baabak** in Azerbaijan and **Maziar** from Tabarestan in North of Iran who started their rebellions in different forms and manner. All these battles had a political theme aiming at the independence of Persia from Arab occupiers.

In spite of these scattered rebellions, in the Abbasid period, **Muslim Persians** gradually attracted the trust and respect of their **Arab conquerors**, starting with **Mansoor**. After him, **Mehdi** took over. He ordered the massacre of **Maani** believers. **Maani,** as mentioned earlier, was an ideologue in Persia, who was born around 216 A.D. and **Shapur** the **Sassanid** king believed in him. His doctrines, based on the religion of **Mehr**, talked about the constant rivalry between the good and the bad in universe. **Maani** had grown popular in the eastern Asia and western Europe.

In 785 A.D. after the sudden illness and death of **Mehdi**, his son **Haadi** took the control, which only lasted for a year. Then, his brother, **Haroon**, took the crown. **Haroon** was referred to as **Haroon Al Rashid** (The brave) in history.[2]

Haroon Al Rashid

It was during the reign of this **caliph, Haroon Al Rashid,** that Baghdad in Iraq became the popular center of The **Islamic Empire.** His court was haven for poets, philosophers, scholars, and artists. The famous book of *The Tales of One Thousand and One Nights* pertains to this period.

Scattered confrontations between the **Byzantine Christians** and **Middle East Muslims** were still going on. However, internally, Persia caused some threats against the government in Baghdad. **Yahya,** a descendant of **Imam Hasan** (the second **Imam** of **Shiite**), rebelled in Gilan (near Caspian Sea). However, **Fazl Barmaki,** a **Persian Viceroy** ruling inside the occupied Persia, diminished this threat from within the country on behalf of the **Arab Caliph (Haroon Al Rashid).** Soon, **Yahya** was captured by the help of **Fazl** and delivered to **Haroon** in Baghdad. This capture is of historical importance because it shows a political division among **Persians** who quarreled and fought for the rule of total strangers inside Persia.

Because of such services, **Fazl Barmaki** and his sons and family members gained the trust of the **Caliph.** Thus, **Haroon Al Rashid** bestowed upon them important governmental and official high positions. As **Philip Khalil** writes in his *History of Arab,* **Barmakian** were the most powerful **Persians** in the Islamic world after the **Caliphs.** There was supreme irony in the fact that **Persians** themselves were helping Arab invaders to rule Persia. **Persians** who were delegated chief positions in their local government usually claimed that they chose to do so to retain the ultimate control over the lives and wealth of their own fellow citizens against the utter control of the **Caliph.** Unfortunately, most of these **Vazirs** would loose their lives when their local power grew beyond the trust and tolerance of the **caliph.** This actually happened to **Barmakian** family.

Islam has strict rules for physical closeness governing men and women. In some cases a mock marriage (Sigheh) would lessen the restrictions to accomodate their simple contacts. **Haroon** had given his sister, **Abbaseh,** in a mock Sighe to **Jafar Barmaki,** his trusted **Persian Vazir.** Thus, **Jafar** could easily enter the private sections of **Caliph's** court (Harem) while women were present. Of course, it was understood that **Jafar** and **Abbaseh** could never be physically together and this relation was not to be construed as a real marriage. Naturally, after a while, the young couple did not care to follow the senseless orders of the **Caliph**. Soon, **Abbaseh** and **Jafar** fell in love and the news of her pregnancy made **Haroon** absolutely insane. Consequently, the whole **Barmaki** family were persecuted and destroyed. This tragic and heinous crime is unfortunately repeated in many ways in the history. Although seldom noticed as an example, it is ultimately proven that betrayal of ones country against the pressures or temptations of invaders is inherently tragic.[3]

Haroon died in 809 A.D. when he was only 43 years old. He is buried in a garden in Khorasan where **Imam Reza** (the eighth **Imam** of **Shiite**) was also buried a few years later.[4]

Ironically, the 7th Century was the time of **Sibuyeh**, the first **Persian Linguist** who wrote a complete dictionary of **Arabic** language, never attempted before. Ironically, the 7th century, amidst the bloodshed, science was taught in schools and the **Abbasid** promoted arts. The 8th Century is the time of the great **Persian Grammarian** and translator called **Ibn Moghafa**; his real name was **Roozbeh** and was born in Firooz Abad in Persia. He reformed and rewrote the entire grammar rules of **Arabic** language that revolutionized the morphology and semantics of it. The famous **Persian Chemist** in the city of Ray, in the 9th Century, is **Muhammad Zakaria Razi**, who discovered a new substance, which he named Alcohol. Also, he discovered and named another substance called Ammonia.[5] It is interesting to know that contrary to public opinion, wine was first made in Pars plateau about 5000 B.C.

1. *Tarikh-e-Iran*, Sir Percy Sykes, Tehran, p.778
2. *Chekideh Tarikh Iran*, pp. 68-69
3. *Tarikh-e-Iran*, Vol. 2, Sir Percy Sykes, translated by M.Taghi Fakhr Dayee, Tehran 1993
4. *Chekideh Tarikh Iran*, pp. 69, 70
5. Concise Encyclopedia Of Iran, by Jaleh Mottahedian, edited by Dr. M.J. Mahjoob, 1998, U.S.A., pp. 285-313

CHAPTER TEN

Taheri (Taherian) Dynasty (818 – 872 A.D.)

History recalls increasing rebels at far corners of **The Islamic Empire**, which continuously threatened the position of the **Caliphs** in Baghdad. Various viceroys, with individual goals and authorities, came to power in Persia and other parts of the Middle East and Asia Minor. Naturally, some stronger **Persian Viceroys** yearned for more independence from the **Caliphs**. However, each reigning **Arab Caliph** was struggling to strengthen his own position within Arabia. For about two centuries some minor **Persian** centers of authority — pushing for independence — came under the influence of each of these **Caliphs**. These centers would constantly rise and fade away.

After **Haroon** the late **Caliph**, the **Islamic Empire** was caught between his two sons - **Amin** and **Mamoon**. They had different mothers. A **Persian Muslim** by the name of **Fazl ibn Sahl** who was the new **Vazir** of this government, stepped forward. The influence of this **Vazir** was detrimental in the nomination of **Amin** or **Mamoon** as the future **Arab Caliph**.

Knowing that, **Mamoon**'s mother was a Persian "kaniz" (maid) given to **Haroon** as a gift, **Fazl ibn Sahl** was more favored towards

Mamoon who was of Persian blood. Thus. **Mamoon** grew stronger in the eyes of the public until he had the confidence to name himself the **Caliph of East**. As mentioned previously, the presence of **Persian Vazirs** in the **Arab** rulers' courts was an embodiment of the **Persians'** resistance against the racial prejudice of their **Arab** invaders. This may be looked at as a degree of peaceful resistance along with the acceptance of the new faith.

Thus, **Persians** had realized that they needed to differentiate between the Arab invasion and the great ideology contained within it. **Persians** understood that ambitious **Persians** in high governmental positions inside Arabic aristocracy would resist and modify these **Arab invaders'** racism and prejudice against **Persians**.[1]

Eventually, there were some changes in the attitude of **Arab rulers** that followed. The basic difference between the **Omavian (Bani Omaieh)** — the previous rulers — and the **Abbasid** Dynasties — the current rulers — was that the latter ruled without extreme racial discriminations. During this period, the **Abbasid** were more willing to learn from **Persians** or other non-Arabs than just simply denying the foreign nations' heritage. This truly gave **Persians** a chance to demonstrate the depth and width of their own culture and civilization .[2]

Therefore, a more lenient diplomacy of **The Abbasid** called for decentralization of power down to local governments. This is another reason for the rise of many smaller kingdoms in this period inside Persia — some founded by **Persians** and some by **Turks** and even other **Arabian** tribes.

One of these smaller kingdoms in Persia during the **Abbasid Caliphate** actually started to form in this period. As mentioned earlier, the next two centuries are filled with such centers of command inside Persia. These small Persian kingships gradually deviated from the absolute control of **Arabs**. **Taherian Dynasty** is one of them with a history slightly over 50 years.

In addition, the position of the Caliph was also threatened from within Iraq. Meanwhile, the Arab **Amin** of the **Abbasid** Dynasty became more restless. He tried to overcome his brother — **Mamoon** — by sending troops towards him. This was a controversy that caused more dissension among Arabs. A **Persian** warrior named **Taher** managed to overcome this army in spite of the small numbers of his soldiers. Later on, he pushed to the heart of Baghdad and killed **Amin**. He is the founder of **Taherian Dynasty**. Under **Mamoon**'s supervision, this dynasty ruled over Khorasan for a short period of about fifty years. Again, history repeats itself. Because **Taher** became increasingly popular in Persia, **Mamoon** gradually turned against him. **Taher** was finally poisoned as an immutable reaction of the **Caliph** against his own **Vazir**. However, to keep the peace in that part of Persia, **Mamoon** chose **Taher**'s son, named **Talheh**, as the Viceroy of Khorasan under direct supervision from Baghdad. **Taher** had chosen Neishabour as the capital of Khorasan for his ruling around 818 A.D. Generally, **Taherian** rulers were not very opportunistic and could not hold out against the strong **Saffarian**'s invasion in 872 A.D.

Continuously, **Mamoon** was facing tremendous pressure from **Shiites** in Persia as well as **Christians** of Byzantium. **Mamoon** decided to subdue the pressures in Persia by nominating the eighth **Imam** of **Shiite**, **Reza**, as his official Crown Prince. Thus, **Mamoon** ordered the marriage of one of his daughters with this **Imam**. Again, after noticing the extraordinary popularity of **Imam Reza** in Persia, he ordered this pious man to be poisoned in 818 A.D.

Meanwhile, **Baabak Khoramdin**, a Persian patriot fighter who had gathered a large group of followers in Persia, had become a more serious trouble for **Arab rulers** of Baghdad for over twenty years. Before **Mamoon** passed away in 833 A.D., he nominated his other brother, **Motasem**, as his successor. **Motasem** ran the government just like **Mamoon**. He was fond of expansion and commercial ties with the world, but had the least tolerance for argumentative confrontations. This period in **Abbasid** Dynasty, contrary to the previous book burning was the climax in the **Caliphs'** patronage of scientists, poets, scholars, physicists, and artists from all over the world. The Islamic lands, Persia and Arabia, in particular, were open to all faiths and their believers as long as the conduct was not threatening the doctrines of **Islam**.

Afshin, another Persian general in **Motasem**'s court, was delegated with the authority to find and eliminate **Baabak** who had been rebelling against the authority of the **Caliph Motasem** in Baghdad. This finally happened and **Baabak** was arrested in Azerbaijan and sent to his death in Baghdad. He is another example of dilemma of **Persians** against **Persians**. It is noteworthy how some

Persians were used by the **Arab Caliphs** against their own people. Later on, just when **Afshin** gathered enough attention, he received his imminent fate. After a fake prosecution on the basis of his **Zorastherian** inclinations, **Afshin** was also executed. In 842 A.D. the **Caliph**'s son, **Vassegh**, traditionally took over the throne. His mother was a **Greek** maid (a concubine as well) in his father's court. The riots in Iran grew tense. The insurgent **Syrians** and **Palestinians** started their scattered resistance against this dynasty, but the **Turkish Vazirs** in **Vassegh's** court were sent to fight these rebels. However, this **Caliph**'s unrestrained and luxurious life was shortened by an early death.

Then **Motevakel** took his place in 847 A.D. He immediately increased the pressure and control on all social layers in his kingdom. **Motevakel** demanded an Orthodox outlook strictly conforming to the rites and traditions of older **Sunni Islam**. He is known to have initiated the support of extreme and Orthodox views in Islamic schools—a dogmatism that backfired in later centuries as an impediment for the social and economical growth in Persia. While drunk, **Motevakel** ordered the destruction of the tomb of **Imam Hussein** the third **Imam** of the **Shiites**. Also, **Motevakel** uprooted the famous holy tree that **Prophet Zarathustra** had personally planted. The tree had been apparently over 1500 years old. These senseless actions brought such unpleasant reactions that his personal guards finally killed **Motevakel** and put his son **Montaser** on the throne. But, **Motaser**'s kingdom was short, too. After about six months he also died. Now the **Turks** in his court had gained so much power that they constantly chose new heirs to the crown and replaced or killed them at their own discretion.[3] During this time the **Turk Vazirs** inside the **Abbasid** courts transgressed the laws and possessed a totalitarian power in government like **Moghs** during The **Sassanid** dynasty.

It is important to remember that **Abbasid Dynasty** brought to the public a substantial interest in science and art. Ordinary people were urged to go to school and learn about the world. Most of the western philosophers' books and theories were translated into Arabic since **Caliphs** and their men needed to know more about the new parts of the world they had conquered. **Persians** had already established this trend in their land and obtained a huge treasure of books and texts that were transferred to the **Arabs** upon their arrival in Persia. Of course, this treasure could be far greater if the earlier tragic book burnings had not occurred. The Persian solar calendar of **Yazdigird** was in use and observed by **Arab kings**. Jondi Shapur in northwest of Khuzestan near Shush became one of the biggest medical universities in the world. It is true that **Shapur I** of the **Sassanid** originally had established it, but it reached its universal fame during this period. The persecuted **Byzantine scientists** had also migrated to the Islamic lands of Persia and Iraq to continue their scientific experiments and teachings in peace. This era had brought a civilization that simply was not available anywhere else in the world.[4]

Christian Europe was caught in dark ages while Middle East thrived with the new religion of **Islam**. It was in this period in Europe, that the dominant **Franks** (a **Germanic** tribe, referred to as **Barbarians**) became the most determined influence upon the character of the age to come. **Christian Orthodoxy** and their first king, **Clovis**—referred to as **Louis**—established the **French kingdom**. It was **Charles Martel**, the mayor of Tours in this kingdom, that resisted the **Muslim** invasion against France in 732 A.D., (During the ruling of **Hesham** of **Bani Omaieh Dynasty**). In Britain the **Vikings**, whom the **Anglo-Saxons** called inaccurately the **Danes**, first arrived in 787A.D. Later, king **Alfred of Wessex** in Britain inspired his country to stand up against the **Danes** (**Viking** raiders) around 880 A.D. (He is the only **English King** who is called The Great; greatness is reserved for **English Queens**). He was a king with futuristic vision who fought enemies of his country as well as illiteracy among his people by establishing a court school and importing professional teachers.[5]

1.   Dar Piramoon-e-Tarikh, By Ahmad Kasravi, 1999, Tehran, p. 59

2.   *Farhang Irani Pish Az Islam*, M. Muhammadi, 3rd edition, 1996, Tehran, pp. 86-90

3.   *Chekideh Tarikh Iran*, Hasan Naraghi, 2nd edition, 2002, Tehran, pp. 70-73

4.   *Farhang Irani Pish Az Islam*, By Muhammad Muhammadi, 3rd Edition, 1996, Tehran, pp. 222, 229

5.   *The Middle Ages*, by Morris Bishop, 1987, published by Harrington Mifflin, N.Y, P.16-34

CHAPTER ELEVEN

Saffarian Dynasty
(870 A.D. – 903 A.D.)

Yaghoob Laith (Yakub ibn Lais), referred to as Saffar (blacksmith), was a young Persian leader in Sistan (south east of today's Iran). In early youth, he led a life like an outlaw with his gang. This kind of behavior was a sort of traditional lifestyle for those who chose to stay as rebels - like the legend of Robin Hood. Later, Yaghoob managed to show a great deal of valor in the court of Saleh (the viceroy of Sistan). But after the execution of Motevakel by his own men (around 850 A.D.), the Arab Caliph of the 9th Century, Yaghoob succeeded Saleh in Persia and became the Viceroy of Sistan. Soon after securing his position, Yaghoob looked towards Kerman and Fars (central Iran). This appeared to be a fight against the rebellious Khavarej who were against the central government of Baghdad. But, his continuous victories on different battlefields had accrued for him more fame among Persians than he expected. Soon, Yaghoob took the control of the entire Khorasan and Tabas (northeast of Iran). Thus, he easily put an end to the short Taherian reign of Khorasan.

Subsequently, in 871 A.D. Yaghoob sent a messenger to Baghdad to the court of Movafagh (Muaffak) who had succeeded Motevakel. Through official requests, Yaghoob had asked permission from the new Caliph for himself to stay as a faithful servant, although he was ruling over all these lands. **Persians** liked **Yaghoob Laith**, because he was the first **Persian** who had taken control of the land from **Arab rulers**. Also, **Yaghoob** was a strong swordsman from Sistan, the birthplace of the legendary heroic **Rostam**.[1] **Persia** during **Saffarian Dynasty** elected its own religious scholars as supreme judges of the nation, and the Arab **Caliphs** could not appoint them to this position anymore. The **Persians** were getting their power back and they installed supreme judges in appropriate and highly qualified governmental positions. The lasting effect of this appointment was Persian control over local government.

Because both the **Arab Caliph** and **Persians** acknowledged his authority, **Yaghoob** found the opportunity to raid Kabul in Afghanistan (this province had formally been under the Persian rule for centuries). Then, **Yaghoob** chased **Hasan ibn Zeid** the founder of smaller **Alavian** kingdom from Sari (in the northern province of Mazandaran). These accomplishments reinforced his political strength. Tired of submission to the **Arab Rulers (Caliphs)** inside his own country, **Yaghoob** campaigned against **Caliph Motamed (Motamid)** in Baghdad in 875 A.D. This was an unprecedented direct battle against the **Arabs** by **Persians**. But, **Yaghoob** did not succeed and had to retreat back to Fars. He started gathering a new army without delay – probably convincing them that this fight is a patriotic battle and has no religious demoralization. About three years later, **Motamed,** worried about **Yaghoob** being a relentless fighter, sent him his personal friendly remonstrance in a dual diplomatic tone to invite **Yaghoob** to peace while saying that this was also to his own advantage. **Yaghoob,** who was terminally sick and bedridden, pointed to his sword next to his tray of a plain food. He had a piece of bread and onion on the tray. He told the messenger to tell the **Caliph** that if he recovered, that sword would rule between **Yaghoob** and the **Caliph**. In case of his victory, **Yaghoob** emphasized, that he would decide about the fate of the **Caliph**, and in case of his defeat, that plain food was all he really needed. **Yaghoob Laith** died shortly after. His strong resistance against those **Persian** writers and poets who used to recite and devise their writings in **Arabic** is well known in the history. **Yaghoob** questioned and deplored the use of any language but Farsi as the dominant language of Persia. He served the heritage of **Farsi** language through his famous patriotic resistance of Arab language domination in **Persian** lands.[2]

CHAPTER TWELVE

The Samanid (Samanian Dynasty)
(873 A.D. – 999 A.D.)

Thus, Farsi language prevailed in Persia rather than the Arabic language of the **Caliphs**. But after **Yaghoob**'s death, his brother **Amro Laith** took the control of Khorasan by a peace agreement that he had to sign with **Caliph Motamed**. After the death of this **Caliph**, a new **Caliph** named **Motazed** took the throne in Baghdad. About this time **Amro Laith** raided Neishabour. In order to attract **Motazed**'s satisfaction and trust, he started towards Bokhara and Balkh in East of Iran. **Ismail**, the son of a **Persian** noble man named **Ahmad** who had founded **Samanian Dynasty** around 873 A.D., ruled this land. This dynasty had the control over this part of the world for over 125 years and its **Persian** rulers claimed to be a descendant of **Bahram Chubin** of the **Sassanid**. But **Amro Laith** could not overthrow **Ismail**. Ironically, he got captured and killed by him later in 903 A.D. Thus the short life of **Saffarian Dynasty** came to its end in about three decades. Their descendants maintained scattered control in Sistan for some more time. However, the **Caliphs** in Baghdad enjoyed the chance to continue their rule in Persia as long as there were internal fights inside this land. These fights diverted attentions away from Baghdad.

Because of his latest services to the **Caliph** and because of politics of his time, **Ismail Samani** received the kingdom over Khorasan and Kerman by the direct order of **Caliph Motazed**. Thus, **Ismail** chose Bokhara as his capital. After him, his 7-year-old son, **Nasr II**, ruled for about thirty years. After him, came: **Noah, Abdul Malek, Mansoor,** and **Noah II** respectively. **Avi Cenna (Abu Ali ibn Sina)**, the **Persian** physician and philosopher born in Hamadan in 980 A.D., lived at the time of **Noah II** and was his personal physician. A few western historians have erroneously referred to **Ibn Sina** as an Arab. The fact that many Persian scholars and seers had produced their writings in Arabic (the officially dominant and politically correct language of the Arab invaders in Persia) seems to have confused some historians in their superficial surveys. After **Noah II, Mansoor II** (and after him **Abdul Malek II)** took the throne. This last king of **Samanian Dynasty** was captured by **Eelak Khan** a descendant of the **Ghaznavi Turks** in Ghaznain and later died in prison in 999 A.D.

Around this period, the dismay and administrative chaos in the courts of Baghdad, the central headquarter of the Islamic domain, had caused numerous scattered bedlams all over the Middle East and Asia Minor, including Persia. **Persian Dynasties**, that flourished in a dispersed fashion and in various provinces, did not last long enough to define borderlines and authorities that could positively be recognized in the history of this period. **Taherian, Saffarian** and **Samanian Dynasties**—three short-lived local governments—had **Persian leaders**, but they were mainly under the control and supremacy of **Arab Caliphs**.

Simultaneously, with the ruling of **Nasr II** (of the **Persian Samanid Dynasty**) the province of Tabarestan (today's Mazandaran) was seized again by **Hasan ibn Ali** (an **Arab** descendant of **Ali ibn Abitalib** the first **Imam** of **Shiite**). This did not take long, since **Mard Avij** from **Al-e-Ziar** tribe conquered that province as well as Isfahan and founded the **Al-e-Ziar Dynasty** in 928 A.D., which lasted over a hundred years in northerly parts of Persia. He was not much attracted to **Islam** and apparently had stayed a **Zorastherian** all his life. **Ghaboos** seems to stand out in many successors of **Mard Avij**. He was a cruel ruler, but had a soft spot for scientists. **Abu Reihan Birooni**, the Persian scientist and writer of *Asaar Al Baghieh*, dedicated his work to **Ghaboos**. **Birooni** is also erroneously referred to as an **Arab** scientist frequently by less than knowledgeable historians. Finally, **Ghaboos**'s noblemen forced him to abdicate and killed him in his castle near Gorgan (North of Iran) in 1012 A.D.[3]

Most of the **Persian kings** of **Al-e-Ziar** (also called **Ziarid Dynasty** 928 – 1042 A.D.) paid a great deal of attention to literature and ethical teachings for the younger generation. One of these rulers was named **Kay Kavus ibn Ghaboos** (the son of **Ghaboos**). He wrote his own book in the ethics and dedicated it to his son the crown prince, **Gilan Shah**. In this book, he advised his son about his future social role as a leader and gave him guidance in righteous ruling of his people and his land. This book was written in 1082 A.D. and is titled *Ghaboos Nameh*.[4] Persia could definitely use more kings with this type of vision.

Famous poets and philosophers of this age are these: **Abu Shakur Balkhi, Rudaki, Kassaie Marvazi,** and **Daghighi. Abu Zeid Balkhi** and **Al Jihani** wrote their extensive books in geography of the world. **Muhammad Zakaria Razi** in science and chemistry in this period and **Muhammad Tabari** in history are very much known to the world, although they wrote their books in **Arabic**.[5] Because of the strict rule of **The Arab Caliphs**, still most books in Persia were written only in **Arabic**.

The **Viceroys** in Persia under the **Baghdad Caliphs** were the major influence on the expansion of science and arts. For comparison, in the western world the equivalent influence seemed to generally belong to the **clergy**, like in **Scandinavian** society, as well as other parts of Europe.[6] The **clergy** in Persia did not contribute as much to civilized arts as the **clergy** in Europe.

Along with The **Al-e-Ziar**, The **Saffarian**, The **Taherian**, and The **Samanid Dynasty**, several other small centers of command formed simultaneously in Persia. The **Daylamite Dynasty** was one of them.

1. *Tarikh-e-Iran*, By Sir Percy Sykes, 2nd Volume, translated by M.T Fakhr D. Gilani,
    1984, 4th Edition, printed in Tehran, Elmi Publishers, pp. 24-26
2. *Chekideh Tarikh Iran*, By Hasan Naraghi, pp. 74-75
3. *Chekideh Tarikh Iran*, pp.75-76
4. *Tarikh Iran Zamin*, by M.J. Mashkur, pp. 175
5. *Tarikh Iran Zamin*, p. 181
6. *A History of Scandinavia*, by T.K. Derry, p. 46

CHAPTER THIRTEEN

Daylamite Dynasty (Al-e-Buyeh)
(934 A.D. – 997 A.D.)

Many historians referred to **Al-e-Buyeh Dynasty** with different names to accommodate the pronunciation of the language of the text. For example, **Daylamite, Daylamian, Al-e-Buyeh, Buwayhid,** and **Buyeh** all refer to the same dynasty. Same trend is followed for some other dynasties and their kings as well.

A man named **Buyeh** was serving in the army of **Mard Avij** from The **Ziar Dynasty (Al-e-Ziar,** 928 – 1042 A.D.). **Buyeh** had three sons: **Ali, Hasan** and **Ahmad.** Later, one of his sons, **Ali,** was appointed to be a viceroy to run the province of Karaj (near today's Tehran). **Ali** responded with brilliance and zest for leadership. **Buyeh** family took pride in its ancestry of heroes from Daylaman tribe in Mazandaran (north of Iran). After the death of **Mard Avij,** these courageous brothers, who were commanders in his army took the control and expanded their territories to the south by conquering a vast area from Karaj to Fars (from north center to south center of Iran) in 934 A.D. Thus, **Ali ibn Buyeh (Ali the-son-of Buyeh)** and his two brothers are known to be the founders of **Buyeh Dynasty** (also called **The Buwayhid**). They originated from Gilan and Mazandaran provinces and are believed to be related to **Bahram Goor** of **Sassanid Dynasty.**

They were of the **Shiite** faith of Islam. Their growing popularity frightened the **Sunni Caliph** in Baghdad. But he could not deny the three brothers' astute expertise and power in overseeing the newly acquired southern territories in Persia. Therefore, the **Daylamite (Al-e- Buyeh)** brothers received the customary title of **Viceroy** from the **Caliph** of Baghdad (**Mostakfi**) in 945 A.D.[1] **Ahmad** earned the prestigious title of **Moez-u-Doleh.**

Around 967 A.D. **Azad-al- Doleh** became the most famous of all **Daylamian (Daylamite)** kings. He was a **Muslim (Shiite)** and a religious king who cared about his subjects. He chose Shiraz for his capital. Subsequently, **Azad-al-Doleh** started a number of renovations and social reforms. The famous Amir Band (small dam), which was built to improve cultivated lands around Kor River and the famous Azodi Hospital of Shiraz, were among his works. He also had a special protective wall built around Isfahan that resisted any possible attacks.[2] Finally Persia finds a chance under its native rulers to see signs of reform and renovation within the land. Also, this marks the nearing end of the interfering power of the **Caliph** (**Caliphate** tradition) within **The Islamic Empire.**

After the death of **Azad-al-Doleh**, the **Al-e-Buyeh Dynasty** began to fall quickly. **Majd Al Doleh**, the only available heir, succeeded the throne when he was only eleven years old. His mother, **Malek Khatoon**, actually ruled southern Persia through her son. She was a learned woman who took control as a Regent with great governing skills.

At this period, **Mahmood Ghaznavi** who was a descendant of powerful **Turks** inside the courts in Baghdad had gathered his own army and power in Afghanistan (around northeast of Persia). He was anxiously looking at southern Persia to expand his control. **Malek Khatoon** was practically the only political barrier between **Sultan Mahmood Ghaznavi** and the **Daylamian** territories in Persia. She delayed all rebels against her dynasty with utmost control and political insight. **Malek Khatoon** had sent **Sultan Mahmood Ghaznavi** a personal letter. She had discouraged **Mahmood** from any invasion against her. **Malek Khatoon** had emphasized that being a woman ruler, she might not withstand a fight with **Mahmood**, but such victory would not bring much glory for him either. She had also cautioned him that in case of any failure, **Mahmood** would inevitably suffer a great loss of fame. This letter must have had an effect on **Mahmood**, since he never attempted this invasion during her rule. When **Malek Khatoon** passed away **Mahmood Ghaznavi** finally found the chance to invade Fars, Ray, and Isfahan in 997 A.D. The **Buyeh** family was eventually pushed further down in southern Persia where **Saljoughian Dynasty** later eliminated what was left of it.

Daylamian kings (**Al-e-Buyeh**) had enjoyed ultimate control of their kingdom and through strong administration had overcome the dissipating **Caliphs** in Baghdad. This in turn helped the growth of science and philosophy as well as Farsi language inside Persia.

As mentioned earlier, **Avi Sina** (**Abu Ali Sina**), the great Iranian physicist, seer, and philosopher of the late 10th Century lived during this time. The English historian, Professor Brown, has referred to this scientist as one of the exceptional scholars that East and West have benefited from. **Avi Sina** passed away in Hamadan in 1037 A.D.; his tomb is still visited by thousands every year.[3]

In this age, Farsi language, referred to as Dari, found more social ground in Khorasan and other eastern states of Persia and gradually spread over the entire country. Arabic letters, however, replaced the Pahlavi style of writing. Many poets like **Ferdowsi** and **Muhammad Sistani** found refuge in the eastern lands far away from the central quarters of the **Arab Caliphs** in Iraq. Many **Persian** poets feigned approval of the viceroys to receive monetary compensation. However, three outstanding poets—**Ferdowsi**, **Rudaki**, and **Daghighi**—refused to dissemble. They lived poorly but maintained their dignity and pride.[4]

Thus, the **Al-e-Buyeh** period marks the beginning of the decline of the power of **Arab Caliphs** inside Persia. The Arabs were dominant in Persia from 650 A.D. up to about 1000 A.D. At any rate, most of these dynasties were short-lived. Soon a new dynasty would take over with stronger roots.

1. *Chekideh Tarikh Iran*, p. 77
2. *Tarikh Iran Zamin*, p. 177
3. *Chekideh Tarikh Iran*, p. 78
4. *Tarikh Iran Zamin*, Dr. M.J. Mashkur, p. 181

CHAPTER FOURTEEN

Ghazna Dynasty (Ghaznavian)
(962 – 1037 A.D.)

As explained before, **Turkish Vazirs** and generals were gaining political power in the courts of **Arab Caliphs**.

In the time of **Abdul Malek** of The **Samanid Dynasty, Alptigin**, a **Turkish** slave, became a chieftain by his own merit in Khorasan around 962 A.D. He resided in Ghazna in the Sulayman Mountains (Solomon Mountains) in today's Afghanistan. Although **Alptigin** started this semi-independent government it was still under **Arab** supervisors. The real founder of **Ghaznavian Dynasty** is **Alptigin's** **Turkish** son-in-law—**Sabaktagin**. He was the one who had managed to gain the governorship position and later, extended his territorial coverage (east and west) and seized Khorasan from **Noah II**—the last **Samanid** monarch in 994 A.D.

Later, **Mahmood Ghaznavi** succeeded **Sabaktagin** and became one of the greatest figures on the stage of Central Asia. His twelve campaigns in India and zeal for Islam earned him the title of "**Idol-breaker**" —he broke all the **Indian gods** statues on his path to India. In 1007 A.D., **Eelak Khan**, the destroyer of the remaining **Samanid Dynasty**, took advantage of the absence of **Mahmood** from central Asia and raided Khorasan. But **Mahmood** speedily returned from

India and in a bitter and decisive battle in Balkh put an end to **Eelak Khan** and all of his men. As mentioned earlier, **Mahmood**'s last campaign was against the **Buwayhid dynasty (Al-e-Buyeh)**. After the capture of Isfahan (south Central part of Persia), he returned to Ghazna where he died in 1030 A.D. A shrine still marks his grave.[1]

Abolghasem Ferdowsi the great literary scholar, poet, and linguist lived around this time. His masterpiece *Shah Nameh* is truly a Farsi treasure that all **Iranians** cherish. **Ferdowsi**'s brave struggle to stay on the path of creating his book in spite of all the negative political pressures is indeed extraordinary. He spent both his life and wealth in standing firmly for the restoration of Persian heritage and culture under the reign of **Arab Caliphs** and their strict **Persian Viceroys**. Unfortunately, **Mahmood** who had a Turkish blood was more involved with his own religious crusades and did not support the ongoing work of this great scholar.[2]

Masud Ghaznavi, the son of **Mahmood** was from the outset unfortunate. Numerous rebellions all over the territories caused him a lot of pain. He was finally forced to abdicate and was killed by his disappointed noblemen in his court. Also, his son could not survive very long; his rule was weakened by dissensions from all layers in the society. Finally **Ghaznavian Dynasty** was stopped by **Seljuk Dynasty (Saljughian** in Farsi) around 1037 A.D.

Thus, **Ghaznavian Dynasty** reigned for 75 years. **Mahmood** (The **Idol-Breaker**) was the strongest king in this dynasty. His many massacres in India and plunder of Indian wealth made him a dominant figure in Asia. However, **Persians** did not benefit from this bloodshed - although, these crusades indirectly helped the growth of Farsi language among those eastern lands. This expansion of Farsi language caused further translations of many foreign texts into Farsi. Therefore, Farsi spread into Indian language and even became the official language in India's judicial courtrooms for centuries.

1. *History of Persia*, Sykes, Vol. 2, London, pp .26-27
2. *Chekideh Tarikh Iran*, H. Naraghi, Tehran, pp. 80-81

CHAPTER FIFTEEN

Seljuk Dynasty (Saljughian)
(950 – 1072 A.D.)

The first of **Seljuk (Saljugh)** leaders was **Seljuk ibn Daghagh** – the name implies that he was the son of a bow-maker. He was a **Turk** from Turkistan, who belonged to the tribes of **Ghoz** and **Khezer** around the Caspian Sea in northern Persia around 950 A.D. Later on, Seljuk converted to Islam. While the **Samanid Dynasty** was still in power, The **Seljuk** tribes gradually spread eastward to an area called Kharazm (in northeastern Persia).

Although not of **Persian** ancestry, the importance of **Seljuk Dynasty** inside Persia is in its unifying influence upon The **Islamic Empire** as a whole. This was in contrast to the short and provincial dominations of the last scattered dynasties. **Saljughian** ruled for about 120 years. The strong rulers of **Seljuk** in Persia were the direct force behind the increase in dominance of the **Arab Caliphs,** but they did not show much consideration for the **Persian** culture against the **Arab** rulers.

Seljuk ibn Daghagh had a son named **Mikail**, who had two sons. Among the two it was **Toghril** who supervised the invasion of Nei Shabur in 1037 A.D. **Toghril** ruled with power out of egotism rather than love for Persia.

While in the city of Nei Shabur, the major judicial headquarter in Persia, **Toghril** showed his bigotry against the **Persian** scholars and inhabitants of this city. He had remarked that Nei Shabur would be a greater city if only its people could be under the ground and its good water on the surface.[1]

The victories of **Toghril** - in the remainder of Persian territories under the **Ghaznavi**, **Al-e-Ziar**, and **Al-e-Buyeh** rulers - strengthened his position as the only monarch of the East. But, he was still under the autocratic power of the **Arab Caliphs in Baghdad**. In 1005 A.D. he visited the **Caliph** to receive the traditional investiture and recognition he deserved. The **Caliph** had ordered **Toghril's** name to be mentioned after his own in the mosques all over the Islamic territories- a sign of great importance. **Toghril** tested his military strength successfully against the **Emperor** of **Constantinople** and demanded the Emperor's tribute and obedience. **Toghril** died when he was over seventy years old. He had brought respect and prosperity to a **Turkish** tribe that had known only the simple lifestyle of a shepherd.[2]

Toghril had appointed **Alb Arslan** (his younger nephew) as the successor to the throne in 1063 A.D. Under **Alb Arslan** the boundaries of **Seljuk Empire** expanded farther. He was a brave warrior and crushed the army of **Diogenes Romanos** (the Emperor of Rome) in 1071 A.D. Also, he defeated the **Fatemi** rulers in Hijaz. **Alb Arslan** was killed in a war against the **Kharazmian** of northeast of Persia in 1072 A.D. Many important leaders coexisted at this period to whom the expansion of the **Seljuk Dynasty** may be attributed. **Nezam al Molk**, a religious seer, is one of them who politically served this king well but his archaic religious ideas caused further damages inside Persia by returning to severe archaic worldviews.

It is important to note that in order to compete with other religions and to keep current with most scientific and philosophical studies, the **Caliphs** in Baghdad of the early 8th Century through the 9th Century permitted full and free investigation of all the world knowledge available- astronomy, mathematics, sciences, philosophies and religions.

Therefore, like a comet briefly flashing across the sky, between the early 7th and the mid-9th Century, the **Islamic** lands were a haven for complete freedom in pursuing knowledge and making that available to all - both in the sciences and the arts. This zenith of enlightenment was reached while Europe was caught in its dark ages (5th to 10th Century). The harsh confrontation of **Byzantine Empire** (eastern Europe) against the sciences of the time resulted in closure of many schools like Alexandria center of science in the 5th Century A.D. Meanwhile in Persia, **Avi Cenna (Abu Ali Sina)** was writing great books in medicine and Law and **Razi** produced his revolutionary experiments in chemistry (these books were in **Arabic** which was the only language permitted by the **Arab Caliphs**).

However, around the 9th Century, **Arab Muslim** leaders (with appalling fanaticism in social and religious matters) reverted to dogmatic guidelines that held back the worldviews and lifestyles of **Persians** for centuries to come. The **Abbasid Dynasty** produced arrogant but narrow-minded **Caliphs** in **Baghdad** (starting with **Motevakel**, 847 A.D.). These tyrant **Caliphs** and their appointed **Viceroys** in the **Islamic** lands gradually returned to censor and control over anything that contradicted the doctrines of **Islam**. These antiquated dogmas provoked archaic and antiscientific thinking and behavior.

By the end of the 11th Century A.D., the effects of the Orthodox views of the **Caliphs**—devised in the previous centuries - finally reached Persia. Three major religious scholars in Persia contributed directly to this negative change: **Nezam al Molk, Moddares**, and **Muhammad Ghazali.**

Nezam al Molk, although a superb **Persian Vazir** and scholar of **Alb Arslan,** unfortunately brought **Islamic Orthodoxy** and traditional views back into lives of his **Persian** contemporaries at the beginning of the 11th Century A.D. He was born near Meshed in Khorasan and his religious schools built all over Persia were designed to train only a breed of **Orthodox Clergy** who were denouncing changes or newer outlooks.

Also, another scholar named **Moddares** reverted to an even older **Orthodox Muslim** doctrine. This Orthodoxy is referred to as "**Islamic Scholasticism**" or "**Moddaresi View**"—the traditional and Orthodox view of the 11th Century in Persia that prohibited any scientific or philosophical subjects to be taught in schools other than the traditional religious themes and theories (*Hadith*).

Muhammad Ghazali, a brilliant graduate of the religious schools of **Nezam al Molk,** was born in 1058 A.D. in Toos. He wrote Tahafatul-Falasafeh (Nonsense of Philosophers) against the method of rational thinking in philosophy. He was another theoretician of extreme archaic doctrines in **Islamic** fields.[3]

This archaic point of view in **Islamic** lands resembled that of **Bishop Cyril** of **Byzantium**, who strictly kept the **Christian** churches away from teachings of the sciences of that age.[4]

On the other hand and with a completely different view, **Omar Khayam**, the Epicurean philosopher, poet, and astronomer also lived during this age. **Khayam** was using an observatory established by **Nezam al Molk** in Nei Shabur. With help from other scientists, he produced the Famous *Jalali Calendar*—named after **Malek Shah**. Finally, **Khayam** died in 1123 A.D. in Nei Shabur in Khorasan.

In addition, around the 10th Century, four **Muslim** scholars individually created their own personal interpretation (named after them as **Hanafi, Maleki, Shafaie,** and **Hanbali**) and brought further restrictions. The backward essence of these sects had negative results on the freedom of thought within the social fabric of the **Muslim** nations. Except for "**Hanafi**", the other three sub branches of **Sunni** sect of Islam; **Maleki, Shafaie,** and **Hanbali** were extremely restrictive. Their followers believed that the traditional dogmas and irrevocable religious laws took precedence over wisdom of the believers. Thus a restraining viewpoint gradually dominated **Islamic** lands that urged blindly acceptance of older standards without questions.[5]

However, the nebulous supremacy of these strict **Caliphs** of Baghdad was doomed by the gradual infiltration of influential **Turkish** generals and officers in their own royal courts.

1.   *Rah Avard*, Winter edition no. 62, Article by Seyyed Hasan Amin, 2002, L.A., pp. 138-145

2.   *History of Persia*, Sykes, Vol. 2, pp. 28 – 31

3.   *Ma Cheguneh Ma Shodim*, by Dr. Sadegh Ziba Kalam, 4th edition, Tehran, pp. 209, 229

4.   *History of the Arabs*, By Philip Hitti, Macmillan Publishers, 14th edition, U.S.A., pp. 315-369

5.   Ma Cheguneh Ma Shodim, 4th edition, pp. 264-268

MALEK SHAH

After **Alb Arslan's** death his seventeen-year-old son inherited the crown. This new king was called **Jalal-U-Din (Malek Shah) of Seljuk** in 1073 A.D. His political confidant and **Vazir** was **Nezam al Molk** who was a great Islamic philosopher and theologian. **Malek Shah,** with the help from **Nezam al Molk,** managed a great deal of timely political maneuvers (lasting a total of five years) against many rebellions within the country. Thus, the **Seljuk Empire** reached its zenith under the supervision of **Nezam al Molk** (this nickname connoted his valuable role; meaning he himself was the order of the land). But **Malek Shah** ordered the dismissal of this great Vazir. **Malek Khatun** (the **Seljuk Queen**) was not very much fond of this Vazir and created the political intrigues against him. **Nezam al Molk** enjoyed a growing fame among **Persians** and this intimidated the king's family. Death usually followed those dismissed by the king. **Nezam al Molk** was confined to a simple and secluded lifestyle without customary protections of his court. He was eighty years old when assassinated by a subservient follower of **Hasan Sabbah.** Shortly after this, **Malek Shah** himself fell sick and died in 1092 A.D.

Hasan Sabbah had ruthless followers who were politically important in the history of this age. This sect is referred to by the name of **Assassins** (derived from the original word of **Hashashin** meaning the users of *cannabis indica, or hashish*). In order to mention the influence of **Hasan Sabbah** and his followers in the Near East and Persia, it is necessary to go back and look at **Fatimid Dynasty** (909 – 1171 A.D.) This dynasty is the promoter of the **Shiite sect** in Persia. This sect is also known as **Sect of the Twelve** or **Ismaili.** The **Fatimid Dynasty,** also referred to as **Fatimi** (attributed to the descendants of **Prophet Muhammad's** daughter, **Fatimah**), was initially established, through propaganda, in 873 A.D. by a Persian ophthalmologist named **Abdula al Kaddah,** from Ahwaz (a port at Persian Gulf). He was a demagogue who wanted to bind together the believers from **Christianity, Judaism,** and **Islam** and lead them under his own rule—emphasizing on the common grounds in different sects (return or resurrection of the savior) and considering number seven (as in seven seas) holy and mystical. The followers used to run their secret societies in Yazd, Kerman, and Tabarestan (north of Persia). Eventually, **Abdula al Kaddah**'s grandson, a Persian man named **Abu Muhammad Obaydulla**, founded the **Fatimid Dynasty**. Soon. **Abu Muhammad Obaydulla** conquered the larger portion of northern Africa and made Mahdiya (near modern Tunis) his capital. Sixty years later, Egypt was added to the **Fatimid** territories. The city of Kahira (now Cairo) was founded on the ruins of the ancient city called Fostat. By the end of 10th Century A.D., the greater part of Syria (including Jerusalem) was also in the hands of the **Fatimid** line until the famous **Salah-u-Din** of the **Crusaders** overthrew their kingdom in 1171 A.D.

Hasan Sabbah was a self- imposed leader. When he joined the **Shiite** followers of the **Fatimid Dynasty**, he led and expanded **Ismaili** sect to include more southern states in Persia. He—following his own autonomy. **Hassan Sabbah** built the famous Alamut fortress in the Alburz Mountain range (northern Persia) in 1090 A.D.—coinciding roughly with the assassination of **Nezam al Molk**. Inside Alamut, **Hassan Sabbah** had beautiful secret gardens with runnels flowing with wine, milk, and honey - resembling the ones promised in heaven, by all the holy books. Only his devoted followers who were his trained **Hashashin (Assassins)** could enter the gardens and live with him. He used a potion composed of hashish to cajole his devotees to submit to his personal wishes.[1]

SANJAR

As mentioned earlier, **Malek Shah** had passed away in 1092 A.D. when almost forty. Four of his sons succeeded him one by one and out of them only **Sanjar** was successful in suppressing the rebellions inside the country as well as Samarghand and Kharazm (Khiva) in 1140 A.D. He was tall and experienced in combat. He was the most merciful king of this dynasty. **Sanjar** had forgiven **Bahram Shah** of **Ghaznavi Dynasty** when he had raged a war against **Sanjar**'s territories. Also, when **Sanjar** surrounded Samarghand in 1130 A.D., he refused to kill **Ahmad Khan**, its ruler, who had declined to pay the agreed tributes. **Sanjar** accepted his request for forgiveness and reinstated him to his position. But, the **Ghoz Turks (Gharakhtaie** tribes of **Chinese-Turks** descent) finally captured **Sanjar** in 1153 A.D. after a series of battles. He was held as a prisoner for four years, but he finally managed to run away. **Sanjar** reached the province of Marv—an area once abundant of green pastures and happy dwellers that had turned into a pitiful ruin. **Sanjar** who was already seventy-three years old could not tolerate witnessing these harsh days for his country and his people. Finally, while in hiding he passed away in 1157 A.D. with sorrow in his heart. He was old and had ruled about forty years. **Sultan Sanjar (King Sanjar)** was a kind leader and had assisted many other kings and rulers in his neighboring land. During his kingdom there was not much left of the **Abbasid** rulers and their residual power had already diminished.[2]

Sanjar is believed to have changed his mind about a serious campaign against the **Assassins** of **Hassan Sabbah.** Historians believe that finding a letter pinned above his bed with a dagger had changed his mind about raiding the Alamut Fortress. In the letter he was praised as a fair king, yet he was strongly cautioned about any antagonistic moves against the **Assassins.**[3]

All historians praise the valor and kindness of **Sanjar.** He was referred to as **Sultan** (king in Arabic) **Sanjar;** and his name was read in the mosques - a tradition well respected among all Islamic lands—for a full year after his death. This was truly an unprecedented compliment.

At this period (1095 – 1099 A.D.) the first Crusade had happened against the **Seljuk Dynasty. Pope Urban II** erroneously had referred to the **Seljuk** race as "accursed **Persian** race", rather than "accursed **Turkish** race." Through emotional lectures in churches, **Pope Urban II** asked for the gathering of **Christian** armies from Europe to take back Constantinople and Jerusalem. The effect was instantaneous on minds already prepared. But, the bloody confrontations in Asia Minor had initially ended in favor of the **Seljuk** warriors. It is of interest to note that the **Crusaders** had opened negotiations in advance with the **Fatimid** rulers who had refused any concession except that three hundred unarmed pilgrims were to be allowed to enter the holy lands each year; but this offer was rejected with scorn and eventually the **Crusaders** stormed Antioch and Jerusalem in 1099 A.D. The deplorable fanaticism of Christendom was vented on the **Muslims** and **Jewish** inhabitants, who were slain by thousands.[4]

Edward Said—a contemporary historian—portrays this incident and many other of this caliber that followed, in some ways, as a door that opened East to West for better and closer understandings. He argues that the subject of Orientalism or study of East for westerners had a fluctuating meaning and purpose in the West. Centuries of physical encounter with Eastern worldview have enabled westerners to realize the weaknesses in their earlier prejudicial approaches to the East. The World Wars (I & II) and Arab-Israel wars have demanded better and more realistic and unbiased studies of the East. Even famous experts like Morroe Berger, a specialist in Political Science at Princeton University, fell in the trap of misjudgments against **Islam** and **Arabs** in particular, and his statements not only seem childish these days, but somewhat tainted with bigotry and racism.[5]

It may well be that the **Crusades** did little else than make **Christians** and **Muslims** much more bitter enemies than they had been before. The people who probably gained most from the Crusades were the merchants, neither the men of religion nor the men of war. The **Byzantine Empire** had been fatally hurt as much by the **Crusades** as by the **Muslims**.[6]

1. *History of Persia*, Vol.2, London, pp. 34-39
2. *Chekideh-e-Tarikh Iran*, pp. 84-85
3. Tarikh-e-Iran, Vol.2, Tehran, p. 71
4. *History of Persia*, Vol 2, London pp. 44-45
5. 'Orientalism' *Shargh Shenasi*, by Edward W. Said, translated by Abdul Rahim Gavahi, 2nd edition, 1999, Tehran, pp. 168, 177, and 516
6. *The Middle Ages*, by Trevor Cairns, 1995, Cambridge University Press, p. 52

CHAPTER SIXTEEN

Kharazmshahian
(1097 – 1231 A.D.)

As mentioned earlier, for almost three centuries there was a perpetual transfer of political power within Persia. These changes were usually results of fluctuation in the political power of immerging **Muslims** with **Turkish, Arabian,** and **Persian** backgrounds.

Anush Tagin was a **Turkish** slave in the court of **Malek Shah** of **Seljuk Dynasty**, who received special attention because of his faithful service. His son, **Ghotb-al-Din Muhammad,** was nominated as Viceroy of Kharazm (northeast of Persia), thus receiving nickname of **Kharazmshah.** Contrary to the **Abbasid Dynasty** it seems that **Turkish** rulers showed more propensity for their own race than **Persians** when choosing viceroys for the states inside Persia.

After **Sultan Muhammad (Kharazmshah),** his son **Atsiz** took the control of Khiva (old name for Kharazm) in 1097 A.D. while **Sultan Sanjar** of **Seljuk Dynasty** was on the throne. But **Atsiz** started two major revolts against **Sanjar** that ended in defeat. But **Sanjar,** being a merciful king, forgave him and only demanded a harsher tribute from him. Reluctant to accept **Sanjar's** supremacy, **Atsiz** sought help from **Turks** of **Kara Khitai** (Gharakhtaie or Ghoz). **Atsiz** died in 1156

A.D. while amidst these fights. However, as mentioned previously, the scathing campaigns of **Kara Khitai** against **Sanjar** (who was over seventy) resulted in his sad death a year later - a result of emotional stress in captivity.

Il Arslan was the heir to his father, **Atsiz**, in Kharazm (Khiva); but his death also came in 1173 ironically by the hands of the same **Kara Khitai** tribes that his father (**Atsiz**) had approached for help against **Sanjar**. Civil war broke between his two sons, and **Tekish** eventually established his supremacy. He also chased and killed **Toghril III** the last king of the **Seljuk Dynasty** and added the greater part of western Persia to his empire. **Tekish** had done this through the instigation of **Nasir** the last **Caliph** of **Islam**, who continuously struggled to get rid of **Seljuk** kings in Persia.

It is noteworthy that during the heyday of the **Seljuk Dynasty** the **Arab Caliphs** were mere puppets, but the cunning **Mustarshid**, who was **Caliph** for seventeen years, took advantage of the raging internal wars in Persia around 1135 A.D. by taking side with the **Turkish** leaders against the rights of the people of Persia. But, **Nasir** who had succeeded **Mustarshid** to the Caliphate (Islamic Empire) in 1180 A.D. instigated **Tekish**, a Turk, to attack **Toghril III**, another Turk, to get rid of this last **Seljuk** king—as said earlier. Although **Toghril III** was slain, **Ala-u-Din Muhammad**, **Tekish**'s son, ironically raged against **Nasir** and threatened to depose him. **Nasir** appealed to the far-off **Chengiz Khan (Genghis Khan)**. In other words, the head of **Islam** in Baghdad is believed to have invited a horde of **Mongol** pagans to attack a **Muslim** state in order to sustain power.[1]

Ironically, **Genghis Khan**, the savior who came at an **Arab Caliph**'s initiation (**Caliph Nasir**), came and destroyed not only the **Persians** but the **Arabs**, too.

Ala-u-Din Muhammad was not satisfied with these victories but pushed towards India and defeated the **Ghoz** rulers there, expanding borders of his empire. He was the only ruler from Persia—of **Turkish** descent - that almost abdicated the Caliphate of Islamic Lands, but this did not last long because **Caliph Nasir** had sought help from **Mongols** to protect his own throne.[2]

The Atabegs (Atabakan)
(1148 – 1329 A.D.)

The singular word "**Atabeg**" (or "**Atabak**") literally means Caretaker. The plural word **Atabegs** (or **Atabakan**) refers to generations of caretakers of kings of **Seljuk Dynasty**. Unlike the **Abbasid Dynasty**, the **Seljuk kings** appointed their viceroys from their own **Turkish** blood (even as young as 15) to govern different provinces and states in Persia. But usually a special (trusted and learned slave) **Turkish** caretaker was dispatched to look over these young viceroys' shoulders. These caretakers were called **Atabegs**. The **Atabegs** of Fars and Azerbaijan (two states inside Persia) gradually gained unusual force and popularity to the extend that they chose not to obey any **Seljuk Kings**. Then, they themselves became independent rulers of specific areas inside Persia. For example, **Atabeg Songhor**, from Fars, is one of those who served **Toghril** (the **Seljuk King**). He even revolted against his own **Seljuk** Viceroy. **Atabeg Songhor** effectively dominated the province of Luristan in 1148 A.D. Eventually, **Atabeg Songhor** passed away but the next two Atabeg leaders did not possess any significant Political ambitions. Until the time of **Atabeg Saad** (about 1200 A.D.) who defeated the **Ghoz** tribes and added province of Kerman to his territories. After the death of **Atabeg Saad** in 1226 A.D., his son, **Abu Bakr,** took over the province of Fars (Shiraz). **Atabeg Abu Bakr** is remembered in history because he initiated peace negotiations with the **Mongols.** This saved a lot of lives on both sides. The great seer and poet of this era is **Saadi Shirazi** whose poetry and prose are cherished amid the heritage of **Persian** literature.[3] One of his poems expressed his belief in the sacredness of humanity. Lines from this poem were chosen to be carved on the U.N. building:

The sons of Adam are limbs of each other,
having been created from one essence.
When the calamity of time affects one limb,
The other limbs cannot remain at rest.
If thou hast no sympathy for the trouble of others,
Thou art unworthy to be called by the name of a human.

The **Atabeg** leaders ruled the provinces of Fars and Azerbaijan. They were relatively better rulers and cared more for the Persian interpretation of the law than the **Turkish Seljuk Kings**. This fact is portrayed in the writings of **Saadi Shirazi** the scholar of this period.[4]

Another line of the **Atabegs** remained in Luristan in southwest Persia until 1329 A.D. who also entered a wise peace treaty with the **Mongols** to save lives.[5]

1. *History of Persia*, Sykes, Vol. 2, pp. 52, 53
2. *Chekideh Tarikh Iran*, H. Naraghi, p. 87
3. *Chekideh Tarikh Iran*, p. 88
4. *Rah Avard*, Winter edition, No. 62, 2002, L.A., article of S.H. Amin, p. 143
5. *Tarikh-e-Iran*, Vol 2, Tehran, p. 82

CHAPTER SEVENTEEN

The Invasion Of Mongols
(1219 A.D.)

Since the fall of the **Sassanid Dynasty** in 650 A.D. by the swords of the **Arab** invaders, Persian history has been filled with numerous short regional kingships appointed by the corresponding Caliphate of the time. Two problems prevented a united Persia. First, the **Arab Muslims** who manipulated Islamic religious language to justify their invasions and massacres. Second, the horrific invasion of pagan **Mongols** who not only took advantage of a weak Persia but also put an end to a corrupt Islamic administration in the Middle East.

History is marked here with a recorded atrocious **Mongol** invasion against helpless civilians. Women were raped, children too weak to work were destroyed, even healthy domesticated animals were not spared. The exorbitant cruelty of **Mongols** towards enemy soldiers was completely unprecedented. **Mongol** cataclysm not only blotted out of existence the entire population of major inhabited towns and states in Persia, but also carried these unbelievable massacres to Russia, Asia Minor, Europe and Central Asia.

The **Mongols** were descendants of **Hun** tribes (in central and east Asia) who were sometimes referred to as **Tatars** (or **Tartars**). They spent their nomadic lives in raising cattle, breeding horses and raiding farms, villages, or towns. Even the dynasty of northern **China** (who shared ancestry with them) regarded these cruel tribesmen with contempt. Nevertheless, **Mongols'** archery and horsemanship was superb due to their nomadic lifestyle. But they had not improved their lives much and still lived in tents and traveled all their lives staying within their own groups with limited contact with outside world. Because of the **Mongols'** values, they could not appreciate civilized living. Books, mosques, and schools were not valued and therefore not considered essential. The inhabitants of the conquered cities were useless except as targets for their greedy raids. All the religious and civil laws of the countries they raided were of no value to them. They brutally inserted their own limited "*Yasa*" laws based on paganism which only contained tribal administration techniques.

Chengiz Khan (Genghis Khan) was born in 1162 A.D. His name was originally **Temuchin**. His father, the chief of his tribe, died in 1173 and **Chengiz** finally succeeded to the headship of the tribe at the age of thirteen. His valor and discipline compensated for his lack of experience. His fame grew beyond that of his father. In 1206 through a historical assemblage of leaders of many tribes, he chose the nickname of **Chengiz Khan** for himself.

The army of **Chengiz** permeated central Asia against **Kin Dynasty** of China in 1218 A.D. This dynasty was the center of a large populated area in Asia. **Chengiz** dispatched an embassy to **Muhammad Kharazmshah** of Persia with gifts and a message expressing hope that the two rulers would live at peace with one another. **Chengiz** (**Genghis**)declared that he would look upon **Muhammad** as his most beloved son. **Muhammad Kharazmshah** cautiously inquired of the three ambassadors about the size of the **Mongol** army. The Persian army was much bigger in size than the Mongols'. Then, **Muhammad Kharazmshah** confidently dismissed the ambassadors with a friendly reply, although he sensed the word *son* to carry a veiled demand to recognize **Mongol** superiority. The governor of Otrar—a border city but still inside Persia—confiscated the second envoy of valuable presents through **Mongol** merchants doubting their true intentions—not a far-fetched assumption. A report was sent to Khiva and **Mongol** representatives were accused of spying. The order for their execution was received from the capital; the governor of Otrar put them to death immediately. About this time, **Chengiz** must have received the dispatches of the **Caliph Nasir** of Baghdad to invade Persia. Therefore, **Chengiz** was on the lookout for a pretext such as the impolitic severity of **Kharazmshah**. Hearing of the ill-fated trading venture, he sent another embassy demanding the surrender of the governor of Otrar to Mongol vengeance - war being the alternative. **Kharazmshah**, blinded by his earlier uninterrupted successes, made hostilities inevitable by putting the third and last ambassador to death.[2]

The following year, 1219 A.D., the scathing attack against Persian borders started. Four sons of **Chengiz Khan** were acting as heads of his troops. **Kharazmshah** forwarded his army of 400,000 men to Otrar, but his army was humiliated with defeat. Shortly after, **Kharazmshah** lost his morale. The **Mongols** surrounded Otrar and did not allow the delivery of food and water for six months. The governor, abandoned by terrified **Kharazmshah**, was eventually captured and tortured to death by **Mongols**.

Chengiz and his men pushed to Bokhara (northeast of Persia) and rode their horses into the mosques and engaged in drinking in celebration of such unbelievable victories. Then the invasion of homes started. Again, the savage conquerors took serviceable men as captives for harsh labor, enforcing front lines of their troops for future raids. The women were the prey of the captors. The cowardly viceroy of Persia, **Kharazmshah,** chose to run towards Neishabour. After months of resistance and struggle without signs of help from central government or the Caliphate in Baghdad, the cities of Samarghand, Neishabour, Isfarayen, Damghan, and Ray were sacked and burned one after the other. **Kharazmshah** was in Ghazvin when he learned about the approaching **Mongols**. All he cared about was his own life. His megalomania had driven him to madness. He ran for an island in Caspian Sea where he passed his last days in misery and seclusion.

Kharazmshah's heroic son, **Sultan Jalal-u-Din** had courageously requested to be sent to Oxus area to rebuke **Mongols** from their weaker point, but **Kharazmshah** had denied this request. However, following the death of this weak king in 1220 A.D., all of his brave sons and on top of them **Jalal-u-Din** who was a paradigm of valor among rulers of this dynasty, moved to Khiva by the sea and, although too late, engaged in gathering of a quick response to stop **Mongols**. It was just about this period that **Chengiz** had finished the massacre of the inhabitants of Samarghand, thousands of civilians were killed and many women taken as captives. The population of Sabzawar, estimated at 70,000, was completely annihilated. Neishabour had showed exceptional resistance causing a lot of casualties to the **Mongols**, thus, after the fall of this city, the additional punishment from the enemy came harsher by flattening the entire city down, including anyone or anything inside, and turning it into a plantation sown with barley for the Mongols' horses.

The second attack from the sons of **Mongol** practically wiped the population off of Zanjan, Ghazvin, and Hamadan, which had stayed safe due to earlier negotiations with a different wing of the vicious **Mongol** warriors. The scattered resistances of **Jalal-u-Din** were somewhat effective, yet enraged these savage raiders to go beyond imagination in vengeance. **Chengiz Khan** openly had ordered the arrest and execution of the courageous **Jalal-u-Din**, but never had this chance. This **Persian** warrior spent all of his life and wealth in gathering armies to counter attack the **Mongols** in many fronts. Even the **Caliph** in Baghdad had reluctantly conferred on him the title of Shah-in-Shah in 1229 and restored his name in public prayers. Eventually in 1231 A.D. **Jalal-u-Din** was killed by the hand of a greedy Kurdish man who had taken note of his valuables about four years after the death of **Chengiz**.[3]

Some political figures such as **Shams-u-Din Khatib**, the governor of Tabriz, saved hundreds of thousands of innocent lives by diplomatic conduct to avoid the wrath of the **Mongols**. **Taymur Malek** and **Shah Mansoor** were two brave commanders other than **Jalal-u-Din**, who showed valor against all odds in fighting the **Mongols**. In some cases, the number of **Persian** soldiers reached 3000 against the army of 200,000 of the **Mongols**.[4]

Chengiz Khan had died when sixty six years old, and took with him the biggest wish he had for capturing **Jalal-u-Din**, who had bravely fought him and killed thousands of his men including members of his family with the most limited resources for more than a decade. Eventually in 1227 A.D., **Hulagu Khan** was elected as the successor to **Chengiz** in **Persia**, who founded the **Il-Khans Dynasty**.

Yakut Hamavi (Yaghut), the eminent geographer at Masoul, wrote a letter which refers in glowing language to the rich libraries, to the many men of science, and to the numerous authors of Marv, and exclaims in his enthusiasm, "Their children were men, their youths heroes, and their old men saints." Also, **Ibn-ul-Athir** the Arab author of the Islamic chronicle of *Al-Kamil,* or "complete", who is also referred to as **Izz-u-Din**, portrays the ruins that this contumacious race (**the Mongols**) left behind and puts the number of victims, in this area, as seven hundred thousand, and **Ala-U-Din Juwayni,** who was the Persian secretary of **Hulagu** and author of *Tarikh-e-Jahan Gusha,* mentions the same fact with a higher figure.[5]

At this time, the last of **Abbasid Dynasty** was an incompetent degenerate who was full of false pride. He was **Mustasim Billah** the last **Caliphate of Islam** who chose to ignore the approach of Mongols and refused to gather his army to defend his own nation. In 1258 A.D. he was captured by **Hulagu Khan** and put to death by being rolled inside a carpet and beaten to death (Mongols usually refrained from spilling royal blood). One million inhabitants of Baghdad were massacred. The destruction of six centuries of **Islamic** literary and artistic treasures along with learned men of all classes defies description. Meanwhile **Hulagu** attacked the **Ismaili** fortress and wiped out the remainders of the sect of **Assassins** who had not previously shown any resistance against the **Mongols** except the last years of leadership of **Jalal-U-Din** who had just joined them. Thus, six hundred years of the **Abbasid** reign was over. The racist **Arabs** were to be replaced by bloodthirsty **Mongols. Hulagu** died in 1265 A.D. His capital was Maragheh in Azerbaijan. **Khajeh Nasir-u-Din Toosi,** the great astronomer and scientist lived and served under his rule.[6]

In the West, **Mongols** had viciously pushed to Poland and Hungry in Europe, and when it appeared improbable that they would attempt to conquer Western Europe, the fear they inspired began to give place to the hope that they would shatter Islam, and rumors also were heard that there were Christian tribes among the new invaders. The Christian missions- from the Council of Lyons held in 1245 A.D.—to the **Mongols** were treated with contempt; the **Pope** in Rome was summoned to come in person and offer his submission.[7]

European Christian leaders in the west did not dare to approach **Islamic** lands by force, although this method was not unfamiliar to them. Instead they preferred to penetrate the **Islamic** territories through taking sides with the **Mongols**. Undoubtedly, Europe was facing its own turmoil—the so-called *Christian Conversion.* The

Christian Crusades were conducted against **Islam**, but Christian Conversion was about forcing **Christianity** against the pagans or non-Christians of Europe. At about 1000 A.D., **Germans**, **Nordics**, **Slavs**, and **Baltic** peoples were forcibly baptized and given new names by order of the European Christian rulers. Those who resisted were murdered or forced to fight. The persecutions and expulsions of **Spanish** and **Portuguese Jews** and **Muslims** were notable examples of Christian intolerance, including public burnings of alleged heretics and secret **Jews** and **Muslims**.[8] It is true to say that the rulers in the **Islamic** lands expressed, unfortunately, the same intolerance against **Christians**.

1. *History Of Persia*, London, Vol. 2, p. 74
2. *History Of Persia*, pp. 75, 76, 90
3. *Chekideh Tarikh Iran*, p. 91-93
4. *Dar Piramoon Tarikh*, By Ahmad Kasravi, 1999, Tehran, pp. 73-79
5. *History Of Persia*, p. 80
6. *Chekideh Tarikh Iran*, pp. 93, 97, 98
7. *History Of Persia*, pp. 92, 93
8. *The Two Faces Of Islam*, by Stephen Schwartz, 2000, N.Y. p. 2

Il-khan Dynasty (Ilkhanan) (1227 – 1335 A.D.)

The title of **Il-Khan** means "leader of Tribe" and was used by the **Mongols** to designate sequence of leaders. This is the dynasty of several **Mongol** rulers as the successors of **Genghis Khan**.

Hulagu (Genghis Khan's son) had died in peace in 1265 A.D. and was buried near Lake Urumia- north of Persia. Genghis and his sons were extremely lucky to have been raging war against a weak Baghdad and a falling Alamut (Assassins' fortress) in Islamic lands, otherwise their hordes would have bean beaten beyond return. **Abaga Khan (Abagha Khan)**, his elder son, succeeded **Hulagu** in 1265 and ruled Persia up to 1281 A.D. He married the daughter of Eastern-Roman Emperor **Paleologus**. Because **Abaga Khan** had shown inclinations towards **Christianity**, this marriage had made **Edward I** of England very hopeful to have a Christian **Ilkhan** ruler who could put an end to the Islamic dominance in the region. But, this dream did not come true.

Among the highlights of this era were these; the travels of **Marco Polo** (the Venetian explorer) and the collaboration of Christendom of Europe with paganish **Mongols** against Islamic territories.

After **Abaga Khan**, his son **Tagudar,** who was baptized at birth, took over in 1281 A.D. The newer generation of pagan **Mongols** in Persia had become somewhat religious. In addition, they seemed more aware of the civilization around them. A few years into his reign, **Tagudar** converted to **Islam** and took the name of **Ahmad**. His elder brother **Arghun** was dissatisfied with the result of election of **Tagudar.** So **Arghun** had initially rebelled against his brother in vain and had to flee. In addition, a strong party in the army, against the conversion of **Tagudar** to **Islam**, joined with **Arghun.** The latter eventually came back from hiding and this time captured and killed his brother (**Tagudar** or **Ahmad**) in Mongol fashion by having his back broken (1284 A.D.). During the reign of **Arghun**, the relations between **Christian Europe** and **Mongols** grew closer, so that a convoy of ambassadors under the supervision of a Franciscan friar was sent with friendly missions from the **Pope**. This mission, hoping to convert **Arghun** to **Christianity** failed due to the death of this **Il-Khan** in 1291 A.D.[1]

The **Mongol Generals** over ruled **Arghun**'s appointments to his throne and usurped the power initially. They chose **Gaykhatu**, his brother, to lead as the new **Il-Khan**. The fight among the rivals for this position followed. Meanwhile, **Gaykhatu** had diminished all coins in the treasury by his lavish expenditures. Even though there was not adequate back-up reserve, **Gaykhatu** ordered printing and distribution of the first bank notes or paper money in Persia in 1294 A.D. Due to his infamous life-style, the public did not trust him or his money. Therefore this paper money was immediately cancelled. Contrary to public opinion, **Johann Gutenberg** from Germany was not the inventor of printing; **Persians** had both the technology and at least ten different printing headquarters about 700 years before **Gutenberg**. The number of printing houses in China was even higher during the 13th Century. Dr. John Wall refers in his articles in *The*

Currency Collector to the fact that **Persians** and **Chinese** had invented this science while Europe was lost in its dark ages.[2]

Baydu was **Arghun's** cousin, who killed **Gaykhatu.** A year later **Baydu** himself was captured under orders from **Ghazan Khan, Argun's** son. Imprisonment of other opponents who were more inclined towards **Islam** followed: **Baydu** was subsequently put to death in 1295 when **Ghazan Khan** took the control.

1. *Chekideh Tarikh Iran,* p. 94
2. *Iran Nameh,* Published by the Foundation for Iranian Studies, article by Ali Sharghi, No. 4 edition, Fall of 1993, U.S.A., p. 61

Ghazan Khan

Except for **Tagudar (Ahmad)** who had converted to **Islam,** all **Mongol** rulers in Persia were pagans (though a few favored **Christianity). Ghazan Khan** is the second ruler in this dynasty that formally converted to **Islam** and took the name of **Mahmood.** He actually called **Islam** the official religion of Persia, but showed his religious zeal by invading churches and temples of **Christians** and **Zoroastrians** inside the country and transforming them by force into mosques. On the other hand, he forbade many irregular taxes. His keen attention to modifying taxations and construction of new and safe routes for travelers is worthy of praise. **Ghazan Khan (Mahmood)** was fundamentally against unlawful taxes or tributes sought by his corrupt officials in his name, and stopped all usury to be immoral and illegal. His famous *Yasa of Ghazan* is a collection of laws and reforms in military, agricultural, and civil laws.[1] This set of laws was actually based on a more civilized foundation than its previous version of Yasa laid down by **Genghis Khan.**

But his improvements did not last - regretfully **Ghazan khan's** administrative genius was shortly afterwards succeeded by puppet-Khans. Under these new **Mongol Il Khans** Persia relapsed into anarchy. During this period, **King Edward I** of England, had dispatched the first **British** ambassador to Persia hoping to make allies of this dynasty against Muslims in Asia. **Ghazan Khan** died in 1304 A.D.

The civil freedom brought by **Ghazan Khan** had a positive effect on arts and handicrafts. The genius of Persia, so strongly expressed in ceramics and textiles, was equally visible in metal work of every kind. **Marco Polo** testifies: " They are very skilful in making harness of war: their saddles, bridles, spurs, swords, bows, quivers, and arms of every kind are very well made."[2]

Major artistic and industrial works in the world at this age were very much controlled by men. Education, trades, and most of the skills were still in the hands of men. Even Europe discouraged female literacy because it would give women the means to write love letters. But **John of Gaunt** (1340-91), the king of England, had married his distant cousin **Blanche** who was an exception to this rule. She could read and write exceptionally well.[3] But, in Persia, the role of majority of women in the society was tragically reduced to bearing children.

Uljaitu

After **Ghazan Khan**, his brother **Muhammad Khoda-Bandeh** became the next ruler in Persia. This new **Il Khan** was known by his title **Uljaitu** (meaning Fortunate). His mother had brought him up as a **Christian**, but later on he converted to **Islam**. He also corresponded with the sovereigns of Western Europe; it is interesting to note that they believed him to be an enemy of **Islam**.

Uljaitu (**Khoda-Bandeh**) did not accomplish anything significant and in 1335 A.D. he died without an heir. The country was caught again in series of fights for acquisition of power, which lasted several decades and caused more poverty and injustice. The uprising **Sar-be-Daran** sect in 1337 A.D., in the province of Khorasan, stands out in this age, which revealed new resistance of **Persians** against the **Mongols** from within the conquered lands. **Hafiz**, the great mystic poet of Persia, lived during **Amir Mubarez-u-Din** around the end of this era. A subtle scrutiny of the conduct of this corrupt **Il-Khan** is expressed elegantly in poetry of **Hafiz**.[4]

Another spiritual leader although in disguise—due to life-threatening fundamentalism of this age—was **Sheikh Attar**. He was a learned spiritual leader who stated as a perfume merchant (attar) in Nei Shapur. **Sheikh Attar** had mastered the **Sufism** of his time, and **Hafiz** owed him the development of Gnosticism in his poetry. **Hafiz** was born in Shiraz. He is the most beloved poet of Persia and is considered to be one of history's greatest lyrical geniuses. This poet wrote with a sweet playful genius unparalleled in world literature. **Hafiz** is rightfully called "the tongue of the invisible" or "Lesan-ul-Ghaib."[5]

My broken heart's sorrows are deep;
painful, disturbed, broken my sleep.
If you don't believe, send me your thoughts
and you will see how in sleep I weep.

Surprisingly, many intellectual literary masterpieces were created during the rule of **Mongols**. Finally, the **Khan of Tartar** started to lose his power in the world. The inhabitants of territories in Persia and Russia were realizing new ways to stop their hundred fifty years of cowed subjection. In 1380, **Dmitry**, a **Russian** hero, advanced with his army against the **Tartar** horde and won a bloody victory. Two years later the **Tartars** made a surprise attack under their new leader. However **Ivan the Great**, the first **Russian** prince to take the imperial title of "Tsar" or **Caesar**, finally destroyed the **Mongols** and freed the country from the **Tatars** yoke. No more tribute was paid to the **Khan** from the **Russians**.[6]

1. *Tarikh Iran Zamin*, Dr. M.J. Mashkur, p. 231
2. *History Of Persia*, p. 207
3. *The Wars of the Roses*, by Alison Weir, Ballantine Books, 1995, New York, p. 26
4. *History Of Persia*, pp.114-115
5. *Love Poems From God*, by Daniel James Ladinsky, Penguin Publishers, 2002, U.S.A.
6. *A History Of Russia*, by John Lawrence, 7th edition, Penguin Group, 1993, New York, p. 89

Tamerlane (Taymur the Lame)

The final days of The **Il Khans** in Persia were coming fast. The most brutal resistance came by the hands of **Taymur (Tamerlane)**. Born in 1335 A.D., he was the son of **Amir Turghay** (the word **Amir** means Ruler in Arabic, also used in Farsi), chief of **Turkan** branch of the **Barlas**, originally a noble **Turkish** tribe. **Taymur (Tamerlane)** spent his early childhood in Khorasan under **Amir Kazghan**. After the death of his father and uncle, **Taymur** decided to tender his submission to **Tughluk Khan**-governor of Mongolia (Jatah) around 1360 A.D. Due to his administrative skills, **Taymur** was appointed governor of Transoxiana (Mavara-ul-Nahr)—a large area in north east of Khorasan beyond Oxus River. Not much later, **Khan of Jatah** (Mongolia) asserted his supreme authority and appointed his own son as governor for Transoxiana; thus limiting **Tamerlane's** rule. In brief, many intrigues that followed pushed **Tamerlane** to leave this chaotic position with contempt. He chose to use his power for his own goals. By attending some campaigns to help a ruler who had sought his expertise in combat in 1363 A.D., **Tamerlane** received two arrow wounds in his foot that made him permanently lame. For this, he became known as **Taymur Lang** or "the lame."

Taymur (Tamerlane) has impressed Europe more than any other Asiatic conqueror. **Chengiz Khan**, a century and a half earlier, was not brought into direct contact with the Near East or with Europe, and had stayed away from the west. It was not until after his death that his descendants subdued Russia and Mesopotamia. **Tamerlane**, on the other hand, overran Persia and Mesopotamia, and subsequently entered Russia and plundered Moscow. Then he turned towards India and invaded this reputed treasure house of the world in 1399 A.D. Neither **Alexander the Great** nor **Chengiz Khan** had managed to penetrate so far into so remote areas. Westwards, too, he took Damascus and weakened the power of the **Mamelukes** of Egypt. Then took over Turkey; thus **Sultan Bayazid I** was captured by Persian army in 1402 A.D.[1]

Tamerlane had acquired the self-esteem he needed as a great leader on the basis of his earlier campaigns. His valor and perseverance in battlefields as well as in council chambers had already brought him supremacy over Kharazm and subsequently in

Herat, Kabul (in Afghanistan), Sistan, Ray, and Mazandaran (in Persia) between 1369 and 1384 A.D.[2] All these events helped put Il Khans supremacy out of Persia.

Tamerlane died of old age in 1405 A.D. in Samarcand, northeast of Persia. Hafiz, the great mystic poet of Persia had a chance to have a historical interview with this king. Tamerlane's object was glory, and as in the case of all conquerors - ancient or modern—his career was attended by terrible bloodshed. As a Muslim ruler, he brought back solidarity to his nation against the intrusions of its enemies. History reflects the truth about ends and means, so that they may be judged without bias. However, one could argue that as a soldier, his heroic invasions called for imperative military exigencies. Except for the patronage of learned men and founding of mosques and colleges, as a ruler of a nation, he failed to bring peace and prosperity into homes.

1. *History Of Persia*, Vol. 2, London, pp. 118-134
2. *Chekideh Tarikh Iran*, p. 97

The Taymurid Monarchs (1360 – 1495 A.D.)

After Tamerlane, as an old tradition, the battle for the throne engulfed many civilians and soldiers who had different leaders in mind. Eventually Shah Rukh, the fourth son of Tamerlane, ascended the throne in 1404 A.D. Having the experience of viceroy of Khorasan and Herat, Shah Rukh competently reigned as the new monarch of Persia and Central Asia for about fifty years. Through his beneficent activities many cities were restored and particularly Meshed and Marv. (The famous Gohar Shad mosque was built in the memory of his beloved wife in Meshed). Shah Rukh's court was a popular place for attraction of artists, scientists, and architects of his age. He was not weak in war either and had repeatedly defeated the rebels of Ghara Kuyunlu (Black Sheep) dynasty in Azerbaijan in 1431A.D. His son Ulugh Beg, who was the governor of Samarcand for thirty-eight years, succeeded him and continued his father's reforms. This monarch (Ulugh Beg), though unfortunate as a ruler, is the author of the famous astronomical tables held to be the most accurate and complete which have been passed on by the East to the West. These texts were initially published in Latin by **John Greaves**, professor of Astronomy at Oxford about 1650 A.D. and reprinted a century later. Moreover, Persia and the world owe the calendar, which is in use to day to **Ulugh Beg** (the names of the months being the signs of the Zodiac).[1]

Tragically, his own son, called **Abdul Latif**, revolted and killed this literate monarch in 1449 A.D. This parricide did not enjoy his ill-gotten throne for long; for **Abu Saeed**, a descendant of **Tamerlane** engaged in a battle with **Abdul Latif**. Though **Abdul Latif** was victorious, he was assassinated shortly after. Subsequently, **Abu Saeed** dominated Transoxiana, Northern Persia, and Afghanistan, killing other potential successors. But, in 1467 he was defeated and beheaded by **Uzun Hasan**, the ruler of **Agh Kuyunlu** (White Sheep) in Azerbaijan. At this time, **Sultan Ahmad**, **Abu Saeed**'s eldest son, succeeded his throne and managed to stay in power for 27 years.

Accordingly, both **Sultan Ahmad** and **Uzun Hasan** governed their territories next to one another in Persia and Central Asia. After the death of these rulers their heirs could not gather the solidarity to continue, thus, the weakening dissension among tribes opened the way for the **Safavi** leaders to reveal their supremacy in mid-15th Century. On the other hand, in spite of all these fights, the goldsmiths and expert metalworkers of Persia were dispatched to go to Venice and train the European metal workers in Nuremberg and England, where interlacing designs in gold of the **Elizabethan** period gives clear evidence of Persian influence. This arrangement was the result of embassies between the **Prince of Karamania** (today's Cilicia) and **Uzun Hasan**.[2]

It is interesting to know that **Zahir-u-Din Muhammad**, also known as **Baber** (Tiger) is a descendant of **Abu Saeed** or **Tamerlane** family who ravaged the entire Pakistan and India through his campaigns from Afghanistan- which was a state of Persia. **Zahir-u-Din** (**Baber**) is the pioneer in establishing Farsi as the formal language of courts of law in India that lasted for centuries after him and through his descendants. **Baber** had many ups and downs during his rule. He was contemporary of **Ismail** (The founder of **Saffavid Dynasty**). After his final combat with **Uzbeks** in 1512 A.D., he left the world of politics forever. Beautiful palaces and architectural masterpieces constructed under his supervision are still seen in Pakistan and India (Taj Mahal is one of them). The support for the arts by this family (**Taymurid Monarchs**) facilitated migration of many **Persian** artists to India and Pakistan during the reign of the **Saffavid Dynasty**, which followed.[3] Even today, being able to recite Persian poetry of **Hafiz** and **Molana** is considered a traditional advantage for the scholars in India and Pakistan.

The dynasty of **Tamerlane** (the **Taymurid**), which lasted nearly a century and a half, included many members who pertinaciously loved art and literature. The lovely 'miniature' art belongs to this era. The splendid buildings remaining from then, even in their decay, still challenge the visitors' admiration.

The agony of life amidst centuries of struggle and bloodshed did, in some areas, result in an inclination towards **Sufism**. Although **Islam** demanded active "Jihad" or "Struggle against vice" from its believers, **Sufism** persuaded submissive meditation through seclusion. This downward journey of man in seclusion had started before the invasion of the **Mongols**. It is true that **Sufism** created an artistic and profound look at life and at the role of man in the universe—all reflected in many glamorous pieces of literature. However, it had a destructive side that contributed to passive reaction of **Persians** towards worldly affairs. As a result, since the early 13th Century, the idle **Dervish** lifestyle grew more acceptable in the society. This negative point of view about **Sufism** is largely accepted among historians - and is believed to have roots in **Christianity** as well. History reveals that the **Assassins** of **Hasan Sabbah** did not show resistance against invaders like the **Mongols**, since they followed a trend of life, "Batenian" (meaning looking inside), that unfortunately did not recognize the imminent danger of these enemies.[4]

The word "*Jihad*" in Arabic means "struggle" and implies the ultimate pious resistance of any **Muslim** against vice and flaws in human nature. *Jihad* can be in the form of quitting smoking cigarettes or refraining from telling lies. *Jihad* does not require a second party— as wars need two parties—because it only portrays ones resistance against his or her own inner flaws. However, because of the political pressures, *Jihad* has been wrongfully attributed only to bloodshed and terror by the western media. **Sufism** also emphasized inner struggle of ones soul through meditation and piety to achieve spiritual freedom.

The master of all **Sufi** poets **Jalal-u-Din Rumi**, was born at Balkh in Persia (now in Afghanistan) in 1207 A.D. His family moved away from the invading **Mongols** and traveled to western Ghunieh (Conia) in Western Persia — now a part of Turkey. **Rumi** was a Muslim ascetic with remarkable spiritual wisdom or *Irfan* (Greek word for it is gnosis). When only 24 years old, **Rumi** was known as an eminent scholar of religion. This highly attained mystic poet, also referred to as **Molana**, may be claimed as yet another of the extraordinary men of whom Khorasan can justly boast.

> 'Tis light makes color visible: at night
> Red, green, and russet vanish from thy sight.
> So to thee light by darkness is made known:
> Since God hat none, He, seeing all, denies
> Himself eternally to mortal eyes.
> From the dark jungle as a tiger bright,
> Form from the viewless Spirit leaps to light.

Persian Poems, An Anthology of Verse Translations, edited by A.J.Arberry, Everyman's Library, 1972

Rumi was, like his father **Baha-u-Din,** a leading theologian.

Sheikh Attar was another devout **Sufi** theologian of this era. Their poetries were divine and their humanity abundant, while their diction helped to preserve Farsi.

Farsi (the language of **Iranians** today) was never lost because of glorious works of **Rumi, Attar**, and **Ferdowsi**. Moreover, the evolution of Farsi language starting from the ancient Parsi (Mikhi) – written from left to right – also referred to as the language of *Avesta*; moving towards medium Farsi of Pahlavi (Dari Style) up to the present or New Farsi, came partially through endeavor of **Al-e-Booyeh** and **Al-e-Ziar** who came from **Persian**-speaking families. The first two and a half centuries after the **Arab** invasion were extremely harsh for the natives in Persia, who intended to safeguard their Farsi language in the societies under **Arab** rulers. However, it was the **Saffarian** and **Samanian** dynasties, being from a **Persian** ancestry that patriotically insisted on use and distribution of Farsi in their land. **Turks** and **Mongols** were mostly illiterate and could not run the official government transactions without their Persian **Vazir** as their *persona grata*.[5] Therefore, Farsi grew stronger in all corners of Persia, in spite of the desire of the foreign rulers.

Persian scholars had opened the way for the evolution of Farsi as well as Arabic language. Ibn Khaldun, the Arab historian, writes in his *Al Moqadameh* or *Introduction to History*, about the founders of grammar of Arab language to be all non-Arabs (**Persians**). He also refers to these non-Arabs as preservers of knowledge who tirelessly wrote systematic works. Ibn Khaldun refers to the famous words of the **Prophet Muhammad**: "If scholarship hung suspended in the highest parts of heaven, the people of Fars (Pars) would reach out and take it."[6]

1. *History of Persia*, S.P. Sykes. London,Vol. 2, pp. 136-138
2. *History of Persia*, pp. 141-142
3. *Chekideh Tarikh Iran*, by Hasan Naraghi, 2nd edition, Tehran, p. 100
4. *Dar Piramoon Tarikh*, by Ahmad Kasravi, 1999, Tehran, pp. 29-64
5. *Majaleh Iran Shenasi*, periodical 5th Volume, No3, article by Jalal Matini: Zaban-e-Farsi va Hokumat Hai-e Turkan, Autumn of 1993, U.S.A.
6. *Iran, past and Present*, by Donald N. Wilber, 9th edition, Princeton U. Press, 1981, N. Jersey, p. 86

CHAPTER EIGHTEEN

Safavi Dynasty (Safavian)
(1499 – 1722 A.D.)

By now Persia is rescued—by the **Taymurid** monarchs—from the powerful **Mongol** rulers who dominated many nations in Asia and Eastern Europe. At this period this rescue is completed by the next Dynasty—The **Safavi**—who realized the vulnerability of the remnants of the **Mongols Ilkhan** (Chieftain).

In addition, opportunistic European leaders (especially **British**) capitalized on the distinctions separating **Shiite** from **Sunni** believers. The opportunistic **British** and **French** politicians devised a military enhancement plan, which would equalize the gun power of the countries of Turkey and Persia. The main objective was to let these Islamic nations destroy each other. This plan was put in process during the **Safavi Dynasty**.

The ancestry of the **kings** of **Safavi Dynasty** goes back to **Sheikh Saffi-u-Din** who was a chieftain in the Ardabil tribes inside Azerbaijan. He was a descendant of **Imam Musa Kazim** the 7th imam of the **Shiites** (unsubstantiated by the consensus of all historians). **Sheikh Sadr-ul-Din**, his son, succeeded him as the new head of the tribe - a man of great prestige who had once asked **Tamerlane** for the release of **Turkish** captives under his rule. These freed **Turks** and their descendants emigrating to Ardabil and Gilan areas, later on, became the members of the group of devout followers of **Sheikh Sadr-ul-Din**. After him, came **Khajeh Ali** and then **Ibrahim, Jonaid,** and **Haydar**—all blood relatives who received the leadership of their growing tribes in Azerbaijan (northwest of Persia).

Sheikh Haydar had married his cousin, the daughter of his uncle **Uzun Hasan,** who had a **Greek** princess as his wife. The name of his cousin was **Martha** and she had born three sons, only **Ismail I** managed to survive and was later appointed the leader of his people in northwest Persia around 1499 A.D.

This period coincides with the discovery of America by the **Italian** explorer in 1492 A.D. His name was **Christopher Columbus**. He was in the service of the **Spanish** monarchy. It was **Isabella I**, the queen of Castile—in central Spain—and the wife of **King Ferdinand V** who encouraged **Christopher** to go on a voyage to South Asia, thus, **Columbus** accidentally landed on the shores of this continent.

Shah Ismail Safavi

Before the **Saffavid Dynasty**, with the exception of the short reign of the **Booyeh (Buyid) Dynasty**, Persia was ruled by a majority of **Sunni** dynasties—mostly **Turks**. However, the **Safavian Dynasty** recognized **Shiite** and ruled with a more active militant nature than the earlier **Shiites**. **Twelver Shi'ism** believes in the hereditary ruling of twelve **Imams** only descending from **Imam Ali**. Thus, these **Shiites** argued that **Prophet Muhammad** had personally chosen **Ali ibn Abitalib**, his own son-in-law - **the Prophet** had publicly announced this official appointment in a place called Ghadir Khom. Therefore, these **Shiites** did not recognize other three **Imams** who had succeeded **The Prophet** through their own tribal influence (the **Omavian** and the **Abbasid Dynasties**). On the other hand, the **Sunnis** believed in the equal legitimacy of all four **Imams**. It is true to believe that the expansion of **Shiite** (**Twelver Shi'ism**) was a counter attack by **Ismail I** against the rule of the **Ottoman Empire** of Turkey and Central Asian **Uzbeks**. But this attitude of **Ismail I** could not purely come from merely patriotic or nationalistic nature, since he habitually wrote in **Turkish** while his enemy **Sultan Salim** in **Persian**.[1]

When elected as the heir to his Ardebil tribe, **Ismail I** was only thirteen years old. This tribe was originally a quietist **Sunni** order— mysticism akin to quiet meditation—with ties to the 14th Century **Mongol** rulers. **Ismail's** first enterprise was the capture of Baku. Now, he was empowered with a better army of about 160,000 men, he defeated **Alvand** the leader of **Agh Ghuyunlu** tribe. Then, he formally sat on the throne in Tabriz (a prosperous city in province of Azerbaijan in northwest Persia). **Ismail I** devoted his full attention to the sect of **Shiite (Shia)** and to the followers of **Imam Ali**. Also, his tribal position enabled him to grow the fame and power he needed to unite all the tribes under a name "**Kizilbash**" (English name) or "**Ghezelbash**" (Turkish name) meaning "Red heads." This magnificent achievement brought **Ismail I** the support of many tribes of Turk inside of Persia; **Ustajlu, Shamlu, Takalu, Baharlu, Zulkadar (Zolghadr), Kajar (Ghajar)**, and **Afshar** tribes—all became sworn upholders of the **Shiite** sect under **Islam**.

It is interesting to know that the word "Tribe" in Farsi is "Eal," which was originally a **Turkish** name spread by the oriental **Mongols**. The above-mentioned tribes or eals belonged to the race attributed to **Turks**. In Iran, today, there are many other tribes or races that have established their ethnical and racial characteristics of their own. The major ones are these: **Kurd** (south of Azerbaijan and Zagros Mountains), **Lorr** (southwest of Zagros), **Baluch** (southeastern provinces- Kerman and Sistan), **Ghashghaie** (north of Persian Gulf around Shiraz), **Turkman** (Khorasan and east Mazandaran), **Ealat of Khamseh** (central Iran), **Kolie** (gypsies originated from Egypt and India and scattered through), **Arab** (Khuzestan and Persian Gulf), and **Shahsavan** (Turks of Azerbaijan).[2]

As a result of the union of the many **Turk** tribes, **Ismail I** was nicknamed **Shah Ismail I**. This youthful king quickly annexed Baghdad and Mosul (both cities are in today's Iraq). Later on, he won the position of Diarbakr and the rest of the land under **Agh Ghuyunlu** reign. Immediately, he headed towards Khorasan. In 1510 A.D., **Shah Ismail I** defeated and killed **Shaybani**, the **Khan** (or ruler) of **Uzbeg**. This defeat of **Uzbeks** gave **Baber** (of the **Taymurid Dynasty)** the green flag to invade Samarcand (Samarghand in Farsi) and Transoxiana (Mavara-ul-Nahr in Arabic). Nevertheless, this victory did not last, since **Uzbegs,** recovering from defeat, returned to northern Bokhara and beat **Baber** who had lost the support of **Ismaili** army in his area. These **Uzbegs** recovered Transoxiana and remained a serious menace to the eastern province of Persia.

Around 1514 A.D., the court of **Sunni Turks** was referred to as **Othman (Ottoman**—originally used as **Osman)**, one of its conquerors named **King Selim**, started a secret search for all of the seventy thousand **Shiite** heretics in his dominion inside turkey. He viciously ordered about forty thousand of these **Shiite Muslims** to be killed to prove sovereignty of his **Sunni** sect. Then wrote to **Shah Ismail I** of Persia (the king of the **Shiites**) in double tone asking his opinion about the massacre, to which **Ismail I** replied that he had given no provocation and did not desire war. **Shah Ismail I** added that the tone of the letters must have been due to indulgence to opium, and he, therefore, sent the royal secretary a box of the drug. Because **Selim** himself was addicted to narcotics [a fact which was probably known in Persia] the sarcasm went home. The war began; **Ismail I** dispatched a limited number of soldiers to the west near Lake Urumia in Azerbaijan. **Shah Ismail I** needed his army at Bokhara area in eastern provinces to check on the **Uzbegs**. This war was lost; **Ismail I** retreated and **Othmans** got the control of Tabriz. This invasion did not hold since **Othmans** had to withdraw due to lack of support in this land and due to their own mutinous fractions. Thus, a long-lasting hatred was established in 1514 A.D. between the two sects of **Sunni** and **Shiite** in Islam. Later on, **King Selim** raided Egypt in 1516 A.D. and made that country a **Sunni** state under the Caliphate of **Turkish Othman**.

Shah Ismail I reestablished Persia as a separate and independent state. For this reason and because he led the establishment of the **Shiite** doctrines as the national religion, he was very much regarded with affection. **Shah Ismail I** passed away at Ardebil in 1524 A.D. His last years were passed mostly in seclusion. It was during his reign that, for the first time, the **Portuguese** expeditions ravaged the port of Hormuz on the Persian Gulf and asked for tribute in 1507 A.D. However, this **Portuguese** invasion terminated in disaster for the invaders a little more than a century later.[3]

Shah Tahmasp I

Tahmasp I, the eldest son of **Shah Ismail I**, succeeded to the throne at the age of ten. His initial combats against the **Uzbegs** and the rebels in Baghdad ended triumphantly. He circled the city of Harat (In today's Afghanistan) to protect it from the invading **Uzbegs** in 1530 A.D. At this time **Sulayman I** was the strong monarch in **Ottoman Empire**. Soon, **Sulayman I** found the opportunity to invade Persia in 1534 A.D. and penetrated all the way to Tabriz with heavy artillery and guns. A treaty was reached in 1555 between Persia and Turkey. **Bayazid** was the crown prince to **Sulayman I**, who had rebelled against his own father and had to flee Turkey with his family. **Shah Tahmasp I** accepted his secret request for refuge. After two years, **Tahmasp I** shamefully decided to sell this guest and his four sons to **Sulayman I** for some prize money. These guests were sent back to **Ottoman** emissaries and were executed immediately.[4]

The **Ottoman kings** of the 16th Century called themselves the head of the **Islamic** World. Their biggest enemy in Europe was **Charles V** The **Holy Roman Emperor** who ruled other European territories such as Spain under direct authority from **Christian** leaders. **Turkish Ottoman leaders** were **Muslims** but unlike the early **Arab Caliphs** had no intention to spread the religion of **Islam**. The **Ottomans'** eyes were only on the treasures and lands of the **Byzantium** Europe. But **Venetians** finally won the naval battle of 1571 A.D. against the **Ottomans**.

At this time, **Queen Elizabeth** had succeeded her father **Henry VIII** in 1547A.D., **although** he had six wives and many heirs. **Anthony Jenkinson** was the first English ambassador to Persia in 1561 A.D.

Apparently, Ambassador **Jenkinson** was badly humiliated in the fanatic court of **Shah Tahmasp I** and was sent back because he was **Christian** and not considered thoroughly clean. **Tahmasp I** was cruel when it came to punishing his men. He was a peculiar man. He was fond of calligraphy and breeding Egyptian donkeys. It is mentioned in the diaries of **Vincenito A. D'Alessandri**, the **Venetian** ambassador that **Shah Tahmasp I** had not left his palace for eleven years. Consequently, **Persians** were not able to present petitions to him. Roads were deemed unsafe to travel and judges were corrupt. Finally, **Shah Tahmasp I** died at the age of 64 after ruling for about 54 years. His sedative lifestyle plus his weak character both directly affected his administration which ended in civil chaos and injustice.[5]

1. *Roots of Revolution*, by Nikki R. Keddie, Yale University, 1981, pp. 9-13
2. *Concise Encyclopedia of Iran*, By Jaleh Mottahedian, edited by Dr. M.J.Mahjoob,1998, U.S.A., p. 111
3. *History of Persia*, Vol. 2, pp.158-164, 186-187
4. *Chekideh Tarikh Iran*, pp. 105-106
5. *History of Persia*, pp.169-171

Shah Ismail II

In 1576, **Ismail II**, the fourth son of **Shah Tahmasp I**, who had been imprisoned by his own father for twenty-five years, took over the throne after much bloodshed. His reign was short, but very much affected by his demented personality. He decided to kill two of his closer brothers, and after the burial ceremonies for his father, continued to ravage the lives of six more princes in his family. **Abbas Mirza**, one of the lucky princes, was only six years old; and his execution was delayed due to Islamic rituals in that particular month of the year- Ramadan. **Shah Ismail II** had a heart attack due to excessive drinking—some historians believe that his close guards had actually assassinated him.

Persia at this particular time is being torn from within, and the degree of external threats from foreign powers did actually seem less damaging in comparison to what the **Persian kings** had managed to do internally.

After the death of **Ismail II**, his elder brother **Muhammad Mirza** (nicknamed as **Khoda Bandeh** meaning the humble server of God) took control in 1578 A.D. His reign was catastrophic because his Vazirs opposed **Khoda Bandeh** as well as each other. Thus, he was forced to abdicate. His sixteen-year-old son, **Abbas**, was chosen to run the country.

Shah Abbas The Great

Shah Abbas was called **The Great** because he enlarged the boundaries of Persia and improved the lives of its citizens. In this period, in other nations, there were other great kings as Sir Percy Sykes puts it in *History Of Persia* who were equally efficient in improving the everyday lives of their people.

Sir Percy Sykes refers to a few characters at this age to be great rulers in Asia and Europe. He admires **Charles V** (the **Holy Roman Emperor**), **Elizabeth I** (The Queen of England), **Sulayman I** of Turkish **Ottomans**, **Akbar** of the **Moghul** Empire of India, and **Shah Abbas The Great** of Persia.[1]

It is interesting to know that **Queen Elizabeth** was born in 1533 to **Henry VIII**. Her mother, one of six wives of the king, was beheaded for committing adultery. **Elizabeth I** had a harsh life as a youth and was even put into prison by her own half sister. However, she was famous for her united and powerful rule. She was the longest reigning **English** monarch.

The second worthy king according to Sykes was **Charles V** Born in 1500, son of **Philip I**. He was chosen the holy **Roman Emperor**. He received this title by bribing the electors for falsifying his hereditary successions.

Sulayman I (The magnificent) was born in 1494 in Turkey. He brought **Ottoman Empire** to its peak, which did not last after him. He had his own son **Mustafa** strangled because he was afraid of his son's growing popularity among his army, which could ultimately threaten his position as king. History recalls that the collapse of the western Empire of Rome had happened around 476 A.D. by the paid barbarians led by a **German** general named **Odoacer**. Now it was time for the fall of the Eastern Empire of Rome–**The Byzantine**–which came much later by the **Turks** in the **Ottoman Dynasty** in 1453 A.D.[2]

These **Ottoman** leaders were mostly older and were tempted by the inexperienced **Persian** rulers who could be taken advantage of with little effort. One of these **Persian** leaders was **Shah Abbas** who took the throne at the age of sixteen. His initial confrontations started with the **Ottomans** from the west and **Uzbegs** from the east. While the whole country was facing interior civil unrest, two of the

Ghezelbash leaders, **Morshed Gholi Khan** and **Ali Gholi Khan**, were chosen by leaders of the other tribes as regents to look after this young king and guide him through major decisions in the kingdom. They used their position to enrich themselves rather then to strengthen the young king and his nation. When **Ali Gholi Khan** was killed by the **Uzbegs** invasion, **Shah Abbas** jumped on the opportunity to blame **Morshed Gholi Khan** for his death. Thus, he rid himself of the two assertive leaders forever.[3]

In 1587, a battle broke between the **Shiites** of Persia and the **Sunnis** of Turkey near Baghdad, which resulted in loss of Tabriz, Shirvan, and Gorjistan to **Ottoman Empire** by a treaty signed in 1590. Persia lost those three western thriving areas to Turkey.

On the other hand, most of the eastern provinces of Persia came under raids of the **Uzbeg** tribes. In 1591 the astrologers had warned **Shah Abbas** of a serious danger that threatened the life of the occupant of the throne. Therefore to divert the effects of the dire prediction, a temporary abdication was arranged by the Shah's men who replaced him with another figure on the throne, probably a non-Muslim. On the fourth day of this poor man's reign he was put to death. **Abbas** reascended the throne on a propitious day as the astrologers saw fit. Interestingly, the victory over **Uzbegs** followed shortly after this incident.

About thirty-seven years after the first unsuccessful dispatch of an English ambassador to Persia under **Tahmasp I**, England stepped forward for such political connection in 1598 A.D. With the military training of these ambassadors, **Shirley Brothers**, Persian infantry and artillery was modernized to match that of the **Ottomans**. Thus, **Sir Anthony Shirley** became very much trusted by **Shah Abbas** and therefore, he was elected as the personal agent of the king of Persia in Europe. This extraordinary closeness to the king was reflected in the official creeds and notes that **Anthony** carried with him visiting different countries.

Shah Abbas who now had obtained a better-equipped and modernized army finally started his long-desired campaign against the **Turks** and released the city of Tabriz from under their control in 1603. More future victories came one after the other, and the cities of Baghdad, Mosul, and Diarbakr were captured and added into Persia within a period of ten years. Particularly, the seizure of the two holy cities of Karbala, and Najaf (currently situated in Iraq), brought **Shah Abbas** tremendous fame and respect among **Shiite Muslims** who nicknamed him **Shah Abbas The Great**. This victory caused a series of peace negotiations in 1612 and 1618 A.D. between **Turks** and **Persians**; conversely more clashes were seen between the two **Islamic** sects of **Shiite** and **Sunni** in the Middle East. This clash made Europe feel safer, because the growing **Sunni** dominance in the Middle East was now being modified by the **Shiite Muslims**. At this time the **British** attaché, **Sir Robert Shirley**, was selected as the Commander-in -Chief of the Persian army.[4] This era can be characterized as the beginning of influence of **British** and other European countries in the internal affairs of Persia through inducement of wars between believers of the two major sects of **Shiite** and **Sunni**.

    Shah Abbas led a domestic life, filled with contradictory indications of both wine drinking and exemplary piety. He transferred his capitol from Ghazvin to Isfahan and made a series of much-needed modernizations in this city. **Shah Abbas** was able to build numerous bridges, roads, and 'Caravanserais' or resting places for travelers. He was against religious fanaticism and was exceptionally against the seclusion of the political leaders so they would be more responsive to their civic duties. However, this trend did not prevail after him. He also employed many **Europeans** to improve arts and the military in his country. **Shah Abbas The Great** ordered transfer of five thousand **Armenians** from Julfa in Armenia to Isfahan in Persia. These **Christians** prospered in peace instead of being treated as slaves or prisoners. Yet he was extremely cruel against the wrong doers, and his own children were not immune. He had doubts about even his son **Saffi Mirza** and ordered his death to feel secure. It is argued that related evidences must have been verified beyond any doubt for him to carry such a cruel sentence against his own son. He died in 1629 A.D. at the age of seventy.

    Persia under **Shah Abbas The Great** grew closer to the western art and technology. He opened a new window for the world to become aware of Persia. These vital renovations and improvements based on technology and science of his time improved many lives. Persia regained much of its power and pride, and **Persians** started to feel peace and order inside the country.

This account of the greatest of Persia's sovereigns since the Arab conquest may be fittingly concluded with Chardin's words," When this great Prince ceased to live, Persia ceased to prosper."[5]

Shah Saffi

By the order of **Shah Abbas**, his grandson who had chosen the nickname of **Saffi** for himself—his father's name—received the throne in 1629 A.D. As if this was a tradition, he pursued the execution of all rival princes and even some princesses. Among these victims were some political figures and their sons; and this made him more detestable in the eyes of his people. First, the madness of **Shah Saffi** and secondly his incompetence permitted invasions of **Uzbegs** from east and **Turks** from west into the borders of Persia causing more bloodshed. He made successful campaigns to recapture Irvan (part of Armenia) in 1636, but Baghdad was lost to **Ottomans**. **Shah Saffi** died about six years later.

Around this period one of the **Persian** prodigies of **Islamic** Law and philosophy was **Mullah Sadra**. He was born in Shiraz into a family of learned religious scholars. This great seer passed away in 1640 A.D. almost in seclusion. His school of Eastern Theology based on inner illumination brought a deep philosophical approach to the universe and its inherent theory of constant movement. This is a part of theory that **Albert Einstein** recipient of 1921 Nobel Prize proved as the theory of relativity.

Shah Abbas II

Abbas II, a boy of ten, took over the throne after his father **Shah Saffi** in 1642 A.D. He had to be under the supervision of his Ministers. But, as was to be expected from an absolute monarch, when he reached maturity, he indulged himself in all vices. His European travelers were invited to share all his orgies. Nevertheless, the country had reached a prosperous state away from bloodshed. Architecture and painting reached higher standards during his reign. The **Saffavid kings** were mostly generous and kind towards refugees or needy. The first **Russian** embassy to Persia happened in 1664 from **Emperor Alexis**, the father of **Peter The Great**. Surprisingly, the **Russians**— northerly neighbors to the **Persians**—had never initiated any commercial ties with Persia until this date. Interestingly, **Emperor Alexis** initiated same political liaison with **King Charles II** of England. Thus, some 800 merchants were accompanying the **Russian** Ambassador into Persia. Of course, this **Safavi king** treated them with his habitual kindness. Later on, it came obvious that these men are merely greedy merchants who showed political approaches to get away with the customs dues. **Shah Abbas II** was justly disappointed at this duplicity and ordered their exile. The **Cossacks** of southern Russia were dispatched by **Alexis** to raid Mazandaran (the northern state in Persia) in retaliation, which did not continue due to resistance from Persia. . This was the first act of **Russian** aggression towards Persia. **Shah Abbas II** died in 1667. It is noteworthy that except **Shah Abbas The Great** most **kings** of **Safavi Dynasty** were kept inside the palace without much connection with the outside world. They were mostly brought up by the supervision of the concubines and eunuchs of the court. This custom, set by **Shah Ismail**, had resulted in many characteristic flaws in these kings and their heirs. **Shah Abbas II** had apparently changed the prevailing Persian tradition of training the heirs with the science of war at early ages. Of course, this was to avoid the risk of rebels from within his family against his power.[6]

Nevertheless the western ties with Persia grew. The commercial treaties of the **Portuguese**, the **English**, and the **Dutch** in the Persian Gulf for direct shipment of the Middle Eastern as well as Far Eastern commodities - including silk and exotic spice—had been established around this period. Finally, the French Prime Minister, **Colbert**, sent a direct embassy to **Shah Abbas II** requesting the same custom rights in 1664 A.D. **Louis The Fourteenth** of France signed a treaty with **Shah Abbas II** in 1708 A.D. regarding mutual commercial activities in the Persian Gulf and its most important port of Hormuzd.[7]

Persian Gulf has always played an important and strategic role in the history of Persia. Recently this historical identity seems to have been neglected by The National Geographic, which printed a map of the world in 2004. In this map a different name for The Persian Gulf is erroneously stipulated—calling it The Arabian Gulf.

1. *History of Persia*, Sir Percy Sykes, Vol. 2, p. 172
2. *The Roman Empire*, by Don Nardo, printed by Lucent Books, 1994, San Diego, CA, p. 84
3. *Chekideh Tarikh Iran*, pp.108-110
4. *History of Persia*, p.179
5. *History of Persia*, p.183
6. *History of Persia*, pp. 208-212
7. *Tarikh -e- Iran*, Vol.2, translated by F. Daie,Tehran, p. 301

Shah Sulayman

After **Shah Abbas II**, his eldest son of twenty, **Saffi**, by the nickname of **Shah Sulayman** was ready to take the throne in 1667. But the **Vazirs** were reluctant to have a grown up successor who would rule on his own terms. So they spread the rumor that **Sulayman** who had spent most of his life inside the palace was almost blind and unfit for the throne. Soon, these greedy **Vazirs** nominated the younger son of the late king for the throne hoping to maintain better control through this young king. However, a faithful eunuch betrayed this mutiny and **Sulayman** became the new **Shah**. This **Shah Sulayman** should not be confused with **Sulayman The Magnificent** the ruler of **Ottoman Dynasty** in Turkey. **Shah Sulayman** started some renovations for the holy shrines in the **Muslim** lands, but this was the extent of his major works. The idle and luxurious life of **Shah Sulayman** plus his lack of attention to the security of the borders opened the way for more invasions of **Uzbegs** over Khorasan and even of the **Dutch** over The Persian Gulf.

On his death bed, **Shah Sulayman** had warned his powerful greedy **Vazirs** that if they were seeking an eventless life in leisure and oblivion, they should aid his son, **Hussein Mirza** to the throne. If they were after the glory and pride of Persia, they were advised to choose his other son—**Abbas Mirza**—as the next king.[1]

The **Vazirs** chose **Hussein Mirza**.

Shah Sultan Hussein

Hussein Mirza known as **Shah Sultan Hussein** succeeded his father (**Shah Sulayman**) in 1694 A.D. **Sultan Hussein** was one of the most detested womanizer kings in the history of Persia. First, because he had many women and concubines in his harem, he could still choose any new woman whom he liked - even if married - to add to his private collection. Secondly, he was not even interested in any major social issues. His entire indifference continued while possible invasions from **Peter The Great** of Russia seemed more imminent. This **Russian Czar** was receiving the reports of travelers and spies witnessing the collapse of the economy and morale in all classes of the society inside Persia. (*Rasm-ul-Tavarikh* by Muhammad H. Assif gives a complete account of the character of this reign)[2]

The society in Persia was in dismay because lies, embezzlement, and sexual indiscretions were openly acknowledged and ignored by authorities. This decline of ethics and piety were not happening just in the **Persian** courts. Also, the **Ottomans** of Turkey who claimed to be the head of the **Islamic** lands indulged in greedy incursions in their neighboring lands. **Europeans** considered these numerous invasions of **Ottomans** to be religiously instigated. But these **Turkish Muslims** were only after monetary gains and had no missionary value for expansion of **Islam**. Finally in their last major battle against Vienna in 1686 A.D., the invasive naval forces of **Ottomans** were harshly destroyed. After this defeat, the **Ottomans** never rose to their original power.

Meanwhile, Persia was also suffering from its unfit kings: for example, **Sultan Hussein Safavi** was egocentrically involved with affairs of his own. In addition, a large number of **Persians** ignorantly sought relief in the nostalgic side of **Sufism** – diminishing patriotism in the society was the unbearable result. (**Sufism** placed greatest emphasis on the relationship between man and God rather than any earthly matters.)

Muhammad Bagher Majlesi (Allameh) and **Mullah Mohsen Feiz Kashani** were two of the renowned **Islamic** scholars. Though not completely against the spreading of **Sufism,** they were weary of its effects. Many historians criticize **Sufism** for its other worldliness, which diminished active citizen participation in the political life of the city. This introspective attitude was especially harmful for the civic leaders and kings who were supposed to stay alert. Although **Sufism** encouraged passivity and idleness, it also encouraged a *Gnostic view* of the universe in a highly poetic and divine language. However, some historians refer to **Sufism** as a side effect rather than the cause of the decline of patriotism and scientific explorations. During the **Safavi Dynasty** of about two hundred years, all the attention in schools was on religious matters. Philosophical or scientific debates were prohibited. This downward trend unfortunately continued through the 19th Century.[3]

Initially one of the reasons that **Sufism** grew in the royal courts was direct support of some **Ulama (Muslim clerics)** who strengthened the belief that **kings** ruled by divine rights. The position of **Ulama** of the 18th Century resembles the power of **Moghs** during the **Sassanid Dynasty** (224 A.D.- 652 A.D.). But later on, the **clerics'** independence from **Shah** also grew, since they gradually introduced the idea of *Vaghf* (inalienable endowment from people to mosques) to support themselves.[4]

Religious corruption gradually spread and people of Persia were forced to join or condemn it. Persia was distracted by these social dilemmas and political confusion. Persia was more vulnerable at this time; **Afghan** tribes invaded Isfahan and related provinces around 1720. **Shah Sultan Hussein** practically handed over his crown to the **Afghan** leader **Mahmud**. The most positive product of the **Safavi Dynasty** is the recognition of Farsi as the official and legal language of the country. Arts, ceramics and delicate architecture of Persia grew fundamentally during this period. Textile and silk industry evolved and Hormuzd in Persian Gulf became a strong port for its exportation to Europe, instead of the way of Turkey. People, especially the inhabitants of the towns inside the borderlines, received a sweet yet false sense of security away from wars and bloodshed. This false and brief security, however, resulted in prosperity in agriculture and trades.[5]

1. *Tarikh-e-Iran*, Vol.2, Tehran, pp. 331-334
2. *Chekideh Tarikh Iran*, pp. 113-115
3. *Ma Chegooneh Ma Shodim*, Dr. Sadegh Ziba Kalam, 4th edition Tehran, p. 270
4. *Roots of Revolution*, p. 16
5. *Tarikh Iran Zamin*, by M.J. Mashkur, pp. 285-289

The Afghans
(1712 – 1730 A.D.)

Afghans, as mentioned earlier, were a segment of the **Aryans** who were occupying the northeastern part of Persia and situated just north of Pakistan. **Afghanistan** had always been a part of Persia, although **Afghans** were mostly of **Sunni** sect. The discontent of the **Sunnis** had started with delegation of a **Turk** prince called **Gorgin Khan** to the governorship of their province. **Gorgin** was an arrogant ruler who had shown no mercy and had killed many protesting **Afghans** instead of attempting to establish a fair relation with them. **Gorgin** captured **Mir Vais**, an unhappy **Afghan** leader, and sent him to **Shah Sultan Hussein** for punishment. Conversely, **Mir Vais** established a wise and diplomatic relation with the king and his court and very soon received permission for pilgrimage to Mecca. He used this chance wisely and persuaded the **Sunni** leaders in Arabia to call the forceful resistance against the **Shiite** believers as 'Rava' meaning 'a necessity'. Upon his return and with further agreements with the **Russian** ambassador of **Peter The Great**, he managed to stir terror and dismay in the reign of **Shah Sultan Hussein**. In 1712 **Mir Vais** had rebelled openly and had resisted several attempts against his own growing power. Finally, his son, **Mahmud**, succeeded him. It was in 1722, when several deadly campaigns of **Mahmud** against **Shah Sultan Hussein** brought the latter to his knees. The glamorous **Persian** army again had underestimated the ragged enemy. This misjudgment resembles the mistake that the **Sassanid** king (**Yazdigird III**) made against the barefooted **Arabs**. Now history repeats itself; unveiling the hidden cannons under cloths on the back of their camels, the **Afghans** took advantage of the element of surprise. The defeat of the **Persian** army came swiftly.[1]

It is sadly noted that the **Afghans** army consisted of only 20,000, yet they were given a chance to cause so much damage. The true cause of downfall of the **Saffavid Dynasty** was the corrupt and idle nature of the **Persian** army and its commanders including the **Shah**. Most of the **Saffavid Kings** were too young to rule and incompetently trained. The **eunuchs** and the **harem women** were the only trainers for the **princes**. This upbringing reflected the cowardice, effeminacy, and corruption of the kings who allowed such a mistake. Sadly, as Sir John Malcolm says; the **Persian Empire** resembled " a vast fabric tottering to its fall."[2]

Unfortunately, in the mid 18th Century, before the **Afghan** invasion, most of the **Persian** seers, generals and **Vazirs** were already killed or exiled by the order of the suspicious **Sultan Hussein**. In addition, the fanatic and thoughtless **clergies** in the country being affected by an earthquake in Tabriz, several months of famine, and an unexpected eclipse, gave **Shah Sultan Hussein** the indications he was waiting for. He cowardly surrendered the crown to **Mahmud Afghan** in Isfahan and in his short speech blamed the stars and divine intervention for his lack of leadership.

The prediction of failure by **Shah Sulayman** came true with the cowardice of **Sultan Hussein**. If the **Vazirs** had chosen **Hussein Mirza**, the **Afghans** would never be able to cause so much damage.

Mahmud Afghan

After capturing the crown of the king in Persia, **Mahmud** (The **Afghan** victor) started cautiously by allowing key political figures inside Persia to maintain their positions, but appointed his own **Afghan** council to watch over their shoulders. However **Mahmud** lacked administrative skills. His immediate order for the arrest and execution of the traitors of **Sultan Hussein** in Isfahan seemed to buy him some time and sense of security. But numerous uprises in the country had him worried about his position. Therefore, brutality overcame his vision and massacres of innocent people of Isfahan was the inevitable result of his wrath. **Tahmasp**, the son of **Sultan Hussein**, who had taken refuge in Ghazvin found his life in great danger. Consequently, in 1723 A.D., **Tahmasp** sent a message to **Peter The Great** seeking help to overcome **Afghans;** and in return for which some northern states and towns were promised to Russia. The **Russian Emperor** made promises that he never intended to keep. Consequently, Gilan and some northern provinces of Persia were invaded and taken over by the **Russian Cossacks**, but no help was rendered to **Tahmasp** against the **Afghans**. At this period, Persia was caught in a state of frenzy and chaos; the borders were unstable and without adequate protection. This made occupation of northern and western states of Persia appealing to the **Russians** and **Turkish** empires that had initiated some talks. However, in 1725 **Mahmud Afghan** was assassinated by his own men, who were afraid of this mad leader, and his cousin **Ashraf** was nominated to succeed him in Persia.

Ashraf

Although **Ashraf** carried a great deal of hatred in his heart towards **Persians**, but his initial attempts in 1725 A.D. were kind. He tried to help the victims of his cousin's cruel ruling very auspiciously. The scattered bodies on the streets were removed and buried with respect. This did not last long; and his savage temper got the best of him. More massacres of the innocent people followed. **Queen Katherine** was the empress of Russia at this time. She had chosen to linger on the previous agreements that her country had entered with the **Turks** about splitting Persia. Therefore, in 1726 **Ashraf** ordered the army to push the **Turks** out of Persian border- states. A new treaty was signed between the two nations for peace.

Meanwhile, a young commander in Khorasan with the name of **Nader Gholi** had approached **Tahmasp,** who was hiding in Mazandaran Mountains. He persuaded **Tahmasp** to recapture Meshed and Heart from the **Afghans**, and he successfully commanded the army himself. In 1729 A.D. a new army of **Persian** soldiers was founded under **Nader**, who invaded Isfahan for the expulsion of the **Afghan** army. In a few battles around Isfahan, the **Afghans** were severely punished and **Ashraf** found no choice but flee towards Shiraz. Before doing this, he killed **Sultan Hussein** who was under arrest at his court. Following this, **Nader** surrounded **Ashraf** troops and killed everyone who resisted. **Ashraf** managed to run away, but he was caught later and his head was sent as a token to Isfahan.[3]

Persia was still an easy target for the **Czar** of Russia. Here is an extract from the will of **Peter The great**. Therein, he recommended attention and constant observation of his descendants or successors to fourteen articles. The article number nine reads like this: "...to approach as near as possible to Constantinople and India. Whoever governs there will be the true sovereign of the world. Consequently, excite continual wars, not only in Turkey, but also in Persia...and in the decadence of Persia, penetrate as far as the Persian Gulf...Arrived at this point, we shall have no longer need of England's gold."[4]

Persia neighbored Russia from the north and was surrounded by **Turko-Mongol** empires; **Ottoman Turks** and The **Mongols** from the west and east. The **Mongols** population in 1700 A.D. was about 100 million, five times that of the **Ottomans**, almost twenty that of the **Saffavid Persians**.[5]

Persia had only one hope to survive under the pressures of **Russians** on the north and **Turko-Mongols** of west and east. This fragile hope lay in the heroic character of **Nader**.

1. *Chekideh Tarikh Iran*, pp. 119-121
2. *History Of Persia*, Sykes, Vol. 2, pp. 236-237
3. *Chekideh Tarikh Iran* , pp. 122-124
4. *History of Persia*, pp. 244-245
5. *A Concise History Of India*, by Barbara & Thomas Metcalf, 2002, New York, p. 1

Nader Shah Afshar

Nader was born in 1688 A.D. into a poor **Persian** shepherd's family. His early years were spent tending flocks and making sheepskin coats. When **Nader** was eighteen, the **Uzbegs** captured both him and his mother. But after his mother's death in captivity, he ran away. **Nader** gained a lot of attention because of his services to the governor of Abivard in Khorasan. He eventually married the governor's daughter. Later on, after the death of the governor, **Nader** succeeded him. Then he joined **Malek Mahmud** of Sistan province against the **Uzbegs**. **Nader's** raids were successfully commanded and his fame started to precede him. Persia was once again gaining the unity it had lost for centuries.

When **Nader** courageously raided Neishabour and defeated the remaining **Afghans**, he attributed this great victory to **Shah Tahmasp** the last king of **Safavi Dynasty**. Then **Nader** proceeded to Meshed and Sari in northern Persia. Finally he found the chance to get rid of the **Turks** who had invaded the northwestern state of Azerbaijan inside Persia and parts of today's Iraq. **Nader** showed his resilience in this campaign and pushed Turkish army back to Iraqi territories. However, because of some sudden uprises in Khorasan, **Nader** had to pull his army back and immediately ride towards Meshed in northeast. Meanwhile **Shah Tahmasp** tried to use this opportunity and finish what **Nader** had started. In 1731 A.D. the battle of **Tahmasp** against the **Turks** ended with embarrassing results for **Persians**. All recently freed Persian territories were immediately lost to the **Turks**—again.[1]

At this period in India, the language of the courts and judicial offices was still Farsi. Also, Islam was expanding its domain over the population in India. **Shah Waliullah**, a religious **Sufi**, in the capitol had his own scholarly circles setting a new standard of fidelity by following sayings and actions of the **Prophet Muhammad** (*hadith*).[2]

In 1732 **Nader** issued a proclamation which protested against the **Turkish** treaty that **Tahmasp** had caused. **Nader** sent an envoy to Constantinople with a clear message, that if the **Turk Emperor**, **Ahmad Pasha**, did not immediately restore the provinces of Persia, a war would be imminent. Then **Nader** approached many **Shiite** governors to join him in denouncing this treaty imposed by the invading **Sunni Turks**. As a result of these maneuvers, **Shah Tahmasp** was politically cornered and powerless in Isfahan; therefore **Nader** abdicated him and put **Tahmasp's** infant son on the throne and traditionally chose himself as the Regent. This child was **Shah Abbas III**. In the following years, about 1733 A.D., **Nader** had two major fights with the **Turks**. Although unsuccessful on his first attempt, his second one came with a decisive victorious result against the **Turks of Ottoman**. In 1735 A.D. he completely expulsed the **Turks** and regained Iravan, Teflis, and Ganjeh. **Nader** pushed the **Russians** out of Gilan and Mazandaran in north. Then by a brilliant ultimatum to the Russian kingdom, he threatened to ally himself with the **Turks** unless Baku and other cities near Caspian Sea were given back to Persia. **Nader** knew that Russia, after the death of **Peter The**

Great, was not in a position to risk a war against both of these strong neighbors.

In 1736, with the death of the infant **Shah**, the accession of **Nader** to the throne came close. He was crowned as **Nader Shah** with a stipulation attached: "Since **Shiite** schism has prevailed, this land has been constantly in disorder. Let us all become **Sunnis** and this will cease." In order to subdue the animosity between the **Shiite** and the **Sunnis** inside Persia, he added: "...of course **Imam Jafar Sadegh** — direct descendant of **the Prophet Muhammad** — would be the head of this new orthodoxy in Persia."

Replacement of **Shiite** with **Sunni** doctrines is the beginning of deeper philosophical and physical conflicts between both **Shiite** and **Sunni** sects inside Persia. Although the sect change of **Shiite** to **Sunni** was formally approved by the meeting of the religious and political leaders, the majority of **Shiite Persians** did not approve of this change. Thus, a new sub-sect of "**Jafari**" was added to the four existing **Sunni** sects (Hanbali, Shafaie, Hanafi and Rabaie). A **Shiite Mujtahid**, a religious scholar, expressed his opposition to the change by advising **Nader** to confine himself to ruling only in temporal matters. To stand against a king took a lot of courage. However, the sudden and mysterious death of this **Mujtahid** made the concession of others much easier.[3]

His religious stipulations were met and **Nader** took the throne in 1736 A.D. and became **Nader Shah** (founder of **Afshar Dynasty**). He may have desired to become the head of the total Islamic lands in the Middle East. His **Sunni** faith had opened the way for his dream and his outstanding command of a united Persia had proven this. Nevertheless, the **Shiite Persians** were still his biggest challenge. The second biggest challenge for him was the funding he needed for his huge army. At this time he invaded the Bakhtiar tribe and added their men to his. Then **Nader Shah** opened a new campaign by the siege of Herat, Kabul and Ghazna in Afghanistan. In 1738, **Nader Shah** was strongly positioned near Delhi in India. His troops came down on **Muhammad Shah** (King of India) who had initially refused **Nader's** envoys seeking surrender of India.

Muhammad Shah, who was a weak and corrupt leader, formally accepted **Nader Shah** in his court. This scenario sadly resembles the meeting of cowardly **Sultan Hussein** with **Mahmud Afghan**.

Consequently, **Nader** took as loot the unbelievable wealth of India. Unfortunately, this priceless wealth did not go to the service of the people. It was ultimately used for more invasions rather than constructive purposes.

Nevertheless, **Nader Shah** of **Afshar Dynasty** retrieved the lost image of Persia in the world because he unified all provinces of Persia again. He had a marvelous memory and was known to be a great tactician. His early years are filled with his generosity; punishment of criminals reduced, taxes were lessened, and debts and tribal feuds were forgiven. However, the fact that the later years of **Nader** were mostly tainted with bloodshed rather than the renovation of the country cannot be denied. Indeed, the whole victorious Persia was laid to waste as if by an enemy. **Nader Shah** attempted, unsuccessfully, to reunite **Islam** by the abolition of the **Shiite** doctrine. His attempts to found a new religion did not go far. He was surrounded by fanatic clergies who could not set aside trivial differences in their doctrines. As an administrator, he failed, too. He sternly opposed the enemies of Persia. However, during the last years of his ruling (in 1740's A.D.) his severe unjustified punishments were regarded as a threat to the nations security. **Persians** gradually forgot the glory that **Nader** had brought them because **Nader** in his late years became melancholically depressed and extremely cruel.

Consequently in 1747 A.D., four assassins attacked **Nader** in his sleep. Two of them he managed to kill in self-defense—before he was struck to the ground. Because of his political and battlefield experience, Persia had expanded again and found its lost glory and unity as an independent nation. But the lives of **Persians** did not improve from the state of poverty that these wars had caused. Sir Mortimer Durand has pointed out the curious similarity between **Nader**, the last great conqueror in Asia, and **Napoleon**, the last great conqueror in Europe. Firstly, Durand notes that these two kings were great conquerors. Secondly, the resemblance continues with the unbridled ambition and power of both which resulted in deterioration of character. Thirdly, they both became ruthless and insensitive to their own people. If **Nader Shah** had died after the campaigns of India, Bokhara, and Khiva, he would have been remembered as the national hero for all time.[4]

1. *Chekideh Tarikh Iran*, pp. 125, 126
2. *A Concise History Of India*, p. 42
3. *History Of Persia*, p. 254
4. *History Of Persia*, pp. 273, 274

Persia After Nader Shah

Persia entered, once again, the frenzied state of rebellion. Although the assassination of **Nader** did not cause much grief among **Persians** who were fed up with his cruelty, it created dissension among the tribes and provinces. For example, in India, **Nader**'s savage character was (and is still) compared to **Genghis Khan**— although his direct victims were not children or women. Besides, **Nader** did not level or burn the cities he ravaged—at least initially. He just concentrated on the treasures. Inside Persia, however, the most immediate reaction after his death came in the form of dissolution of the robust Persian army.

Ahmad Khan Durrani was an **Afghan** chieftain under **Nader**. He was the only leader who stood up to avenge the fallen **Nader**. At last **Durrani** was defeated and retreated to Kandahar (Ghandahar), where he founded his own smaller kingdom. Also, he seized the jewels of Delhi among which was "Kuh-i-Nur", or "Mountain of Light" (Later on, the **Queen of England** received this unique priceless diamond from a **Ghajar King** as a gift) "Kuh-i—Nur" is now a part of the royal jewels collection in England. **Ahmad Khan Durrani** continued the trend of **Nader** by raiding India, Panjab, and Kashmir for more treasures.

On the other hand **Adil Shah**, nephew of **Nader**, succeeded him on the throne in 1747 A.D. Rather than rebuilding the country, **Adil Shah** ordered the massacre of the family of **Nader**, except **Shah Rukh Mirza** who was 14 years old. **Adil Shah** raided the **Ghajar** tribe in north of Persia and killed many of their princes—this action would guarantee his dominion over Persia. He was finally captured, blinded, and killed by his own brother, **Ibrahim**. Then **Ibrahim** was killed by his own men.

Thus, **Shah Rukh Mirza** ascended the throne at age of fifteen; he too was captured and blinded by a **Shiite** clergy rival from Meshed.

This **Shiite** rival was also defeated and blinded in no time by **Yusef Ali** who was a chief commander in **Shah Rukh Mirza**'s army.

The blind **Shah Rukh Mirza** was restored to the throne with **Yusef Ali** as Regent. Two chiefs of Arab and Kurd provinces defeated **Yusef Ali** and, of course, blinded him. Needless to say, the two chiefs quarreled, and one of them was defeated and added to the long list of blind men.

In no time, the other chief was defeated by **Ahmad Khan Durrani** of Afghanistan and the city of Meshed surrendered. Then **Ahmad Khan Durrani** proceeded to Herat and Sistan in southeast Persia.

The horrific condition that the ordinary people in Persia had to live in amidst all the chaos plagued the nation in this period. So many mistakes were committed repeatedly because the public's awareness of the history was obscured and limited.

Meanwhile, **Muhammad Hasan Khan Ghajar** had maintained his ruling in Astarabad (north of Persia). Since **Nader Shah** had killed the father of **Muhammad Hasan Khan Ghajar (Fath Ali Kahn Ghajar)**, he opposed **Ahmad Shah Durrani** successfully and occupied the entire Caspian provinces in north.

Zand Dynasty
(1750 – 1794 A.D.)
Karim Khan Zand

On the other hand, another courageous and young commander under the ruling of **Ali Mardan Khan** the head of **Bakhtiar** tribes, gathered fame and force and waited his turn to come forward as the governor of southern Persia. This man was **Karim Khan Zand**, the founder of brief dynasty of **Zand**.[1]

Karim Khan Zand had been a simple soldier in the army of **Nader Shah** where he showed honesty and discipline that opened many doors for him. **Karim Khan Zand**'s growing popularity in Isfahan areas (south central Persia) made **Ali Mardan Khan** so Jealous and paranoid that **Karim Khan Zand** was forced to ride off with his followers in order to avoid execution. **Ali Mardan Khan** (the **Bakhtiar** chief) was shortly assassinated. Thus, **Karim Khan Zand**

swiftly returned and took the command of the entire area. He was famous among his people in southern Persia for being a kind and benevolent king. Because **Karim Khan Zand** had just abolished absolute power, he asked his people to refer to him as "**Vakil**" meaning Regent rather than **Shah**. He successfully ascended the throne in 1750 and reigned for twenty-nine years. He not only ruled well, but he was popular for his sense of humor, justice and kindliness. Although illiterate, his knowledge of administration of his land was superior. Shiraz and Isfahan enjoyed the most perfect tranquility and happiness under him for three decades. In 1779 A.D., the nation mourned his death of natural causes. Sir John Malcolm admired **Karim Khan Zand**'s humanitarian rule and believed that his particular reign looked more like a miracle considering the age and place that he lived in.[2]

After **Karim Khan Zand**, the central power was weakened by the dissension among the rivals for the throne. Again Persia was once again at the mercy of the unchained ambitious cruelties of rivals. Among the early claimants of power, the name of **Zaki Khan** stands out. He was half-brother to the late **Karim Khan Zand**. When **Zaki Khan** usurped the government, he tricked his opponents and executed anyone who doubted his rule. His cruelty to subdue his opponents was far greater than his men could tolerate. Therefore, his soldiers killed him in 1781. Now, **Sadegh Khan** and **Ali Murad** were the next in line for the throne. They wanted their share.

On the other hand, in the north , **Agha Muhammad Khan Ghajar** had his own followers. During the ten years of struggle that followed in southern Persia, **Lutf Ali Khan Zand**, the grandson of **Sadegh Khan**, received sufficient fame and popularity to take the control of the southern provinces including Shiraz. At this time, **Agha Muhammad Khan Ghajar** initiated a raid against Shiraz but was resisted harshly and had to retreat back briefly to his place in Tehran.

The balance of power between Ghajar and Zand tribes was soon to be changed by a strong figure in Shiraz. **Haji Ibrahim** (also called Kalantar) was the Magistrate of Shiraz during this time; he had rendered good service to **Lutf Ali Khan** and his family in Isfahan, but later on, he found it imprudent to continue to serve **Lutf Ali** who had changed his attitude during later stages of his reign. This mutiny against **Lutf Ali Khan Zand** caused him to flee to the coast of Bushire by Persian Gulf. Thus, in his absence **Ibrahim** took the control of Shiraz in 1791 A.D.

In 1792 **Lutf Ali**, who had gathered a new army, raided Shiraz, which was under the ruling of **Haji Ibrahim**. Again **Lutf Ali** was victorious against the **Ghajar** troops that had come to the help of **Haji Ibrahim**. However, for some reason, **Lutf Ali** did not follow **Agha Muhammad** that night, — reckless information had been given to this young hero from one of his confidants who had assumed that the **Agha Muhammad Khan** had fled his tent. **Lutf Ali** did not proceed to corner and arrest **Agha Muhammad**. By the next morning, new help had arrived for **Agha Muhammad**, who had actually spent the horrific night waiting to be assassinated inside his tent. Because of this negligence, it was too late for courageous **Lutf Ali** and his limited army to continue to fight the bigger army of **Ghajar**. Nevertheless, in 1794 A.D., **Lutf Ali Khan** raided the garrison of Kerman. **Agha Muhammad Khan** knew that this enemy couldn't be ignored, so he followed. **Lutf Ali** resisted both the surrounding **Ghajar** army and famine for four months, but finally decided to run away by nighttime with just a few soldiers. He traveled hundred twenty miles to the east towards the city of Bam, where one of his supporter's brother owned the governship. But the governor of the town had heard no news of his brother's well being, therefore he assumed that his brother was caught by **Ghajar**. Trying to win the favor of **Agha Muhammad**, he committed the unspeakable treachery of handing **Lutf Ali** to **Ghajar**. The gallant **Lutf Ali**, according to one account, was blinded by the hands of **Agha Muhammad Khan** and then sent to Tehran, where he was hung in 1794 A.D.[3]

All of this was a direct result of **Haji Ibrahim**'s interference. In fact, Sir Percy Sykes called **Haji Ibrahim** "The king Maker" and compared his political genius to **Bismarck** of the **German Empire**.[4]

The numerous crimes committed by **Agha Muhammad Khan** are despicable. For personal revenge, this founder of **Ghajar Dynasty** ordered the massive blinding of the public in Kerman.

These cruel acts of tyrants were not unique to Persia, unfortunately. There are incidents of utmost cruelty all over the world. However, Europe had already passed through its dark ages; but it had managed to enter the new era of scientific exploration and modernization about this time. French revolution had opened the doors for a new democratic state. Sciences and arts of the Renaissance Period were starting to improve the lives of people in the West.

At this period coming out of the Dark Ages, Europe was facing a period of social freedom. **Russian Kings**, ever since the line of **Peter the Great,** had tried to westernize their people to be accepted in the family of European states. On the other hand, European nations were getting rid of older regimes that enforced their unilateral laws over the people. **Denmark** got rid of the tyrannical rule of **Christian VII,** by executing him and his German advisor and physician **Struensee** in a palace coup in 1772. At this time **Sweden** was enjoying prosperity under **Gustavus**, who abolished torture and provided freedom of press and worship. Unfortunately, positive figures in the history of the world are not always recognized in time. **Gustavus** was assassinated at a masked ball in 1792. English men had already checked the power of their kings in their revolutions of 1688-89. Of course, aristocrats of Europe, though only about 2 percent of the population in France and under 1 percent in Russia, resisted the reforms.[5]

Contrary to Europe, reforms in the East, appeared at a slower rate and usually faced a more severe resistance from its aristocracy. **Jean Jacques Rousseau**, the 18th Century French political philosopher, believed that men arrived at truth and virtue intuitively rather than rationally. Whatever the reason, the enlightenment and awareness of the public in the eastern world was not happening fast at this time.

The role of men and women in society were subject to these fluctuations. But men enjoyed more social power then as well as now. **European** women were considered inferior to their men, and women's Enlightenment followed that of the men. Even women in **The United States** could not vote until 1920 and **French** women received this right in 1944. Married women in **England** did not have the right to personal possessions until 1870. However, **Muslim** women had this particular right since 750 A.D.—either in their father's house (*Jihaz*) or their husband's (*Mahrieh*). It seems that civilization continues to make its way sooner or later be it intuitively or rationally.[6]

In addition to the European Enlightenment, another type of enlightenment developed in Persia. The **Zand Dynasty** was popular precisely because it did not indulge in power or prestige. The **Zand**

Kings preferred to be called **Regent** and public servers rather than **Shah**. For about forty years, the **Zand Dynasty** also contributed to the development of trade in bazaars, construction of shrines for worshipers, and construction of rest areas (Caravanserais) for travelers and their animals. **Karim Khan Zand** personally made sure that all and every neighborhood inside Shiraz was filled with music and that food and wine was abundant for all citizens. Persia under these kings, indeed, received a much-needed break from all the previous turmoil.[7]

1. *Chekideh Tarikh Iran*, p. 133-136
2. *Tarikh-e-Iran* , Vol.2, Translated by M.T. Fakhr Daie, Tehran, p. 429
3. *History Of Persia*, By Sir Percy Sykes, London, pp. 285-287
4. *Tarikh-e-Iran*, Vol.2, Tehran, Translated by F. Daie, pp. 444-446
5. *Modern Europe: A Popular History*, by Thomas P. Neill, 1970, Doubleday & Co. pp. 11-24
6. *Rah Avard*, No 48 edition, Fall Quarter, 1999, Los Angeles, article by Dr. Ali Mazrooie;
    "Islamic & Western Values," p. 66
7. *Tarikh-e-Iran* , Vol.2, Tehran, pp. 435-437

CHAPTER NINETEEN

Ghajar Dynasty (Ghajarieh) (1780 – 1924 A.D.)

Agha Muhammad Khan Ghajar (or **Agha Muhammad Shah**) is referred to as one of the most contemptuous tyrants in the history of Persia. An unbiased study of his life story reveals some of the dark areas of his character as well as some positive points. **Adil Shah (Afshar Dynasty)** had massacred **Agha Muhammad's** eight elder brothers in the **Ghajar** tribe. Then **Adil Shah** proceeded to castrate **Agha Muhammad** when he was only five and not a threat to the throne. This misfortune speaks for **Agha Muhammad's** wicked character as the Eunuch-Monarch for life. He had spent his boyhood at the court of **Zand**, in Shiraz. **Agha Muhammad's** sister was married to **Karim Khan Zand** who treated him with respect and kindness.

When **Karim Khan Zand** passed away, **Agha Muhammad Khan** rushed to the north towards his own tribes to siege a troop of followers calling himself the "sole ruler" of northern territories in 1779 A.D. As said earlier, Persia, at this period, was divided between many rulers—each one with his own regional and tribal support. Fortunately, the **Russians** and **Ottomans** were too involved with their own internal conflicts to take advantage of the chaos inside

Persia. During his reign, **Agha Muhammad Khan** actually improved the roads and towns all over the nation. This increased overall safety and trades prospered: whereas under **Nader Shah** (Afshar Dynasty), the country had been depopulated.

In 1795 A.D. **Agha Muhammad** raided Georgia or Gorjistan, which under **Heraclius** had separated from Persia after the death of **Nader Shah**. This land was between Russia and Persia. Teflis fell and **Persians** took many captives and killed those who resisted. Iravan was conquered next. Russia, under **The Empress Catherine**, was too involved with bigger internal problems and did not attempt any interference. The sudden death of **Catherine** brought her son, **Paul**, to the throne of Russia. **Paul** chose to halt any invasions against northern states of Persia. As mentioned earlier, **Lutf Ali Khan**—the last courageous king of the Zand Dynasty—was finally caught with deceit and bribe and blinded by **Agha Muhammad Khan** around this period.

The official coronation of **Agha Muhammad Khan** took place in 1796 A.D. in Tehran. Briefly after, this new king rushed to Khorasan and killed **Shah Rukh** (the last king of **Afshar Dynasty**) and received more of the hidden treasures brought from India. A year later, **Agha Muhammad Khan** was killed by the hands of two of his servants, who were sentenced to death by him the night before, but persecution was postponed to the next morning.

It is true that the character of **Agha Muhammad Khan** had disastrous outcome for many **Persians**, as well as Persian enemies, yet his patience and courage secured him the throne of Persia in spite of his physical disabilities. His passion for power and unification of scattered tribes made the **Ghajars** the royal tribe. This was possible because his love for power was bigger than his desire for revenge. **Agha Muhammad** had forgiven all the **Ghajar chiefs** who had killed his father and/or had insulted him personally.

All of **Ghajar kings** abolished the scattered tribal rulings inside Persia. Nomadic tribes who were almost autonomous were suppressed and brought under a central command. **Shiite** became the official **Islamic** sect and Persia became one unified nation– the **Ulama** of **Shiite** (**Muslim Clerics**) gained more power over the society. The **Ghajar kings** did not allow much propaganda for **Sufism**. Ironically, **Ghajars** had themselves originally come from a **Sufi** ancestry. The **Ghajar** tribes had converted to **Shiite** after they were brought to Persia from Turkey at the time of **Nader Shah**. One reason for this imposition was that most **Sufis** were of **Sunni** sect. Fundamentally, **Sunnis**, like the **Khavarej** group (who had caused all The **Prophet**'s successors a lot of dismay), mostly abolished the combined mixing of the religious leadership and the monarchy in this country. On the other hand, this unfair censorship made future stern oppositions against freedom of speech and religion more permissible. Consequently, the Persian mystic poetry, inspired through **Sufism**, gradually diminished and **Jaami** (born in Khorasan in 1414 A.D.) seems to be the last great poet since the **Saffavid Dynasty** in Persia. **Jaami** managed to create beauty of rhyme, allegory, and mysticism in his poetry. After him, this trend in literature was gradually replaced by a more tangible style of prose regarding down-to-earth issues.[1]

   …What sorrow if Your blade cutting my head apart
   The real sorrow if my head and Your blade afar…

Fath Ali Shah of Ghajar

Each time a king is killed the struggle between the rivals for the succession to the throne begins again. This time, the fighting was in progress before the body of the deceased **Agha Muhammad Khan** was buried. The army was mostly broken up and dispersed. Through the support of **Haji Ibrahim Kalantar**, an army was sent along from Shiraz to Tehran in support of **Fath Ali Khan** (the nephew and the official heir to the deceased **Agha Muhammad Khan**). By the assistance of some **Ghajar** chiefs, the accession of **Fath Ali** came through in 1797 A.D. Later on, the political support of **Haji Ibrahim** along with his monetary aid, resolved many oppositions that rose.[2]

During **Ghajar Dynasty** the first official Prime minister in Persia was **Haji Ibrahim Kalantar** in 1800 A.D. He was officially selected by **Fath Ali Shah**. This man served the king but was eventually ordered to be killed by the intervention of foreign delegates inside the Persian court. The next three of the following prime ministers were all direct recipients of salaries or bribes from **English** embassy to protect its rights inside the region against Russia.[3]

Before this period, around 1798, England was strengthening its colonizing domain in India, and **Lord Wellesley** was its Governor-General of Bengal. From the north, **Paul the Tsar** of Russia was building garrisons inside the border states of Persia. However, **Fath Ali Khan of Ghajar**, like some other kings before him, was indulging himself in his feverous obsessions with his harem concubines.

In the meantime, **Napoleon Bonaparte** of France had approached **Fath Ali Shah** in order to gain his cooperation in allowing **French** army to travel through Persia to drive the **British** out of India with the help of **Shah Zaman** of Kabul (Afghanistan). Fortunately, **Mirza Bozorg (Ghaem Magham)** was the thoughtful **Prime Minister**, who acted brilliantly and jumped on this opportunity to renovate the Persian army at the hands of French specialists without promising anything to the **French**. **Mirza Bozorg** wanted to use this unique position of Persia as a tool to take advantage of the rivalries of the **British, French,** and **Russian Empires**.

The permanent **British** association with Persia began in 1979. The British had established their political domain over India. The Eastern India Company was a front to hide their colonizing interests in India. **Mehdi Ali Khan**, a naturalized **Persian** inside the **British** embassy (acting as the Eastern India Company's Resident at Bushehr) was instructed by the **British** government to take measures for inducing the court of Persia to keep **Shah Zaman**, ruler of Kabul, in perpetual check to preclude him from raiding against India. This was an important diplomatic triumph for Britain, as it has always been a plot of the **French** to get rid of the **British** presence in India **Mehdi Ali Khan** had angered **Fath Ali Shah** by letters reflecting accounts of atrocities committed by the **Sunni Afghans** on the **Shiites** of Lahore (Pakistan). Therefore, a continuity of hostilities between Persia and Afghanistan was achieved. This hostility was used in order to infiltrate the **French** maneuvers against **British** position in the area.[4]

When **Mehdi Ali Khan** witnessed that **Fath Ali Shah** of **Ghajar** is eager to raid Afghanistan anyway—even without any financial aids from England—he refused to mention that such financial credit was already obtainable from **British** government. **Captain Malcolm** of England congratulated **Mehdi Khan** personally in Bushire for this service to England. Very soon, **Fath Ali Shah** invaded Kabul, and **Shah Zaman** had to retreat back to Afghanistan and forget the invasion of **British** territories inside India. Now, England felt at ease from this imminent threat. The mission was a success in 1800 A.D. Although **Captain Malcolm** was a young officer of the **British** army, he gained a great respect from the **Persian** court at this time because of his gallantry in these battles against **Shah Zaman**. As mentioned before, **Fath Ali Shah** who owned his throne to **Haji Ibrahim** became seriously alarmed at his growing fame; and ordered **Haji** and all his family killed around 1802 A.D. During this period there was a rivalry between the **Tsar** of Russia and **Charles II** of Britain and **Napoleon** of France. India was the prize. Because of the lack of a wise **Persian King** during this period, Persia did not benefit as a mediator state.[5]

Europe was alert to opportunities to expand its political power and wealth in the vulnerable Middle East. At this time, The United States was getting ready to declare its freedom from England. **Thomas Jefferson** along with other scholars drew up the Constitution to establish freedom of all U.S. citizens. In 1801 A.D., he was inaugurated as the third President of the U.S. The same year in Russia, **Paul I** the **Czar** was assassinated; **Alexander I** succeeded him. In Europe, **Napoleon** had captured Rome; France was at the zenith of its power.[6]

1. *Tarikh-e-Kamel-e-Iran*, by Dr. Abdullah Razi, 1970, Tehran, pp. 459, 460
2. *Chekideh Tarikh Iran*, pp. 140, 141
3. *Jam-e- Shenasi Nokhbeh Koshi*, by Ali Reza-Gholi, 18th edition, 2001, Tehran, P. 94
4. *History of Persia*, Vol. 2, pp. 298-300
5. *Chekideh Tarikh Iran*, p. 143
6. *Timetables of History*, by Bernard Grun, Simon & Schuster publishing. New York, 1975

Changes in other parts of the world would sometimes directly affect Persia. For example, in 1805 France attacked Russia (a mistake that France soon regretted). A year later, after a quick success in Europe France ambitiously challenged England's presence in India. Subsequently, a **French** envoy, **Monsieur Jauberet**, appeared at Tehran with a proposal requesting cooperation between France and

Persia to stop Britain and to get the **British** out of India. This continued with a second French envoy who was seeking the support of the **Persian King** in Tehran. So **General Gardanne** plus seventy (commissioned and non- commissioned) officers, appeared in Persia in 1807 to train the **Persian army** on **European** military aggressive preparedness. As a gesture of friendship, France promised Persia to persuade Russia to return the occupied lands to Persia. But during this time, France had made peace with Russia. However, restoration of lost territories back to Persia was not even discussed as promised to **Fath Ali Shah**. This huge oversight made the **Shah** furious. Actually this flaw smoldered and became a serious grudge of the **Persians** against the **French**. As a result, England won the confidence of Persia , soon after the **French** envoys had to leave.[1]

The disappointed **General Gardanne**—whose mission had failed so far - wrote in his memoirs that **Persian** statesmen are greedy and usually do not accept even the most beneficial proposals, unless those proposals contain a personal monetary gain for these Persian statesmen.[2] The fact that **General Gardanne** singled out **Persian** statesmen as requiring personal monetary gains (bribes) definitely should not be interpreted as a flaw of **Persians** only. Bribery, in history, has always been a by-product of economic injustice and hardship. For the wealthier ambassadors and/or opportunistic authorities in any government, bribery is often more of greed than need.

Still Russia maintained a controlling hand over Persia. After the loss of Gorjistan (Georgia) to Russia in 1800, Persia had a more direct confrontation with Russia. **Abbas Mirza**, the heir-apparent and Governor—General of Azerbaijan (bordering Russia on the north), was dispatched to block the **Russian** army with untrained Persian army. **Sir Henry Rawlinson**, an instructor of **Persian** troops, wrote that the system of army in Persia lacked discipline, budget, clothing, food, carriage, equipage, and command. Helpless **Abbas Mirza** was aware of these difficulties; he also learned that simple change of attires for the soldiers did not necessarily inspire the fighting spirit. At this time, **Mirza Bozorg** was the clever seer and consultant to **Abbas Mirza** in Tabriz around 1810. **Mirza Bozorg** was also involved in conducting some of these needed renovations inside the country. He was the father of **Mirza Abolghasem** (known as **Ghaem Magham**

Farahani, who later became the valuable prime minister to **Fath Ali Shah** and **Muhammad Shah** up to 1835). **Ghaem Magham** was against the intervention of fanatic **Muslim Clerics** in the total control of the government's affairs. **Ghaem Magham** was the man of the future but born at the wrong place and time. He believed that solidarity of a country's rule is based on democracy. **Ghaem Magham** always mentioned that Persia needed education and justice to overcome its enemies. He knew that borders needed to be secured against the enemies and people needed to be educated to realize the value of freedom. **Ghaem Magham** used to say that the country needs soldiers, not prayers. Later on, he lost his life for his rightful beliefs and conducts. This idea of democracy and justice for all was not new to **Persians** of the 18th Century: **Cyrus The Great** had established this thoughtful trend of ruling in 550 B.C. But his democratic vision was seldom maintained for long periods.

Ghaem Magham was a buffer between the king and his people. Since **Fath Ali Shah** had 270 active heirs, each had some hope for leadership. **Ghaem Magham** was the best Prime Minister that could actually maintain the control inside the country. The **Shah** knew this very well and was actually the only supporter of this great man. **Ghaem Magham** had fired many corrupt members of the government - including some princes that were a financial burden to the taxpayers. Naturally, this benevolent yet bold decision resulted in hostilities toward **Ghaem Magham** from within the system. On the other hand, the **British** had finally seen an untouchable (not susceptible to bribes) and faithful **Vazir** in the **Persian** court. **Ghaem Magham** was the fifth **Prime Minister** of Persia. The other four were merely puppets of **British** government who openly received salaries from that nation to uphold **British** interest in the region.[3]

In spite of the efforts of Persian soldiers and politicians, finally, **Russians** annexed Erivan (Irvan) in 1804, and **Abbas Mirza** could not withstand their army. **Fath Ali Shah** himself had to go to **Abbas Mirza**'s aid and push the **Russians** back. At this time the **Russians** raided Gilan (at the Caspian Sea). The **Shah** sought the Fatva of *Jihad* (the order of religious war) against the **Russians** from the **Sunni** leaders. However, all attempts failed and a disastrous treaty called '*Gulistan*' was signed in 1813 A.D. This treaty surrendered a great area of **Persian** soil to the **Russians**. Gorjistan, Daghestan, Baku,

Shirvan, Gharabagh, and Abkhasia were given to **Russians**. In addition to the actual lands lost, **Persian Navy** was forced to forfeit its right to sail even on Caspian Sea, the common waters between Persia and Russia. Meanwhile, **Haji Mirza Aghasi**—who later became the incompetent prime minister of **Muhammad Shah**—in order to facilitate decisions, foolishly argued in the **Persian** court that the salt water would not be really of any significant worth to Persia. The **Persian** government was hoping that it could find the strength it needed from the **British** military reforms to retaliate soon.[4]

Thus the size of Persia shrank again at this time. In return, Russia promised military support to **Abbas Mirza** to guarantee his smooth succession after his father, **Fath Ali Shah**. Except for **Abbas Mirza,** who cared very much to see the result of the reforms in military and in the agriculture, the **Ghajar kings** and their men usually seemed more worried about their own position rather than prosperity of the nation. This is actually a characteristic of the rule of any self-centered tyrant. In addition, the Treaties of *Gulistan* and *Turkomanchai* allowed **Persian** lands to be given away to Russia in exchange for a promise of military support—which did not ever happen. The borders for more **European** products were opened to the favor of Europe. The imported products promised an easier life style for the **Persians**, but total elimination of tariffs had a devastating effect on the suffering internal economy of the nation.

Fortunately for the **Persians**, Russia was dealing with a bigger issue. The army of **Napoleon** had invaded Russia in its first encounter on 6th of September 1812. The battle of Boradino had 74,000 casualties in one day. In order to starve the **French**, many villages and crops on the path of the **French** army were destroyed by the **Russians** themselves. The army of **Napoleon** was estimated to be about 500,000 strong. In October, **Napoleon** retreats with only 20,000 soldiers left (in about a month France had lost 480,000 soldiers).

Most of the **kings** who cared more for the expansion of their territories, rather than the welfare of the people, eventually fell. **Napoleon Bonaparte** abdicated finally and was banished to Elba in April 11, 1814. Subsequently, **Louis XVIII** took the throne in Paris.[5]

In Persia around this time, **Fath Ali Shah** was also facing serious rebels from several parts of the country. The **chiefs** of Khorasan, who never liked the **Ghajars**, rose against the crown prince—Viceroy,

Abbas Mirza. In 1827, the **Russian** soldiers occupied Tabriz and **Persians** had to bear the burden of another tragic treaty called *Turkomanchai* signed in 1828. Now. Irvan and Nakhjavan also were given to Russia. Years later, **Fath Ali Shah** refused to part with his money as he had promised in this treaty. Therefore, Russia was preparing to invade again in order to collect the promised money. **Sir John Mc Donald**, the **British Ambassador** stepped forward, and this threat was resolved with minor amendments to the original treaty. The loss of Persian territories not only brought financial dismay for the nation, it also shattered the patriotic spirit of the **Persians** in the international community.

Amid al these responsibilities as Crown Prince and Viceroy, **Abbas Mirza** was also the chief commander of the **Persian** army. Although he had not stopped the unfair and unwise treaties, he was the first leader who recognized the need to gain the knowledge and expertise of the West. He was a pioneer in dispatching **Persian** students to receive higher education abroad. **Abbas Mirza** even put ads in papers in London inviting investors and specialists to Persia to modernize the agricultural industry.[6] (Rice, wheat, and barley would be abundantly grown and distributed in Persia)

Ironically, **Abbas Mirza** who had received a promise from the **Russian** Government regarding assistance to his succession, died in 1833. In the following year, **Fath Ali Shah** (his father) passed away after 37 years of pitiful ruling. It is recorded that at the time of death, he had about one thousand wives and over 2000 grand children who, with great ethnical differences, could not tolerate each other.[7]

During this period of devastating political mistakes and economical hardship for Persia, Europe in the 19th Century revolutionized the outlook of its middle class. In 1816, many inventions such as Kaleidoscope by **Sir David Brewster**, and discovery of electromagnetism by **Danish** scientist **Hans C. Oersted** was pushing Europe ahead, while Persia was caught in a pitiful state under greedy leaders of **Ghajar**. By 1821 in South America, Peru proclaimed independence from Spain, and soon Guatemala, Mexico, Panama, and Santo Domingo followed.[8] Meanwhile, Persia suffered from the lack of appreciation for their long-suffering ethical leaders who fought without support to protect their nation against shrewd politicians and greedy foreign ambassadors.

Muhammad Shah

After **Fath Ali shah** again the struggle for power followed the death of this king in 1834. Through the intervention of the **English** and **Russian** ministers, **Muhammad** the son of late **Abbas Mirza** received the throne in 1834. Unfortunately, execution of **Ghaem Magham** (the valuable **Prime Minister**) came as one of the major disasters caused by this incompetent new king. In the past Persia tried to prevent political corruption and improve quality of life. However, new products (better sewers, water systems, schools, artillery, etc.) were brought in Persia but their value was neither taught nor understood. History has shown that renovations or reforms, without fundamental change in the attitude of people towards their democratic rights, are unfruitful.

In addition ethical and responsible leaders were left without public support. There were three major reasons for the increasing number of enemies of **Ghaem Magham** that resulted in his execution:

First was putting limitation on the salaries of the **king** and his royal courts men.
Second was his stern opposition against any wars with any of Persia's neighbors.
The third was his strict resistance against the intervention of ambassadors of foreign countries with the internal affairs of the nation.[9]

1. *History of Persia*, Vol. 2, p.303
2. *Chekideh Tarikh Iran*, p.145
3. *Jame-e-Shenasi Nokhbeh Koshi*, by Ali Reza-Gholi, 18th edition, 2001, Tehran, p. 95-101
4. *Tarikh-e-Iran*, Vol.2, Translated by F. Daie, Tehran, pp. 492-493
5. *Timetables of History*, Bernard Grun, New York, 1975
6. *The If's of Iran's History*, by Dr. M. Javanbakht, 2002, Isfahan, pp.122-125
7. *Chekideh Tarikh Iran*, p. 148
8. *Timetables of History*, by Bernard Grun
9. *Khaterat Ghaem Magham Farahani*, by Dr. A. G. Farahani, Baharestan printing, 2001, p. 42

Bernard Lewis points out the fact that renovations would not necessarily bring prosperity. Modernizing the countries of Middle East has been going on for some centuries. The military and economic reforms – starting in 13th Century by **Shah Abbas The Great** – brought no success, but unhealthy dependence on super powers. But worst of all was the political modernization or reform that ended with empowering of a string of shabby tyrannies, which only looked modern in their manipulative and suppressive appearances.[1]

These tyrannies usually oppose any intellectual controversy, only like-minded politicians become successful. Around this time **Haji Mirza Aghasi** (a fanatic and ignorant figure inside the court) was selected as the sixth Prime Minister of Persia. The reason for his selection was not that he was competent but rather that he used to be the new king's tutor. In 1837, **Muhammad Shah** (who had better relations with the **Tsar** in Russia) received some assistance from that country to invade Herat in Afghanistan. **Ghaem Magham** had resisted this useless action during his service. This occupation, in his absence, did not last more than a year. Because Britain had warned the **Shah** that invasion of Heart would result in invasion of the Persian Gulf by the British. Later on, in 1840, the rising of **Agha Khan Mahallati**, who was a descendant of **Ismaili** tribes, brought some threats against the central government of **Muhammad Shah** by gaining control of Yazd and Kerman. **British** envoys had used the seriousness of this uprising to convince the **Shah** to withdraw his animosity towards Afghanistan. This withdrawal would insure the interest of the **English** in the East.

During the **Ghajar Dynasty** the influence of the **Muslim Clerics** in running both internal and foreign affairs of Persia alarmingly increased. This political control sometimes came as a *Fatva* (religious order). **Dr. Mc Neal**, the **British** envoy, could not gain the consent of the **Shah** to retreat from Herat without the useful insight of the **Clerics**.[2] This influence had its roots in the **Sassanid Dynasty** and continued its growth till the end of the **Pahlavi Dynasty** and beyond.

After **Muhammad Shah** died in 1848, the throne was handed to his crown prince **Nasir-u-Din** - only sixteen. Persia, in the middle of the 19th Century, was on verge of bankruptcy. For example, agricultural industry fell in dismay and the subsequent lack of adequate crops brought Persia to its knees. In some areas inside the country people had to get their nourishments from the remaining food for the cattle.[3]

Also, the poor army with a pay of years in arrears was too far from what it used to be. As Rawlinson recorded, the traditional primary cavalry of the tribes that **Persians** had successfully used during **Nadir Shah** was lost, while the promised renovations had not fully fall into place.[4]

1.   *What Went Wrong*, by Bernard Lewis, Harper Collins Publishers, 2002, New York, p. 151

2.   *Iran Dar Rah Yabi Farhangi*, Homa Nategh, printed by Payam, London p. 138

3.   *Amir Kabir Va Iran*, by Fereidoon Adamiat, Kharazmi Publications, 1976, Tehran, p. 165

4.   *History Of Persia*, Vol.2, p. 338

Nasir-u-Din Shah

After the death of **Mohammad Shah** there was no opposition to the succession of the heir, **Nasir-u-Din** in 1848. Disorders, however, broke out in the provinces. It took this young king about six weeks to get to the capitol of Tehran. **British** and **Russian** ambassadors advised the incompetent **Haji Mirza Aghasi** to withdraw from his position. These assertive foreign ambassadors believed that some of the disorders were because he lacked control during the thirteen years of his inadequate service as Prime Minister.

The increasing domination of foreign ambassadors threatened the solidarity of Persia. The lack of worthy political figures hurt the country beyond imagination. Ali Reza-Gholi refers to the fact that during the last 200 years of the Persian history, the country has witnessed about 87 Prime Ministers—out of which, unfortunately, only a few deserve such an important position. Furthermore, out of the nine kings who ruled Persia since the beginning of the 19th Century, four were exiled by the hands of foreign delegates who dominated legitimate government of Persia, one was hung, and the rest died with agony caused partially by their own tyrannical rule and luxurious life style.[1]

Fortunately for Persia, the wise and strong **Mirza Taghi Khan** was chosen by **Nasir-u-Din Shah** to fill the position of Prime Minister.

Mirza Taghi Khan had come from a humble background. His father was a cook and afterwards steward of **Ghaem Magham** (the competent and just **Prime Minister** of **Mohammad Shah**). It was **Ghaem Magham** who had seen a great future in **Amir Taghi Khan** and had trained him personally. At a younger age, **Amir Taghi Khan** had entered St. Petersburg as the Persian Ambassador at the time of **Khosro Mirza** (a **Ghajar** Prince). His persistence and good will won **Amir Taghi Khan** the prestige and power within the government.[2]

October of 1848 was truly a fortuitous time for Persia. **Amir Taghi Khan** (nicknamed **Amir Kabir** meaning The Great Leader) was appointed as the new **Vazir (Prime Minister)** by **Nasir-u-Din Shah**. Thus, another brilliant political figure in the history of Persia began his extraordinary protocol of development and renovation of the country. Persia had been waiting for this figure while the rest of the world was advancing fast. At this time Europe had already entered the era of industrialization. Also, rulers were no longer looked upon as an extension of divinity in Europe, but as an earthly authority of great importance for the benefit of the people to whom rulers and their governments would be accountable. A new worldview based on individualism and social liberalism had caused expansion of sciences throughout all classes inside Europe. **Montesquieu**, **Voltaire**, **Diderot**, **Jean Jacque Rousseau**, and **Adam Smith** were building on the birth of the Renaissance; on the other hand, Persia was struggling with poverty. This poverty was caused by lack of incentives to work. Hard work and honesty did not guarantee just compensation in the absence of law and democracy. Fereidoon Adamiat emphasizes in his book that **Mirza Taghi Khan** was indeed noteworthy for three major reasons:

> First, expanding literacy throughout the nation as well as in industries in order to training new work forces.
> Secondly, laying foundation for political independence of Persia.
> Third, uprooting corruption among the civil workers and government employees. [3]

A miracle was needed and Prime Minister **Amir Kabir** (nickname for **Mirza Taghi Khan**) met that challenge. He managed to subdue the rebellions of **Salar**, another **Ghajar** prince in Khorasan. A second major problem for **Amir Kabir** was the rebellion of **Baha** (**Bab**) believers. This protest was actually against the extreme tyranny of the regime of **Ghajar** that even threatened **Amir Kabir**. The rebellious **Bahai** leader was **Seyyed Ali Mohammad**, the son of a grocer in Shiraz, who had studied under the celebrated **Muslim clerics** in Iraq around 1840's. At the age of twenty-four **Seyyed Ali Mohammad** proclaimed himself the Bab or "Gate", thereby intimating that he was the "Gate" through which **Muslims** might attain knowledge of the **Twelfth Imam**. Finally, **Seyyed Ali Mohammad** was ordered to execution at Tabriz in 1850. Two years later, the life of **Nasir-u-Din Shah** was threatened by the revengeful **Bahai** believers with no result. Browne reflects on **Bahai** doctrines: "…they formed together a system bold, original and, to the Persian mind, singularly attractive; but, taken separately, there was hardly one of which he (**Bab**) could claim to be the author, and not very many which did not mount to a remote antiquity." This new doctrine under **Islam** has had a great number of followers. Their act of bravery in wars against the suppression of the government, and the tortures they endured in the jails gained them sympathy not only from their fellow-countrymen but also from the **Europeans** residing in Tehran. (Probably this heroic behavior produced many converts to the new doctrine).[4]

Single-handedly **Amir Kabir** was trying, among many other things, to put an end into unlawful incarcerations and torturing of prisoners. But, these fundamental changes were too slow. The majority of **Persians** did not realize the value of the human rights and some were blinded by religious prejudice. They neither demanded social liberties from their government, nor supported **Amir Kabir** who heroically fought for it.

The history of the world portrays much bloodshed, but along with that also appeared delightful moments of heroic actions. One example is the moment when a suppressed people finally stands up on their own feet in order to bring the necessary changes, although final outcomes may vary. For example, in 1841 in the U.S., slavery was very profitable. U.S.S. "Creole", carrying slaves from Virginia to Louisiana, was seized by the slaves. They rerouted the ship and sailed it to Nassau where they became free.[5]

However, in Persia, the lack of coordinated resistance by the masses reaction against a tyrannical ruler was still to come.

Unfortunately, a tyrannical regime in Persia has always been replaced by a new one, and still the same crimes occurred. Ali Reza-Gholi believes that direct confrontation with criminals is only a temporary solution. He stipulates that true social and ethical sources of these crimes have never been identified in Persia. Whereas, in more developed societies, the social sources of crimes are identified and then corrected by preventive measures. **Amir Kabir** knew this fact and was expressly referring to "Hoghugh-e-Sabeteh." These were social primary rights that referred to the essence of human dignity , which today, basically translate to the Human Rights. **Amir Kabir** demanded the upholding of law and justice to protect the rights of citizens from his selected viceroys. His letters to the governor of Gilan reflect this sensitivity to the issues of Human Rights (Hoghugh-e-Sabeteh).[6]

Amir Kabir was truly a blessing for Persia. But, in 1851, **Nasir-u-Din Shah** became extremely intimidated by the increasing fame and power of this great Vazir— although **Amir Kabir** was like a father to him. **Amir** had indeed an extraordinary popularity within the army. This **Persian** army had him to thank for its salary, uniforms, and trainings. Therefore the jealous **Shah** unwisely ordered **Amir**'s demotion to Commander of the Army. Subsequently, **Mirza Agha Khan (Etemad-u-Doleh)** was appointed new Prime Minister **(Vazir)**. The shameful execution of **Amir Kabir** in Kashan that happened two months later was a calamity for Persia: it ceased the progress which had been so painfully achieved.

Amir Kabir, during four years of his extraordinary service to Persia, made unbelievable achievements in different fields. He pioneered free vaccination of public against smallpox a reality in Persia. When **Dr. Cormick** from England printed an article about smallpox, **Amir** arranged for its translation and distribution. In order to vaccinate everyone, he ordered training of a huge task force, equipped with the right knowledge and tools and dispatched them to all corners of Persia. Also, he established the first public hospital in Persia. In addition, the construction of Karaj aqueducts to transfer water to Tehran during summer time was another brilliant work designed by him. Then he established the Post Office inside the country during this short time. **Amir Kabir** was versatile in public and administrative reforms. He is credited with building of some of the greatest Bazaars and trade markets inside Persia. Construction of Toop Khaneh circle and Sabzeh Meidan (major roads and trade centers) were some of his achievements in Tehran. He had also ordered renovations of Khajoo Bridge in Isfahan. He was the founder of *Vaghai-e-Ettefaghieh*, in February of 1851, one of the earliest weekly papers in Tehran that educated people about the latest news of the world and the developments inside the country. The list of **Amir Kabir's** outstanding service in all areas goes on and on.[7]

One of the most important far reaching actions that **Amir Kabir** accomplished was preventing Persia from being manipulated into any wars or political friction with its neighboring nations. **Britain** had finally managed to enter a new treaty with **Afghanistan** in 1855 regarding security of its borders. **Afghanistan** was strategically important to **Britain** since a continuous check against **Russia** and **France** would be crucial for keeping **British** interest in **India**. **Amir Kabir** had previously resisted the useless wars with neighbors of Persia, but his execution gave **Nasir-u-Din Shah** the opportunity to order surrounding of Herat in **Afghanistan** in 1856, even if it cost lives, money, and prestige. **England** hated **Amir Kabir** because of his political achievements, which resulted in a lasting truce with governments of Herat and **Russia**. **Britain** was worried about these possible allies against its growing power in the area. Soon, after the invasion of **Persia** against **Afghanistan**, **Britain** jumped on the excuse to invade the Persian Gulf ports of Bushir and Khoram Shahr to support Herat. Consequently, **Persia** had to withdraw immediately. **Nasir-u-Din Shah** was not much interested in following the steps of his missing **Vazir** (**Amir Kabir**). No major renovations were accomplished in Persia by this king. Instead, foreign countries — **Britain**, **France**, and **Russia** - had to provide a meager level of technological advancement in Persia required for manipulating Persia's resources. For example some years later, in 1864, the Telegraph was brought into the country via Baghdad. This new communication connected all of Persia with the southern states along the Persian Gulf. This benefited the foreign embassies more than the people of Persia and this was the primary reason for its development.

This era coincided with the assassination of **Abraham Lincoln** in April of 1865 and the succession of **Andrew Johnson** as the 17th president of the United States. The U.S. was struggling to emancipate slavery, and Europe was busy launching ships to expand its slavery market all over the East.

Meanwhile in Persia in 1871, by the advice of **Mirza Hussein Khan** (Sepah Salar or Chief Army Commander), a **British** fellow named **Reuter** gained the concession to establish the rights to Rail Road, Mining and Banking headquarters in Persia. These **British** advances made **Russians** furious. On the other hand, **Nasir-u-Din Shah** who was traveling did not receive the hospitality he expected from his hosts in England. Upon his return to Persia, and by the passive reaction of the **Persians** against the latest treaties, he voided the unilateral agreements that were signed in his absence. But not much later, he signed an agreement to allow establishment of a British Bank, the first Imperial (Shahanshahi) Bank, by the supervision of **Reuter** in 1889. [8]

Another important concession, but less fortunate, signed by **Nasir-u-Din Shah** was the Tobacco Contract n 1890. This hasty agreement gave full control of the production, sale, and export of all tobacco in Persia. **Shah** was to receive one quarter of the profits. This affected the position of tobacco growers, sellers, and smokers alike. First, a public indignation and then fanaticism was aroused. **Haji Mirza Hasan Shirazi**, the leading **Mujtahid (Cleric)** interdict on smoking. He said because tobacco is both grown and packed by the hands or money of **non-Muslims**, therefore **Muslims** should not smoke that tobacco under any circumstances. This order was obeyed throughout the land the royal palace being no exception. Finally, **Shah**, fearing imminent and more serious uprises, cancelled the concession and agreed to pay compensation to the extent of half million sterling. This sum was borrowed from the Imperial Bank (Shahanshahi), and may be considered to constitute the beginning of the Persian National Debt. Ironically, **Nasir-u-Din Shah** was the most educated **Ghajar** king and spoke French and had some skills in painting and poetry. However, towards the end of his reign he became indifferent, egotistical, and reactionary; yet, he was the best ruler produced by the **Ghajar Dynasty**. He traveled a lot and had, inadvertently, opened the doors to Europe and its advanced technology for the **Persians**. In 1896, **Mirza Reza Kermani** assassinated **Nasir-u-Din Shah**, just before the fiftieth anniversary of his kingdom. This was done by the order of **Seyyed Jamal-u-Din**

Assad Abadi. (The title of "**Seyyed**" that was added to the front of **Persian** names showed a line of ancestry going back to **The Prophet Muhammad**, but most of these claims were not verified). [9]

Ghajar Dynasty is somewhat the gateway for Persia into the modern era. But the highlight of this era is actually based on the existence of a seer like **Amir Kabir**. He and a few of his nominated ministers, who did share his vision, established many schools. The most famous was Dar-ul-Funun (the house of sciences), which was inaugurated by **Nasir-u-Din Shah** despite the death of its founder **Amir Kabir**. Although some clergymen inside the court pretended to walk on the same path with **Amir**, most of the men in the government feared **Amir kabir's** innovations and detested his honest and simple reforms. Unfortunately the ordinary people, who lacked a basic education, were mostly ignorant about his ideals and did not support him.

Amir Kabir was not the only influence from within the government for renovations, but he was truly an honest advocate who realized the absolute importance of **Persian** heritage and independence as a fundamental basis for growth. Conversely, there were others like **Malkum Khan** who showed emphatically positive attitude to the **West**, but lacked the nationalism and morality. Hamid Algar and Fereidoon Adamiat—oriental historians—clearly portray the glibness that the **Mujtahids** (**Clerics** or **Ulama**) of the time commonly used on the **Shah**. It is doubtful that **Mirza Malkum Khan**—a religious figure, an interpreter and an advisor to **Shah**—had any member of religious classes in mind when he suggested that: " by following the principles of **European** governments, known to our **Ulama**, we might find true progress in our civilization." These half-complete doctrines and lack of moral seriousness from many religious and non-religious government members who were greedy and enamored of money was just an act of charlatanry.[10]

1. *Jame-e-Shenasi Nokhbeh Koshi*, p. 104
2   *History Of Persia*, Volume 2, London, pp. 339, 340
3. *Jame-e-Shenasi Nokhbeh Koshi*, by Ali Reza-Gholi, 18th edition, 2001, Tehran, pp.110-113
4. *History of Persia*, Vol. 2, pp. 341-344
5. *Timetables of History*, by Bernard Grun, 3rd edition, publisher Simon & Shuster N.Y, 1975

6. *Jame-e- Shenasi Nokhbeh Koshi*, pp. 120-127
7. *Amir Kabir va Iran*, by Feridun Adamiat, 7th edition, Kharazmi, 1983, Tehran, pp. 332-344
8. *Chekideh Tarikh Iran*, pp.154-156
9. *History of Persia*, Volume 2, p. 370-374
10. *Mirza Malkum Khan*, by Hamid Algar, 1973, U.C. Berkeley Press, pp. 18, 29, 260

Muzaffar-u-Din

In 1896, **Muzaffar-u-Din**, the eldest son of **Nasir-u-Din Shah**, took the throne with deliberate assistance of **Russian** and **British** ambassadors in Tehran. The grand **Vazir** or Prime Minister of the time, **Mirza Ali Asghar Khan** (**Atabak Azam**), also helped this transition. The earliest thing the young **Muzaffar-u-Din Shah** did, after his coronation, was a voyage to Europe, which was said to be for medical treatments. Like The Imperial Bank (Shahanshahi) of the **British**, The **Russian** government created a counterpart inside Persia. The " Banque d'Escompte de Perse" was established which did not function like a regular bank. These two banks, the **British** and the **Russian**, were not necessarily for profit. Surprisingly, they both acted mostly as a political instrument to enhance the financial grip of Russia and England on Persia at any cost. This was achieved by lending large sums on real estate and other methods creating larger deficits for Persia. Very soon, all of the customs rights, except for the Persian Gulf area, were assigned to the **Russians** in return for some large loans of 32,500,000 roubles (almost 3, 500,000 English pounds). Persia was in debt more than its annual revenue, which was only about 1,500,000 pounds at that period.[1]

As a result of all the financial dismay in Persia, some enlightened political leaders and patriotic **Mujtahids** (**Clerics**) started a rebellion protesting against the absolute power of **Shah** over the lives and fortunes of the people. This was the beginning of the "Constitutional Movement", which allowed the **Clerics** to directly interfere with the politics and temporal affairs. Many educated and active **Persians** living or studying outside Persia found the opportunity to unite their voice against the absolute monarch and his family. This became a foundation for the coming constitutional Movement. Even some papers and articles were published outside Persia. *Ghanun*, the Farsi newspaper, which was being printed in London under the direction of **Mirza Malkum Khan** and **Seyyed Jamal-u-Din Assad Abadi**, was covertly distributed over all corners of Persia, causing scary thrills in the court of **Ghajar**.

These public rebellions inside Persia grew. After a series of bloody conflicts between the people and the government army in 15th of August 1906, the triumphant people of Persia marched on the streets asserting their rights to vote for their own parliament members as well as founding of a new Ministry of Justice. Thus, a lot of power was taken away from the **Shah** and invested into public and civic entities. (This movement was not unlike that of the Magna Charta of England during **King John** in 1215 A.D.). A few months later, **Muzaffar-u-Din Shah** who had reluctantly signed the new declaration passed away in 1906 of an old sickness, and his crown prince, **Muhammad Ali Ghajar** took the throne. He was much opposed to losing civil and political domination as a king. He probably found these demands a direct threat to him. This succession of power in the kingdom, once again, was arranged for by the intervention of the same foreign ambassadors inside the country. The numerous written documents about the cooperation between these two foreign countries, France and Russia, and their embassies inside Persia reveal the depth of their control over the internal affairs of the country. The constitutional revolution of Persia may be regarded as the highest positive movement inside the country in this period. The cooperation and perseverance of people, inside and outside the country, brought a new sense of unity that opened the way for further changes.[2]

Muhammad Ali Shah

The country was gradually shifting to a new legal era that promised more social freedom. The elected ministers and even the **Grand Vazirs** (Prime Ministers) did not have to fear an execution after they fell. Now a milder spirit prevailed among all layers of official positions. (The administration of Persia was conducted on lines similar to those of **Darius** of the **Achaemendis Dynasty).** Persia was again divided into provinces under governors appointed by the **Crown.** Unfortunately, **Ghajar Dynasty** cannot be credited for any public work, neither for maintaining or training a well-organized army. This recent Constitutional Movement faced little resistance from a weakened military; this ironically benefited the nation.

Now a council of the nobles in the Senate and Parliament would control the activities of the **Shah** (just like the **Parthians** of the 3rd Century B.C.). All classes in the country opposed the selfish and corrupt rulings of less patriotic statesmen. Initial demonstrations (*Basts*) came in 1905 against the unpopular **Ayn-u-Doleh,** the **Grand Vazir (Prime Minister).** People realized he had approved loans to cover the expensive journeys of **Muzaffar-u-Din Shah** as well as allowed a corrupt and oppressive government.[4]

When **Muhammad Ali Shah** took control in 1907, he showed clearly that he did not like the new constitution and its founders. He refused to invite the newly elected parliament representatives to his coronation ceremony. At this time, he had entered secret negotiations with the **Russian** and **English Ambassadors** for more loans. When later on parliament rejected it, **Muhammad Ali Shah** became furious. He called in **Mirza Ali Asghar (Atabak Azam),** who was once his **Grand Vazir,** to take up his old role again and withstand the pressure from the social reformists. **Atabak Azam** had been traveling outside the country during this time, to avoid prosecutions. But this new delegation did not last since he was gunned down upon his exit from one of the parliaments meetings; the assassin shot himself, too. The political pressures had dejected the people so much that they mourned for the assassin. However, this new era had come to the people without proper edification about the foundation of democracy and its true meaning because the majority was illiterate. People in towns did not form a solid opinion because of the lack of a regular public assembly. They were unaware of the extent and the content of all their demands from their government. Media was controlled and the illiterate majority could not read the articles, anyway. Most of the peasants in rural areas were not involved or aware of the basic doctrines or struggles between different political and social factions inside the capital. On the other hand, the factions inside bigger cities were not regularly meeting or exchanging ideas amicably either.

Sir Percy Sykes reflects on the status quo like this: "**Persians** have not learned to work together. Internal discord, personal advantage, pecuniary or other, and personal animosities influenced the Assembly. Many of the leaders were unpractical extremists or mere visionaries, filled with anarchical ideas, which they had not digested, and yet ready to preach to their listeners on any subject. **Persians** are easily swayed by eloquence, and thus the views of the extremists gained the upper hand in the Assembly and ruined its chances of success."[5]

Because **Persians** were acclimated to a total lack of participation in their government, (worsened by too much reliance on foreign advisors) they could not take advantage of their new opportunity to be a partner in government. But when it came to matters of national security and solidarity even Russia and England were considered outsiders. For example, because the hunger for the strategic control of Persia and its economical rewards were too much to be forsaken, both Russia and England became involved. After the defeat of Russia by Japan, a new agreement was hastily reached between England and Russia in 1907 regarding Persia. By this agreement Persia and all of its resources were to be equally shared between the two nations without intimidating its government. Russia would take the North, and England would take the South. A narrow strip between the two would stay neutral. But, even that narrow neutral zone was greedily desired by England because it was next to their interests in the South. All **Persians** naturally detested this demeaning agreement and called it absurd.[6]

But such national agreement in Persia was rare. The distance between divine right of kings (absolutism) and democracy was too wide to be bridged so suddenly. As a result of the upheaval of conflicting ideologies, an unfruitful assassination attempt against **Muhammad Ali Shah Ghajar** in February 1908 resulted in direct confrontations between two major groups: **Persian Royalist Army** and the Nationalists of The Constitutional Movement (**Mashruteh Nationalists**). On June 23, 1908, the **Russian Cossack Brigade** and **Persian Royalist** troops surrounded Parliament, where the **Nationalists** were in session voicing their unity against any intrusion, Russia, England, or whoever. Artillery fire was opened on the Parliament and casualties were inflicted on the **Nationalists**. Some

Mashruteh Nationalists (Constitutional Nationalists) were captured by the **Shah's** soldiers and hung. **Sattar Khan** and **Bagher Khan** from Tabriz (in Azerbaijan) drove back the **Royalists** (pro-Shah activists) who stood against the new Constitutional Movement. **Ayn-u-Doleh** assumed command of the **Shah's Royalist** forces and surrounded Tabriz. Each side showed more cruelty to overcome the other.

These so-called inevitable killings and uprises are being studied in more detail by Dr. M. Ajoodani. Referring to the bloodshed in this period, Dr. Ajoodani finds lack of freedom as well as absence of social equality as a primal source for brutality on both sides. Even the **Socialist Democrat** groups inside Persia lacked basic understanding of freedom within their doctrines of Communism. Their perpetual reliance on foreign socialist authorities in Russia and Europe to define Persian Socialists' role inside Persia proves that they did not even possess patriotic understanding of their own Constitutional Movement. **Ehtesham-ul-Saltaneh** the head of the Parliament wrote in his memoirs that this brutal and senseless reaction of **Muhammad Ali Shah** (the bombardment of the parliament) actually backfired and strengthened the resistance of the **Constitutionalists** (Mashruteh Nationalists). Because of different interpretations regarding the civil society in Persia, after the fall of the tyrant **Shah**, the gap between the revolutionary allies widened: pro-Mashruteh **Ruhanioon** (**Muslim Clerics**) on one side and pro-Mashruteh **Reformists** on the other. **Taghi-Zadeh**—a member of the parliament and one of the leaders of Democrat Party as a spokesman of the **Reformists** started his scrutiny of the ex-allies, the fanatic **Muslim Cleric**. He was referring mostly to **Ayat-u-Lah Behbehani** who was later assassinated. The forceful censorship and brutal confrontation from within the society was criticized by **Ayat-u-Lah Mazandarani** in an article in *Habl-ul-Matin* Newspaper Number 15 in 1911. He openly criticized the **Reformists** because they could not witness the **Clerics** take over the political power in Persia after the death of the tyrant **Shah**. Ajoodani insists that civil society of Persia had not evolved enough to grasp the meaning of Democracy or 'personal freedom'. Therefore, what was focused on during this period of the Persian history was 'Independence' of the country from the super powers rather than 'social Freedom' which is an internal civic issue. Thus, blindly copying other nations was not the solution for internal problems in Persia.[7]

The chaos was growing mostly because of mixed messages from **Reformists** and **Conservatives** about their understanding of Democracy. Around the same period a successful revolution in Turkey naturally acted as a powerful stimulant to the **Constitutionalists**. Meanwhile, the resistance in Tabriz allowed other parts of Persia to gather their forces and revolt also. Famous leaders such as **Tonekaboni (Sipahdar)** from the Mazandaran region in the north and **Haji Ali Gholi Khan (Sardar-i-Asad)** of **Bakhtiari** tribes around Isfahan in the south joined the revolutionary lines against the government. (Of course, for these two leaders this was a politically correct decision because the people in these regions were truly antagonistic towards any signs of wavering from their **Khans**— tribal heads—or wealthy landowners).

In April 1909, to show that it took no sides, Russia withdrew its troops from Azerbaijan. Because **Muhammad Ali Shah** had counted on the **Russian Cossacks**, he now had no hope for suppressing the revolting people of Tabriz. Finally, in July 1909, after a march of armed desperados (**Mujahidin**) reinforced by the courageous gunmen of all the tribes from north and south, and after some bloodshed, **Muhammad Ali Shah** was forced to take refuge in the Russian Legation and was formally deposed by the victors. To the credit of the **Nationalists,** there was little persecution of the **Royalists**; the majority of whom hastily disowned the fallen **Shah**. Thus, **Ahmad Mirza**, his twelve-year-old crown prince, was nominated to take the throne.[8]

Ahmad Shah

Ahmad Mirza became **Ahmad Shah**. Because this new king was under aged, **Azud-ul-Mulk**, a respected old head of **Ghajar tribe**, was appointed as Regent to the throne. **Sardar-i-Asad** was the Minister of Interior and **Sipahdar** the Minister of War. The ex-**Shah** (his father) finally agreed to receive a pension of 100,000 tomans (about $35,000.00) and leave for Odessa (a city on the Black Sea). His departure cleared the air. Russia began to withdraw its troops from Ghazvin and all of Azerbaijan. The new assembly met in November, when **Sipahdar** read a speech, at the side of **Ahmad Shah**'s Throne, full of good intentions.

Now, the first difficulty to be faced by the victorious **Nationalists** was the disbanding of the **Mujahidin**. These were the courageous and worthy soldiers who, after the cessation of hostilities, assumed a demanding position and started threatening the new government for pay. On the other hand, the "**Revolutionists**" (active nationalists) showed a bitter face to the "**Moderates**" in the judiciary meetings that followed some internal conflicts. These confrontations resulted in hanging of **Sheikh Fazl-u-Lah Nuri** who was against the Constitutional Movement. **Sipahdar** (Minister of War) found it necessary to resign, as also did the president of the Assembly, who was a "**Moderate**."[9]

Ayn-u-Doleh, a commander loyal to the throne, had again been asked to step into service. He wisely paid monetary dues to get away from more severe outcomes. With the confusion about the meaning of the free press, unfortunately, some of the newspapers had indulged in name-callings and harassments of the men of power. **Sipahdar** used this as an excuse to confiscate and shut down many of these papers in order to stop the insanity. The new regulations for disarming the public brought more complications between the government troops and the revolutionary militia of **Bagher Khan** and **Sattar Khan**. Many lost their lives. Several uprises such as the ones in Yazd, Isfahan, as well as the one in Kashan under the leadership of **Nayeb Hosain Kashi**, had resulted in total chaos within the country. These rebels were mostly without any positive outcome towards return of solidarity and peace to Persia. Public was generally unaware of the meaning of democracy or their human rights. Ordinary people were easily misled or confused by differing arguments and could not easily distinguish between right and wrong.[10] Their habitual reliance on foreigners to guide them through these harsh times did not help the situation.

In 1911, ex-**Shah**, **Muhammad Ali**, attempted a return. It was utterly detested and resisted by the people. The **Russians** supported the ex-**Shah** more than the **English**, who had a better grip on Persia during these last years. The ex-**Shah** initially gained some advancement in Gorgan (in north) but was utterly defeated. He finally fled back to Europe. In the same year, it was to the credit of the Democrat Cabinet that an arrangement was made with America to supply disinterested financial advisors to improve the financial status of Persia. For example, **Morgan Shuster** led some advisors, but could not understand the delicacy of the situation inside Persia and made more enemies than he could handle. His hasty interference with Customs in the Persian ports as well as denial of any authority from **Belgian** officials (who had been there for centuries) caused him more trouble.

However, **Shuster** had noticed the rise in radical movements of people inside Persia against the injustice. In his writings of 1912, *The Strangling Of Persia* he had showed admiration for the **Persian women** who, as he noticed, were specifically rising to a social level in their organized protests that had not been seen before. In August of 1907, some widowed and separated women demanded their arreared social wages and alimonies from the government in a demonstration in the Toop-Khaneh Square in Tehran. Newspapers such as *Habl-ul-Matin* wrote extensively about this phenomenon.[11] This book is re- published in 1996.

The **Russian** Government was determined to oust the **American Shuster**. In November 5, 1911, Russia presented a 24-hour ultimatum demanding an apology for some insults to its **Consul-General**. After **Persian officials** arranged for this, another ultimatum regarding the dismissal of **Shuster** was delivered to Persia. On top of these, Russia had demanded that future loans be issued only with direct supervision and permission of the two countries of **Russia** and **England**. This action of Russia was an effort to limit America's influence. After a Persian parliamentary debate over this, the **Nationalist** assembly refused the second ultimatum with the cry of "Death or Independence." People in Tabriz and Rasht attacked the **Russian troops** in the streets. Consequently, more **Russian Cossacks** began to march on Tehran, and **Persians** realized the bitter necessity of submission.

Finally **Sardar-i-Asad** and **Seyyed Hasan Moddares** along with three other political leaders were chosen to deliver the acceptance of these conditions to the **Russians**. But, people had realized that Russia was just trying to tighten its grip over Persia. Consequently, **Russian Cossacks** proceeded with the arrest and execution of many protesting **Muslims**. Among them was **Haji Mirza Ali** (Saghat-ul-Islam) who was hung during the holy month of Ashura in December of 1911 in province of Gilan.[12]

In March of 1912, Russia boorishly and insensitively bombarded the Shrine of **Imam Reza** at Meshed. Also, some of the treasury of the tomb was taken by the **Russians**. This attempted intimidation of **Muslims** backfired. The whole **Muslim** world denounced this irreverent act of **Russian** government. However, this incident did not cause much deliberation in **England** because the tragic catastrophe of the "Titanic" had absorbed the attention of the **British** public.

Ahmad Shah, now about twenty years old, officially celebrated his coronation in July of 1914. This coincided with the outbreak of World War I. Persia had announced its neutrality. Germany invaded Russia. **Russians** used this excuse to raid northern Persia. Parliament Assembly in Tehran asked **Ayn-u-Doleh** to take over again as the Prime Minister. In the summer of the same year, **English** troops surrounded Bushir in the South. Because they wanted a share of Persia, the **Germans** sent their council to assist Persia in its resistance against the interests of the **British**. The integrity and solidarity of Persia was being violated. The **Turks** from the West took advantage by invading Hamadan and looting the Russian Bank. **England** and **Germany** were facing each other in the Persian Gulf and raced for supremacy. It was the **Russian Revolution** of 1917at this period that gave Persia a chance to breathe and focus on dealing with its social problems. The new Soviet Government led by the **Bolsheviks** (Communists) under **Lenin,** showed no interest in pursuing its affairs in the area, and soon withdrew all of its troops from Persia and cancelled all earlier agreements and treaties.[13]

Meanwhile, post-war Europe continued its achievements in science and civil reforms. In 1918, women over 30 in Britain legally received the right to vote. Women in Persia were not only prohibited from voting, they were restricted to their household duties. Unfortunately, fanatic **Muslim Clergies** permitted almost no social roles for women. This religious containment was against the earlier active role of women in the society in Persia. Around this period, the fast pace of industrial and social renovations of the West gradually delivered its impact on the East. In Persia, the students who had finished studying abroad brought back with them the news of modernized societies. Once again, Persia was beginning to compare its social status with that of the outside world.

Some Persian men also formed rebellious political organizations, such as "Jangal Movement" (in the northern forests in Persia) that gathered followers around 1921 but eventually lost concession among major members.

Unfortunately at the beginning of the 20th Century, Persia had an inadequate leadership when it needed it most. **Ghajar kings** were faced in all their realms with the perennial problem of how to maintain an ample central authority. The **kings'** love of luxury at the price of diminishing financial resources of the nation made Persia troubled water with fishing opportunities at the mercy of **European** colonists.

1. *History of Persia*, P. Sykes, Volume 2, pp. 374-376
2. *Chekideh Tarikh Iran*, Hasan Naraghi, pp. 157-159
3. *History of Persia*, pp.381-384
4. p. 394-401
5. p. 408
6. *Chekideh Tarikh Iran*, p. 161
7. *Mashruteh-e-Irani*, Dr. Mashalah Ajoodani, 3rd edition, Akhtaran, 2004, Tehran, pp. 23, 125, and 411-442
8. *History Of Persia*, pp. 415-420
9. pp. 421,422
10. *Chekideh Tarikh Iran*, p. 163
11. *The Iranian Constitutional Revolution*, by Janet Afary, 1996, Columbia U., pp. 233-266
12. *Chekideh Tarikh Iran*, p.164
13. *History of Persia*, pp.423-430

CHAPTER TWENTY

Pahlavi Dynasty
(1925 – 1978 A.D.)

The Constitutional Movement of 1906 A.D. in Persia produced an opportunity for the people to understand the choices they could have for a free Persia (free from both foreign and domestic injustice). It was around this period that a universal desire for change was felt. A new hero was deeply needed.

Back in March of 1877, **Reza** was born in Alasht in province of Savad Kuh in Mazandaran. **Reza** was the only child born into the family of **Abbas Ali Savad Kuhi** and his second wife **Nush Afarin**. Like his own father, **Abbas Ali** was at the employment of the army. When **Reza** was about nine month old, **Abbas Ali** passed away. Therefore, the brother of **Nush Afarin**, **Hakim Ali Yavar**, accepted the responsibility to care for this family. He helped to raise **Reza**, but **Hakim Ali**'s life was short, too. He passed away when **Reza** was seven years old. Then the second uncle **Abolghasem Beig** who had reached the status of a colonel in the army of **Nasir-u-Din Shah** took **Reza** into his guardianship.

Reza treasured his ancestors' way of life; and at the age of fifteen he also joined the **Persian Cossacks Army**. He was tall and strong, yet his young age kept him away from the leadership positions that he wanted. However, after five years of perseverance and dedication in performing his duties, he proved himself to be worthy of nomination for the cavalry division. Then at the age of twenty, he was appointed to the supervisory status in the cavalry under the name of **Reza Khan Savad Kuhi**. His thirty-four years of proud service in the military and close contact with people in many provinces all over Persia enabled him to gather the information and the experience to truly feel the urge for a change in the way of governing the country.

In 1914, **Reza Khan** was delegated the authority to gather and lead an army in Hamadan. Three years later, he was made colonel in the Army in the capital city of Tehran (during the reign of **Ahmad Shah Ghajar**). At this time, he was called **Colonel Reza Khan** at the age of forty when he married **Nim Taj**, a girl from Irvan-lu tribes of Azerbaijan. Their first child was a girl named **Shams** who was born in 1918. **Colonel Reza Khan** was focused and straightforward. He showed his natural leadership, which brought him the position of the Commander of Tehran Battalion in 1919. **Nim Taj** (his wife) had twins in 1920—a girl named **Ashraf** and a boy named **Mohammad Reza**. Around this period, **Colonel Reza Khan** efficiently resisted the rebels of Mazandaran and Gilan in 1921 and scattered the army of **Mirza Kuchak Khan Jangali** in Rasht. Then, his new title became **Reza Khan Mir Panj (General Reza Khan)**.[1]

However, the **Persian Cossacks** under **Reza Khan Mir Panj** had to retreat from the heavy artillery of the **Bolsheviks** in Mazandaran (in the north) and find refuge near the **English** army near Ghazvin (in the north center).

In February 21 1921, a segment of the **Cossacks** under the command of **Reza Khan Mir Panj**, marched into Tehran. This army was to put an end to the recent uprises and revolts in all corners of the country, while reinforcing the central command for **Ahmad Shah** of **Ghajar**. All major government offices and buildings were immediately taken under control and a new declaration was announced expressing the coup and a martial law engineered by **Reza Khan**. A few arrests were made according to a black list of the VIPs and government officials. The nomination of **Reza Khan Mir Panj** as the **Sardar Sepah** (the Chief Commander) and **Seyyed Zia-u-Din Tabatabaie**, the publisher of *Raed Newspaper* as the Prime Minister caused many protests inside the government.

One of these protests came from **Dr. Mohammad Mosadegh** who was the governor of Fars. He telegraphed his resignation to **Ahmad Shah** in protest of the recent arrangements. Because **Ahmad Shah's** position was reinforced with the coup **Russia** and **England** retrieved their armies from the occupied **Persian** lands, as promised earlier. Subsequently, the previous agreements of 1907 between these two nations against Persia were nullified. The people of Persia celebrated. At this time, the **United States** had sent **Dr. Millspaugh** to aid Persia to manage its financial crisis.[2] But Persia's problems were not only financial.

Sardar Sepah (Reza Khan) took over the position of the Vazir Jang (Minister of War)—the incumbent had also resigned. This enhanced **Reza's** control even further. At this time, **Seyyed Zia-u-Din**, the newly elected Prime Minister, infamous for running a so-to-speak "black cabinet' (or corrupt **Royalists**), was denounced and fired. **Ghavam-u-Saltaneh** was the Prime Minister and the only powerful figure that was against the growing powers of **Reza Khan**. In the fall of 1924, after some premeditated plans, **Reza Khan** arranged for the arrest and exile of **Ghavam-u-Saltaneh** to Europe. Now **Ahmad Shah**, who only cared to stay outside Persia, selected **Reza Khan** as the new Prime Minister. **Ahmad Shah** did not like to have to worry about internal affairs unless it affected his throne.[3] **Ahmad Shah** had left Persia for Europe in 1923 and stayed there till his death in 1930. Therefore, **Reza Khan** (Prime Minister) was the highest authority in Persia.

In 1924 there had been a recent revolution inside Turkey (neighboring Persia from the west). Therefore, the political reforms of this period in Turkey had made many **Persians** very much inclined towards a regime with democratic control. Also, the media inside Persia were showing a great interest in a democratic reformation against the tyrannical rule of monarchies. Hence, the papers unofficially nominated **Reza Khan** as the first President for the country. On the other hand, at this time the **Turkish** parliament issued more radical orders for its people to abolish not only the monarchy in the state, but also the influence of religious clerics over the political issues. This new development aroused a lot of antagonistic reactions from the intimidated **Muslim clergy** in Persia. These religious scholars (**Mullahs**) also influenced the wealthy merchants in all bazaars in the country—persuading them to stay with the monarchy regime. This was not a difficult task, since most merchants were losing a great deal of income because of the ongoing strikes and dissentions over the internal power. Accordingly, **Reza Khan** who originally desired a democratic and presidential government corrected his position immediately by joining the winning **Mullahs**. In 1925 he even denounced **democratic government** (run under one elected president) and called it against the **Shiite** doctrines.[4] Therefore, **Reza Khan** wisely took side with the majority who under the **Clerics** (**Mullahs**) preferred a monarchy rather than a presidential government.

Reza Shah Pahlavi

This political upheaval continued in the parliament until **Reza Khan** requested and received complete power in February 1925 to run the nation on a transitional basis. Finally, in December of 1925, **Reza Khan** was officially elected as the new King (**Reza Shah Pahlavi**) by the majority in the parliament. **Reza Shah** shared the same visions with **Mustafa Kamal (Ata Turk)** the president of Turkey. They both believed in renovations inside their countries while maintaining their heritage and independence. But Persia, unlike Turkey, did not abolish **Clerics'** influence in politics.

Persia of 1925 did not possess even a mile of paved road. The country suffered from a long period of oblivion and idleness. There were only five high schools and twenty-six elementary schools in the entire country. It was during the rule of the **Pahlavi Dynasty** that Persia managed to move forward in some ways. Changes came fast; new roads, transportation, schools of higher education and hospitals were built. After six decades by the year 1989 A.D., Persia had produced 30,000 graduates from its own universities; this figure grew to 300,000 in 2002.[5]

Many giant steps were taken in social and economical reforms during the reign of **Reza Shah**. Persia was ready to move into a new era of modernization. In 1935 **Persia** became known as **Iran** by the official proclamation of the United Nations. This was certainly not the only change for this ancient country.

The unification of **Iran** under **Pahlavi Dynasty** did not happen overnight. Instead, some resistant tribal chiefs rebelled. This had to be dealt with swiftly. **Sheikh Khaz-al** was one of the most influential rebels. He was an extremely powerful and independent leader in the southern parts of Persia near the **Arabian** borders. After the nominations of **Reza Shah,** this southern tribal chief was still reluctant to accept the central command, because he had enjoyed many years of independent supremacy over this part of Iran— enjoying the attention and protection of the **British** as an extra advantage. For years **Sheikh Khaz-al** received the attention and assistance of many **English Ambassadors** or representatives. But his rebellion caused his name to be on the black list of those VIPs during the siege of Tehran in the Constitutional Movement. Therefore, **Sheikh Khaz-al** was arrested and sent to Tehran. However, he was not dealt with in any harsh manner. Shortly additional revolts followed in the region of Khuzestan (in the south). At this time, some of the newly appointed commanders sent to replace **Sheikh Khaz-al** dealt with the locals unfairly. **Reza Shah** found out about the harsh treatment of the people and prosecuted all of these cruel commanders including the State Governor. **Reza Shah** sent the clear message that government officials were to serve the people not to suppress them.

Reza Shah Pahlavi ruled for sixteen years, during which he caused a lot of social reforms which enabled Iran to penetrate the international market. First, in 1929, he promoted trades by creating paved roads and railroad tracks. This new system of roads and railroads connected major cities inside Iran and grew very popular. Second, a **German** company was authorized to establish the first air travel lines inside Iran. Third, **Reza Shah** ordered the establishment of an official record of all births, marriages, and divorces within the country. Fourth, in 1931, the minting of golden coins and printing paper money was re-established with the supervision of the **Iranians** rather than foreign advisors. **Reza Shah** reformed the old and inadequate classes for the young and established numerous schools where kids (female and male) had to go to for their compulsory basic education. Women were told to come out of their homes and freely take more serious roles in developing their country. The compulsory Hejab (head cover) for women was abolished. Many students were sent overseas for higher education, while government gladly paid for their expense in return for their future service. In January 1928, Port Anzali in the province of Gilan (in north) that was seized by the **Russians** was returned to Iran to show good faith. It was named Port **Pahlavi** to commemorate this king.[6]

Iran needed such a strict and wise ruler to stop the numerous internal wars and to bring together a nation that was on the verge of complete disintegration. **Reza Shah** knew this. Naturally, he held onto the absolute power to uproot all his enemies. He knew a soft appearance would jeopardize all his reforms. He did not hesitate to confiscate all the barren lands especially in the northern areas where water was abundant. The punishment for the uncaring wealthy landowners was the government confiscation. All of these neglected lands were turned into crop-yielding fields (mostly under the ownership of the government); and occasionally, they were added to his personal possessions. This strict control—sometimes not completely legal—cured the country of many existing problems; yet, it also permitted future political and social restrictions. This type of confiscation even for social reforms resulted in chaotic legalities.

Additionally, **Reza Shah** established the first truly Iranian National Bank (Bank-e-Melli)—unlike the **British** and **Russian** Imperial Banks. Also, he formed the national customs tariffs. Among the industrial programs, he made textile, cement, and sugar industries flourish inside the country. He was in process of establishing the first steel manufacturing plant with the aid of **Germans**, but the break of World War II in 1939 brought a delay. **Germans** under command of **Hitler** were busy invading Holland in 1939. No significant modernization happened anywhere in the world and six million lives were lost in a period of six years. **Reza Shah** did not stay idle; he opened many schools in all levels, including universities in major cities—a forgotten trend for centuries. Also, he revived a government-sponsored program that would provide scholarship to those who wanted to continue their education either at home or abroad.[7] This trend was also forgotten after the death of wise prime minister **Amir Kabir**.

Consequently, **Iranian** students brought in the western technology. For the first time after centuries, more **Iranians** were put in charge of their own social institutions. These changes occurred along with a lot of freedom in many aspects of life (legislative, judiciary, and executive offices were creating newer freedoms in religion, education, work environment, children's welfare, and women's rights). Unfortunately, the older generation and a non-literate majority were very hard to convince or educate about the importance of these reforms. Some social freedom was introduced (for example change of traditional clothing of men and women for a more active role in society, inviting women into the work force, putting more police on the streets, and developing public transportation for use by both sexes). But the means to protect and enhance these social reforms were harder to create because majority of people could not understand and therefore accept the outward appearance of change. Once again, the slow edification of the people gave way to the return of misuse and vice in the government. Most of the public institutions were collapsing because of excessive costs in addition to embezzlements by the authorities. **Iranians** needed to learn to respect one another. They were to learn to try to live amicably and abide the newer civic laws even though these laws seemed shocking to the older generation.

Still **Reza Shah** preferred **Germans** to assist Iran with its fast modernization. **Iranians** had not forgotten the mischievous and unilateral agreements between the **Russians** and the **English** for dividing Iran between them. Around this time in December 07, 1941 **Japanese** planes hit hard at the Pacific Fleet of the United States in Pearl Harbor in **Hawaiian** island of Oahu. The **Germans** waged war on Europe.

Because of the break of the World War II, the **English** and the **Russians** feared the closer relations between **Iranians** and **Germans**. Thus, a sudden invasion against the **Iranian** borders from north and south was put to work. The **Iranian** army that just had gained some skill and firepower could not resist both of these powerful invaders and was destroyed in the summer of 1942. The dissention inside the country finally showed its face. Ordinary people were unaware of the political turmoil inside their land; the foreign powers still kept **Iranian** government under pressure. **Reza Shah** was forced to resign and was exiled to Johannesburg in Africa where he stayed heart broken until he passed away in 1951.[8]

The newness of the changes and the departure of **Reza Shah** created a ripe atmosphere for old abuses. Sir Percy Sykes who was personally in Iran at this time writes: "Iranian land owners and ex-government employees (the wealthier segment of society) were trying to deceive or bribe their co- workers to gain all types of extra credits and fortune for their own families. Today the army officers and their children misuse these chances; they constantly add to their own wealth, while they actually look down on the same people they rule in these provinces. They steal what belongs to the people and spend it in Tehran or Europe."

In spite of the above, as a historian with decades of experience in this part of the world, Sir Percy Sykes had maintained high hopes for **Iranians** although he feared that Iran, in the absence of **British** troops, might be caught in the hands of **Bolshevists** or taken over by some of the tribal forces inside it; but none of his worries actually took form.[9]

1.   *Reza Shah Pahlavi,* by Nader Paymai, 2002, Washington, pp. 3-9
2.   *History Of Persia,* Sir Percy Sykes, Vol.2
3.   *Chekideh Tarikh Iran,* by Hasan Naraghi, p. 167
4.   *History of Persia,* Vol.2
5.   *Jame-e-Shenasi Khodemani,* by Hasan Naraghi, Akhtaran Printing, 2003, Tehran, pp 114
6.   *History Of Persia*
7.   *Kholaseh Tarikh Gozashteh Iran,* by Dr. Zia-u-Din Hayat, Pezhvak, 2002, San Jose, p. 80
8.   *Chekideh Tarikh Iran,* p. 169
9.   *History Of Persia,* Volume 2, p. 849, pp. 538-540

Muhammad Reza Pahlavi

In the summer of 1941 **Muhammad Reza**, the oldest son and one of eleven children in this family, took the throne. **Forughi**, the Prime Minister, officially announced the resignation of **Reza Shah**. It was only at this time that some of the parliament members gathered courage to talk about their concerns about the **ex king**. Some even called him a thief. Numerous hostile reactions resulted from the men in the government—justified or not—and thus added to the chaos. This negative and untimely criticism caused the country a great deal of dismay, whereas an unbiased and democratic parliament might have been able to continue these reforms for the benefit of all **Iranians**.

Reza Khan had left his crown prince, **Muhammad Reza**, numerous deeds to real estate property all over Iran. (Some were neglected barren lands, ironically situated in the northern provinces where there was plenty of water. These were purchased or taken from the landowners and turned into crop-yielding cultivated lands).[1] If this had not been done there was no guarantee of any improvements—these lands could still be neglected property today.

Thus, the young king inherited a land of economical and political turmoil. His father was exiled, and he missed his father's support and advice. His knowledge of his people and their true necessities was trivial in comparison to his father's. Iran had just gained a middle class, unprecedented before the Constitutional Movement of 1920s. Out of 148 parliament members of the early periods only 15 belonged to this class. The rest were from the elite and wealthy families of army generals, landowners, and government figures. Less than five percent of the population was aware of the political issues of the time.[2] Illiteracy was the primary cause of people's indifference—not their apathy.

Because the new King was inexperienced **Reza Shah** had personally appointed the Prime Minister of this time, **Muhammad Ali Foroughi** to guide the young king. In the summer of 1941, allied forces occupied Iran during World War II. It was **Foroughi** who invited the heads of the superpowers into Iran for a peace conference. **Franklin Roosevelt**, **Churchill** and **Stalin** joined this historic meeting and decided the course of the war. For this matter, Iran was called the 'Bridge to Victory'. It was agreed that all forces would be withdrawn from Iran within six months after the war. By 1946 Russia had not fulfilled this promise. It maintained its forces inside the country and gained a lot of control through the free press, which provoked rebellions against the regime of **Shah** in Azerbaijan and Kurdistan under direct support of the Proletarian Party (Hezb-e-Tudeh). But, finally all these **Russian** maneuvers were countered by the Prime Minister of that time, **Ghavam-u-Saltaneh**, under direct supervision of the United States. **Russians** had to withdraw. The followers of Hezb-e-Tudeh (Proletarian Party) lost their status among the community. At this time, Iran got the chance to breath and stand on its feet to take steps towards its cultural and economical independence.[3]

Therefore, the new **Shah** had a long agenda to attend to. The personal lifestyle of this new **Shah** was very much affected by his **European** education. Like most kings before him, **Muhammad Reza Shah** was surrounded by corrupt politicians who were under the spell of foreign embassies in the country. He himself lacked the experience and the advisors that he could go to were mostly corrupt. This made his task in leadership much harder. His lack of experience and self-confidence, plus the corruption of politicians around him gradually caused him to lose the trust of many hardworking and honest government officers. Even his honest army commander, General **Razmara**, was forced to resign in 1944. **Ali Razmara** had provided the army with great service and much-needed modifications. Unfortunately, the pressure of false propaganda and the influence of the worried and corrupt officers of the time kept this great figure confined at his home for over fifteen months. He was reinstated after major accusations (a coup being one of them) were proven unjustified. **Razmara** had shown brilliance in running the army; because of his dedication and rightful discipline he resembled the late **Reza Shah**. Later on, **Razmara** was even promoted to the role of the Prime Minister in the summer of 1950, yet assassinated in the spring of the following year when he was 49 years old.[4] Iran lost a great humanitarian leader, and the **Shah** lost a true friend and counselor without even knowing the worth of his loss.

But **Muhammad Reza Shah** had realized the value of the oil and strategic ports in the Persian Gulf. Up to the winter of 1950, oil had been available to **English**, **Russian**, and **French** purchasers on their terms. The Oil Movement of Iran officially announced the Nationalization of Oil Industry, and National Party of Iran (Jebhe Melli) under the supervision of **Mosadegh** passed this law through the parliament. **Dr. Mosadegh** was instantly nominated as the Prime Minister. He had requested that his nomination be announced after approval of this important law. This would minimize the resistance of corrupt parliament members.

But, the **British Empire** immediately caused international legal barriers for exportation of the oil from Iran. The lack of income from oil quickly caused the collapse of the national budget and dissatisfaction of people followed. Tudeh Party, under the Russian influence, took advantage of these internal conditions to gain some control again. Soon, negative propagandas started against the nationalization of oil. **Dr. Mosadegh** was losing face. Among the **Muslim scholars (Mullas)** only **Ayat-u-Lah Kashani** stood by him— mostly for his hatred towards the **English**. Many supporters of the nationalistic moves by **Mosadegh** in the previous year started to withdraw from their earlier position; they were also alarmed by the recent progress of the Tudeh Party. **Seyyed Zia Tabatabaie** was one of the **Mullas** who started negative propaganda against **Mosadegh**. In the winter of 1951 **Dr. Fatemi**, an important cabinet member of **Mosadegh** and the Minister of Foreign Affairs (he was also serving without expecting regular pay) was targeted for assassination, but was only injured. The pressure from the **British** and the **Americans** was building. Being afraid of loosing majority in a biased congress and parliament, **Mosadegh** ordered the closure of both. By 1952 even **Ayat-u-Lah Kashani** had stayed away from **Mosadegh**. Consequently, the U.S. Government being afraid of losing grounds to communism made arrangements with **Shah** to order the removal of **Dr. Mosadegh** from office. **Muhammad Reza Shah** did so and left the country at the advice of **American** embassy. Upon a fabricated coup d'etat, **CIA** and **British** embassy facilitated the return of **Shah** to the throne in 1953. **Mosadegh** was taken into a solitary prison for three years and then exiled.[5]

Dr. Fatemi was arrested and put through court martial while being bed ridden and hospitalized. He was executed in Tehran in 1954 on the basis of unjustified accusations in regards to a coup d'etat against **Shah**.

In the absence of **Mosadegh**, many **Mullahs** (or Muslim Cleric) regained their power to enforce the older traditional doctrines concerning women's right versus men's. For example, in *Tehran Mosavar* a weekly paper dated April of 1953, appeared the article that showed **Ayat-u-Lah Kashani** (a **Mullah**) vetoed the proposition to women's right to vote in the constitutional debates.

However, in Iran the lack of freedom of speech as well as by general illiteracy was causing major set backs in democratic reforms initiated by **Mosadegh**. The majority was kept in the dark; illegal arrests and false accusations took innocent lives. There was no tolerance for any opposing political view.

This was the social problem in Iran. While across the continent at this period in 1957, the United States was in a different civil turmoil caused to some extent by the ambivalence of President **Eisenhower.** The segregation of schools was still a big issue, and reluctant state authorities, such as in Little Rock in Arkansas, needed to be forced by law to open their school doors to the black children. Education Department in Little rock opposed integration and even closed schools for one full year.

At this time, **Pahlavi Dynasty** caused its own awakening of **Iranians.** Some of the needed reforms were unprecedented since the fall of the country's economical structure during the **Saffavid Dynasty** (of 15th Century A.D.). For example, one of these reforms was free and compulsory education for boys and girls. Nevertheless, several shortcomings caused the fall of most of the reforms structure. The three major factors for the constant failure of many social reforms inside Iran are these:

First, the internal political misery and chaos—worsened by lack of freedom of speech. This was a way to suppress opposing political views against the foreign powers, who interfered with the internal affairs in Iran. Sometimes, foreign delegates even appointed or abdicated the **Iranian kings** (especially during the **Ghajar Dynasty**).

Second, its cultural modernization reform (especially during the **Pahlavi Dynasty**) was wrongfully shaped to absorb mostly the facade of fashion and glamour of the West rather than its technology or civilization.

Third, the country's economy was shaped to grow towards consuming imported industrial goods rather than producing them. Iran became dependant on many new products without being able to manufacture them. The use and utility of many of these new products sometimes enforced an abrupt change in the lifestyle of **Iranians** contradictory to their traditions.[6] For example, one of these false advertisements concerned the introduction of western dress codes or fashion along with false propagandas targeting the young about the quality of life in the western world especially Hollywood.

Meanwhile, the young **Shah** had started off with modesty and willingness to listen and to learn. But people around him took advantage of him. Foreign countries confused and even countered his high ideals. In spite of all of these difficulties the GNP of Iran around 1971 had grown 400 percent during two decades and average income raised from $200 to $ 2000 per year. For example, cars, machines, shoes, household gadgets, and clothing factories were built. More Iranian goods were exported and agricultural equipment and better seeds were imported. **Reza Shah** had established one university. Now, his son (**Muhammad Reza Shah**) established more than 23 with about 8 million students all over Iran. This was a giant leap for the country.

But as mentioned before, there were other shortcomings. The reign of **Muhammad Reza Pahlavi** may be divided into three major periods:

The first period started from the summer of 1951 when the **Shah** had to leave Iran. But as a result of a coup d'etat (planned by **CIA** and **British** intelligence) he returned to power in the summer of 1953. During this period, the young **Shah** was surrounded by various old and experienced political figures with complicated agendas. Iran was practically raided by many foreign powers. People seemed to like the non-arrogant young king who was trying to undo some of his father's stern rules. At this time **Muhammad Reza Shah** was open to new ideas and had no thoughts in personal accumulation of wealth and power. This period ends with the Nationalization of Oil Industry under the magnificent leadership of **Dr. Muhammad Mosadegh** — the nationalistic Prime Minister at the time. This was a political achievement for Iran towards true ownership of its natural resources.

The second period starts immediately after the 1953 coup with the fall of the cabinet of **Dr. Mosadegh**. The accumulation of wealth by **Shah** and his family members along with other dignitaries gradually took a routine form. Because of the general illiteracy the average **Iranians** did not know what was going on. The political dignitaries took advantage of official information for personal gains. In an illegitimate referendum with the help from corrupt **Iranian** politicians along with the U.S.A., a new set of reforms were introduced and implemented under the name of 'White Revolution' in 1960s. As a result of this reform, some rapid yet shallow improvements were made in the lifestyle of the rural communities and in their educational and judicial system. These changes were a positive move, but did not last long enough. The base for such renovations or reforms was not made ready, yet. Rarely can social reforms be sustained in an environment that lacks the respect for human rights.

This period continues with more social problems as these social reforms were being made. For example, the younger educated generation in Iran was gradually questioning traditional worldviews of the **Islamic** fundamentalists. Thus, a new class of philosophical-political activists gained popularity among the younger generation who was growing weary of the old fanatic regulations. Still the need for inner enlightenment was present, but the new generation could not agree with all external physical details. Some **Islamic** scholars tried to connect the loose ends of the old fundamentalist views with the new thirst for religion. **Dr. Ali Shariati** and **Jalal Al Ahmad** attracted the attention of many college students who were lost between the **Socialists** and the **Islamic Extremists.** Yet all factions, social or political, were watched severely by the **Savak** (the secret political police). More censorship of the press and a perpetual breach of human rights in judicial courts and inside the corrupt system of the government followed — for which even the silence of people may partially be blamed. Although the **Shah** was trying to be alert to corruption, there were too many places he could not control. Even the **Shah** and his family succumbed to temptation for monetary gains. In addition, there was a lot of stealing in the government, at different levels, which shattered the trust in the heart of a majority who did not speak up or who were simply afraid to do so. Consequently, the reforms of the 'White Revolution', though truly needed, barely scratched the surface. (The 'White Revolution' was a set of new plans and programs that extended education and social reforms into the doorstep of the rural families.)

The third period reflects the zenith of the totalitarian control of **Muhammad Reza Shah,** which included incarceration of numerous political activist and their jail tortures. His people did not know him closely and he had failed to gain the respect and popularity that his father had among people. Some of the **Shah**'s closest men believed that he ironically lacked the strong inner self that he strived to express. The law and order existed to some extend but was a false sense of security because it only protected a special segment of the society. **Savak** (the secret police) was trained by the governments of **U.S.** and **Israel** inside Iran to find and uproot any form of political resistance or rebellion at any price. The absence of true law and order gradually diminished the middle class and increased the poverty. The greedy top officials in the government glibly flattered the **Shah** for their own gains on one side and caused further suppression of the people on the other. This corruption infected the minds of those who were employed to serve the needy rather than become the recipient of the goods and services themselves. When it came to facing any criticism about his rule, **Shah** (like the kings before him) blamed the **European** super powers for every single conflict.[7]

Thus, **Muhammad Reza Shah** was indulged in his own world and gradually drifted farther from his people. Many years later, this distance with the people he governed became a pivotal point of his apology to the people of Iran. This happened in last days of his rule in the winter of 1978 when he admitted the shortcomings in his rule and asked for a chance to make good. But the apology had unfortunately come too late. **Iranians** denied his request by further demonstrations against him. Even his **American** allies abandoned **Muhammad Reza Shah** when he needed them most. **The United States** felt the danger of losing Iran to the **Communist Russia**. Worse than that was the potential break in the flow of oil from this region. The attitude of the U.S. towards Iran suddenly changed.

Previously the U.S. was a friend of Iran and **Iranians** loved the **Americans**. This friendship had existed from before the World War II. The United States had maintained a helping hand for Iran to defy its poverty and keep its distance from Russia. At that time, the United States did not have close ties with Libya, Iraq, and Egypt. But Iran and Israel were its trusted allies in the Middle East. During the unrest of the late 1970s in Iran, the U.S. tried to secure its own position and investments in Iran and this did not necessarily mean to stick by its old friend, the **Shah**. Meanwhile, the U.S. had a bad and costly experience with Turkey (hundreds of millions of Dollars) against the **Russians'** communistic influence and did not want the same problem with Iran. However, the attitude of the people of Iran gradually changed against both the **Americans** and the **British** after their 1953 coup. The hypocrite interference of the U.S. in the affairs of the Middle East, as a whole, became detested.[8]

The U.S. support of the tyrannical and dogmatic governments in the Middle East in order to resist progress of communism in the area resulted in more suppressive regimes like the **Taliban** in Afghanistan and the **Baas** regime of Iraq under **Saddam Hosain**. Later on, the U.S. had to change its policy towards these two ex-allies in order to save its own position in the world as well as ties with **Israel**.

The United States was facing pressure from some international human right activists such as **Dr. Israel Shahak**, a retired professor at the Hebrew University in Jerusalem and a Holocaust survivor. He was chairman of the Israeli League for Human and Civil Rights. **Dr. Shahak** traveled to the U.S. in 1975 before the house subcommittee on International Organizations and Movements of the Foreign Affairs Committee. He testified of abuse of **Palestinian** rights; but these and other reports received were locked up and any efforts to see them were met with refusal by **Edward Kennedy**, chairman of the Senate Judiciary Subcommittee on Refugees. The **American public** was kept in the dark. However, the media around the world covered the suffering of **Palestinians**. The first one appeared on June 19, 1977 in the London Sunday Times.[9]

The problem of interpretation of Democracy was not unique to **Iran**. The issue of Human Rights looked universal, but was politically manipulated by many governments. At this time, the U.S. Government had found it necessary to enforce these rights only in Iran rather than anywhere else in the Middle East. This was used as an excuse for **American** government to interfere in internal affairs of a troubled Iran to protect its own interests.

Human Rights were an issue in Iran for several centuries. It is only fair to claim that a few decades of industrial and agricultural renovations within Iran during **Pahlavi Dynasty** had caused truly much broader and more positive reforms not seen in earlier dynasties. Some of these reforms were a direct result of the "Constitutional Movement", which started the wheel for the social improvement at the end of **Ghajar Dynasty**. But, in addition to cultural and traditional barriers inside the country, it was also the financial corruption within the government and the society that eventually brought these wheels to a halt. In other words, renovations were essential and brought economical progress, but the social awareness and public education to realize the need for such changes was not emphasized enough.

It was during 1970s; following some direct interference of the **U.S.** through its Human Rights programs, that a new wave of dissatisfied protesters from within the universities and major factories around the nation brought **Shah** more dismay. At this period, **Iran** had been one of the fastest growing nations in the eastern hemisphere. Nevertheless, the mental unreadiness of its huge illiterate population and the strangeness of all the westernized standards caused Iran to hesitate. These conflicting standards in Iran resulted in a break in the unity between its people and the government.

Conflicts rose and **Shah** thought of new changes in his government. Prime minister **Hoveyda** was removed in July 1977 and **Jamshid Amuzegar** (leader of **Rastakhiz** party and pro-Shah) replaced him. **Amuzegar** cut the government subsidies to the **Ulama (the religiousClerics)**. That certainly caused discontent. (**Pahlavi** regime had brought three different apologetic **Prime Ministers** into service during the last five months of its reign). All failed to calm or satisfy the frenzy in the public. In December of 1978, **Shah** appointed yet another new Prime Minister **Shapur Bakhtiar**. He had influential tribal ties, but this had adverse results and did not work.

Shapur and two other **Jebhe Melli** leaders had already written an open letter to the **Shah** criticizing the breach of human rights in the country, but this letter was not a protest against the position of **Shah**. Now, after his acceptance of the prime minister position, even his own National Front colleagues denounced **Shapur Bakhtiar**. People gained more self-reliance and courage through strikes and demonstrations. **Shapur** was a well-known socialist democrat who had over twenty-five years of active service in leftist organizations like **Jebhe Melli** (National Front). After a strike broke out in the entire aviation industry, **Bakhtiar** ordered all airports closed and all flights cancelled. This **Prime Minister** liked to enforce the constitution law against the selfish ruling of the **Shah**, yet continuous strikes were getting out of hand. **Bakhtiar** even wrote an open letter to **Ayatollah Khomeini**—a prominent possible leader—regarding an interview and debate about the best ways to run this country for the sake of the people. But, it was left unanswered.

The police was ordered by the **Shah** not to get involved or use force to break the demonstrations as much as possible. This humanitarian gesture from the shaken monarch was not very much appreciated and mostly construed as a weakness. Nothing seemed to matter to the frenzied **Iranians** who had finally found a chance to raise their protesting voices against the person of **Shah**. The police resistance grew weaker; **Iranians** had made an emotional and hasty choice that **Shah** had to go, but had no general concession about who or what to have in his place in order to survive this crisis.

Bakhtiar tried to bring all political heads around a table, but he was forced by military commanders and the angry mob to resign in 1979 after about 37 days of service. He was treated like a traitor by his own peers and as a **Royalist** at the service of the **Shah** by most of the **Muslim** activists. He did not receive much sympathy or cooperation from the public; he could not bring different leaders of the opposition to a table to discuss a common solution. This has been an alarming characteristic unique to the third world countries—lack of organized political debate and rally—and has had disastrous effects on their future. This flaw is now a part of their history and, sadly enough, is still mostly neglected.

Meanwhile, the United States government under **Jimmy Carter** was watching the Middle East affairs very closely. The movement inside Iran was too strong for America to get mixed with politically. It was wise to wait and see. On one side, the OPEC meetings, which held the authority of production and distribution of oil to the world within the scope of the oil-producing nations, was threatening to the western world. On the other hand, the invasion of Afghanistan by **Soviets** in the 70's seemed very unsettling. To punish the **Russians** the U.S. embargo against the **Soviets** cut the sales of grain. The human rights issues were demanding the U.S. Government to question the totalitarian leaders in the area, and all the recent demonstrations against the **Shah** of Iran proved that he was one of them. **Shah** was an old friend of the U.S. But with the new turmoil in Iran, the U.S. was hesitant to act until the conditions inside Iran would indicate which of the two powers (**Shah** or a newly appointed figure) would emerge as the most powerful.

The lack of a functioning democratic system defined by these basic Human Rights: freedom of speech (the right to disagree publicly without the fear of punishment), freedom to assemble, and respectful treatment of prisoners (especially political) along with a right to attorney and a fair trial with unbiased judge, resulted in the unresolved contempt of the people for the authorities. As mentioned earlier several prime ministers tried to alleviate this situation, but they all failed. Even some of the soldiers started to fraternize and even joined with protesters on the streets.

The revolution was forming. Finally, **Muhammad Reza Shah Pahlavi** was forced to leave his country with a broken heart. At the same time, **Jimmy Carter**, the U.S. President could not support the **Shah**—especially when all propagandas about human Rights issues were going on in the world. The **Shah** was seriously ill (with a limited amount of time left to him because of cancer) and this was not yet publicized in Iran. His requests to come to the United States both for treatment and political support was denied. Therefore, **Shah** of Iran had to reluctantly wonder between friendly countries. Egypt opened doors to him and offered sincere sanctuary.

Muhammad Reza Shah in exile witnessed scenes of protesting crowds around his palace in Tehran. These images must have haunted him. Meanwhile, in the winter of 1978 in Iran, most of the people (some unknowingly and some reluctantly) chose to lay all their trust into a new system—the **Islamic Republic.** Finally, in the summer of 1980, **Shah** passed away in a forced seclusion in Egypt, where he was surrounded by a few of true friends. His physical body was deteriorated by cancer, but his spirit was shattered long before that.

1. *Reza Shah Pahlavi*, by Nader Paymai, p. 172

2. *Zendegi Nameh Siasi Mehdi Bazargan,* Dr. SaeedBarzin,Tehran,1976, Markaz print, p. 47

3. *Kholaseh Tarikh Gozashteh Iran*, by Dr Zia-u-Din Hayat, pp. 81-82

4. *Khaterat va Asnad Sepahbod H. Razm Ara*, 2004, Tehran, Shirazeh Print, pp. 162-198

5. *Jame Shenasi Nokhbeh Koshi*, by Ali Reza-Gholi, 18th edition, 2002, Tehran, p. 179

6. *Kholaseh Tarikh Iran*, p. 83

7. *Chekideh Tarikh Iran*, pp. 170-172

8. *Rah Avard*, editor Hasan Shahbaz, periodical printed quarterly, No. 48, Fall of 1999, Los Angeles, article by Hosain Hazed, pp. 266-275

9. *A Time for Peace*, By Judith I. Shadzi, Saratoga, CA, p. 141

CHAPTER TWENTY-ONE

Islamic Republic

Meanwhile, during the winter of 1978 and spring of 1979, some socialist groups, mainly college students, engaged in publicizing of the news and figures about the atrocities committed by the **Pahlavi Dynasty** and the **Savak** (the Iranian secret police). These newspaper articles, not always accurate, deepened further hatred towards the old regime. Some **ex-Savak** officers and major army figures were executed. Some executions lacked the most basic judicial qualifications (legal hearings with attorneys). These unfortunate retaliatory reactions are an unavoidable part of any revolutionary period. Many Iranians hoped that, after **Savak**, the chaotic status quo would be only temporary. But the series of unjustified incarcerations and possible executions continued by a new line of politicians.

Different political factions and activists inside Iran maintained high hopes for a better Iran. An accepted leader who could be respected and trusted by all political parties was yet to be found. But the fact is that **Muslim Clerics** (**Mullahs**) had found their place among the majority through centuries of **Shiite** doctrines.

Therefore, the religious faction (**Ruhanioon**) under these **Muslim Clerics** since the Constitutional Movement of **Ghajar Dynasty** found it absolutely imperative to fight the tyrannical power of the monarch and his foreign allies. However, the necessity of bringing a much-needed social justice and freedom to the people was not always a priority for these **Clerics**. For many of them, like many of their fanatic followers, this revolution was centered on the same old problem of defending an **Islamic** land against the aggression of sinners and corrupt politicians from inside and outside Iran. The revolution for most of these **Clerics** who made the religious faction called **Ruhanioon** was about change of power rather than protection and upheaval of Human Rights. Therefore, a civil struggle from within Iran seemed likely to resemble the bloodshed following the victory of the **Constitutionalists** (Mashruteh Nationalists during **Ghajar Dynasty**).

Many different people went into the revolution with different goals and expectations. Ideal Democracy did not mean the same to all. Thousands of hopeful **Iranian** students outside the country came back to Iran to join the revolution- many of them were not necessarily ready to put the control in the hands of the religious leaders. Millions of **Iranians** who took part in demonstrations on the streets of Tehran, Isfahan, Shiraz, Tabriz, Yazd, Hamadan, Kerman, Abadan, Rasht, Meshed, and many more hoped that injustice—both before and during the uprises—would finally be stopped by a democratic government. Yet "Democracy" did not mean the same to all of these revolutionary factions. In 1978 Iran had 10 million students in its elementary and high schools, and there were 200,000 students studying in its colleges and universities who only knew that they were against the **Shah**. These were young voices against the **Shah**'s regime. But these 200,000 young voices who responded to the slogans and notes mostly lacked the historical knowledge of the past or a precise language to properly evaluate serious political issues without bias.[1]

On the other hand, skeptics among older generation and the businessmen in Bazaars of Iran were all involved in their own political debates as to whom to trust. Each group innocently involved with its own interpretation of buzzwords like Freedom, Independence, Justice, and Social Freedoms.

Ayatollah Khomeini

Ayatollah Khomeini was an aged **Shiite** religious leader who had been in exile in Baghdad since 1964. The title **Ayatollah** is given to highly skilled and knowledgeable cleric in Islamic laws. **Ayatollah Khomeini**'s bitter opposition to the ex-Kingdom of **Pahlavi** on the issue of Capitulation Laws (permitting foreign delegates to stay above the law inside Iran) and "The White Revolution" had made him politically a target of the secret police or **Savak**. Now in February 1979, **Khomeini** was flown back to Iran. This happened quickly after **Shah** had departed from Tehran in winter of 1978. Millions of **Iranians** were anticipating his arrival. They hoped that this **Ayatollah** would be the savior—although he was vague about many social issues (including the women's rights). Still, **Khomeini** seemed to be the only figure that a majority of **Iranians** would trust as a leader. However, many **Iranians** had not heard his name before or had forgotten about him (mostly because he had been in exile out of Iran for about fifteen years). Meanwhile, numerous politicians, reformists, and even socialist activists were accompanying him on the same plane; among which were **Bani Sadr, Ghotbzadeh**, and **Ibrahim Yazdi** as his entourage. Naturally, all political groups had their own dream of the type and characteristic of a new regime in Iran.

The public was barely familiar with the new term: **Islamic Republic**. Some did not trust it, although **Dr. Ali Shariati**, a humanistic theologian, had paved the way for a major segment of the younger generation in 1970s and had introduced a new wave of "Modernized Socialistic Islam" . **Ahmad Khomeini** (the son of **Ayatollah**), in a newspaper interview in 1979, referring to the critical role of **Dr. Shariati** puts more value on his teachings towards a foundation for Islamic rule than his own father's work.[2]

The suggestions from secular party leaders in Iran regarding the addition of the word "Democratic" to the name of **Islamic Republic** was rejected by **Ayatollah Khomeini** in 1978; **Khomeini** believed the word "**Islamic**" implied democracy.

This remark from the new leader did not raise enough doubts in the minds of the secular political activists. These secular political groups inside Iran formed a significant section of the revolutionary force. Through decades, many **pro-Soviet activists** and guerilla groups inside Iran had gradually formed **Marxist groups** as well as **Muslim Socialists** (referred to as **Mujahidin-e-Khalgh** or Fighters of the People). Eventually, all of these active groups reluctantly gave in to the dominion of the **Islamic Clerics** hoping that the power of religion and the unity of these groups would topple the regime of the **Shah**. Only then, and because of the fact that **Mullas'** (**Muslim Clerics**) knowledge of running the nation is limited, doors will eventually open for the educated **Socialist Activists** to gain the leverage. Thus, these **Pro-Soviet activists** were counting on the fact that most of the educated people in bigger cities in Iran were not necessarily looking for a religious regime. It is true to claim that all **Iranians** who did not want to continue to tolerate the **Pahlavi** regime, were generally hoping for a better government based on democracy and justice. But, they mostly did not know which political party or known politician to turn to. However, a segment of the population insisted on segregation of religion and politics (the **Secularists**).

Obviously, the **Mullas (Ruhanioon)**, mostly **Shiites** enjoyed the most supporters—especially in the provinces where Politics had become the hottest issue. Initially **Mullahs** communicated in the mosques with the entire public and this tribune gave them a venue to promote their own agenda. Consequently, **Mullas (Clerics)** promised everyone (including the **Secularists**) a democratic regime although this word was not defined. Thus, **Mullas** openly received the cooperation of all other political groups and organizations to seize the major centers of media and pulpit to introduce an interim government.[3]

On the other hand, other groups who wanted to stay in touch with people had to maintain contact with **Mullas** and **Ayatollahs** in particular. To join with the majority, the **Socialist Activists** sided with **Khomeini** mainly because he was against the U.S. Meanwhile, some of the Ayatollahs like **Beheshti**, **Motahari**, and **Montazeri** resented any super-power interference and reasoned the public that **Islamic Republic Of Iran** would have social justice for all. However, many of these promises, like the existing rights to divorce and voting rights for women were not completely confirmed in detail by these leaders of the **Islamic Republic**—although majority of hopeful individuals in Iran had voted for **The Islamic Republic**.

Therefore, promises about democratic changes were given. The **Mullas (Ruhanioon)** needed more time to assert their total control while maintaining a kind of consensus between all activists. This maneuver seemed especially crucial because there were many civilians with guns and ammunition. Maintaining a calm atmosphere was imperative for the new political party of **Hezb-u-Lah** (the party in support of **Ruhanioon**). They had the votes of the majority of **Iranians** who trusted anything that derived from within the **Islamic** doctrines. But other Muslim Activist groups including **Mujahidin** and **Feda'iyan** had their own followers all over Iran who were active and armed. Nevertheless, the majority lacked the simple political and historical information to choose wisely between these groups.

This naiveté was fostered by fanatic views both in schools and in the neighborhoods of cities and provinces during **Pahlavi** and **Ghajar Dynasties**. Furthermore, during **Pahlavi Dynasty** the media presented political news supporting only a traditional monarchy which was based on a divine right of kingship. Choices or pros and cons of different kinds of governments were never discussed publicly. Sadly enough, for many years in the past and even now in 2005, the public assumed that academic excellence automatically included political knowledge. The truth was that the educated people were not necessarily better informed than non-educated people about political entitlements and social reforms. Knowing the power of media, the regimes of **Pahlavi** and **Ghajar** had stiffened their control over people's right to know by regulating and censoring the press. Even public debates (especially during **Pahlavi Dynasty**) were controlled anywhere and especially in Religion and Politics. Consequently, the public mind—educated or not—was neither trained to seek alternative sources of facts nor analyze alternative data. A bitter reality had surfaced at this time: unity among **Iranians** was almost impossible to achieve. Therefore, no consensus in Religion or Politics was possible. History remembers similar chaos during the Constitutional Movement of the **Ghajar** period.

Ali Reza-Gholi studied the root of all these problems in his 2001 book *Jame Shenasi Nokhbeh Koshi*. He points out that since the coup d'etat of **Seyyed Zia Tabatabaie** in 1921 until the fall of the political cabinet of **Bakhtiar** in 1978, Iran had changed 45 Prime Ministers within 57 years. Except a few none of these ministers had the honesty or courage to admit his weaknesses in finding solutions for social problems. They were mostly incompetent Prime Ministers except for **Ghaem Magham, Amir Kabir**, and **Mosadegh** who stand out among the true leaders. Reza-Gholi believes that greedy plots of super powers inside Iran could never have been conceived - much less execute–if **Iranians** (politicians as well as common people) were not ignorant, indifferent, or greedy. Therefore, the roots of the current social problems are inherent in internal causes.[4]

Amazingly, the **Mullas** followed the same policy of keeping the public uninformed about the details of their political plans. The winning **Mullas** even organized a special monitoring task force under the name of **Pasdaran**. It had authority to police the towns, but was mostly assigned to follow and protect their own people and their own political faction.

But this totalitarian attitude of some **Mullas** did not surface at once. Looking back, during the earlier days of the Revolution, in the spring of 1979, **Bazargan** was chosen as the **Prime Minister** of the interim government of the **Islamic Republic**. This happened about four days after the arrival of **Ayatollah Khomeini**. **Bazargan** was an educated politician of Jebhe Melli party who had studied in Europe and could play the role of a buffer between many political groups. **Bazargan** was negotiating with **Savak** and the **United States** for an orderly transition of power between **Shah** and **Khomeini**. Partially under the effects of the western civilization, he was a promising figure to bring **Muslim clerics** and other **Social Activists** (Muslim or non) closer together. But this did not happen. **Bazargan**'s failure to stand firmly against the illegal and unauthorized imprisonments and executions of some officials and political leaders of protesting factions shattered his position among the public. Thus, the **Muslim Clerics** found the road open to further illegal acts when this prime minister failed to impose or uphold the law to protect the citizens. As a result, many critical decisions, political and/or social, were made without proper investigation or permission. Many innocent lives were lost, and many important documents were destroyed.

Many government documents or correspondences simply vanished before and after the revolution. **Ibrahim Yazdi** was the Minister of Foreign Affairs in the cabinet of **Bazargan**. Later on he wrote in his diary that a large contract for purchase of arms from the

U.S. was made by **Pahlavi** regime. The U.S. was concerned. This purchase contract had to be cancelled by Iran in order to release the U.S. from return of the deposit. As a result of the push from **General Huyser** during the last days of the cabinet of **Bakhtiar**, Iranian authorities were provoked to nullify this agreement. After all **Americans** had left, **Sullivan**, the U.S. Ambassador, had to stay back in Tehran until mid winter of 1978 to make sure that this military contract was cancelled by **Iranians** under the new regime. Apparently, this action would constitute as a breach of contract by **Iran**. As a result, the **U.S.** found the excuse to hold nine billion dollars ($9,000,000,000.00) of Iran's money that was already deposited into its account for the damage incurred.[5]

With the gradual increase of the power of the fanatic **Mullas** inside **Iran**, the **Pro-Soviet Activists** felt uneasy. Meanwhile, the **Ruhanioon** needed to keep all the activists (Muslim or non) on their side a little longer. The younger members of the **Pro-Soviet Activists** had not been able to easily mix with **Pasdaran** (**Muslim** police force and most of them extremely religious). The **Mullas** tightened their grip on major social activities, and **Pasdaran** helped them to police this control. In addition, the media was not fully allowed to cover all aspects of the lives and ideologies of the elite political figures. Neither were people permitted to confront major representatives with their political questions or concerns.

These oppressive actions of the interim government was not fully explained to the naïve public. Surprisingly, sometimes these protesting voices were heard. There were oppositions from within the system scrutinizing the actions of the government. One of the arguments was that democracy is the ruling of people by the people, while Aristocracy is the ruling of an elite group inside the society over others. **Clericalism** is a kind of aristocracy, and some **Mullas**, like **Hojat-ul-Islam Tabasi**, had openly pushed for it in their speeches. Contrarily, **Ayatollah Khomeini** had expressed his refusal of this unilateral approach towards the control of people. He had labeled this as one of the flaws of the previous dictatorship and against the constitution.[6]

Public seemed to lose faith in extreme Islamic interpretations by some Mullas. But the new government needed to maintain its hold on the public mind. Towards the end of 1978, some **Muslim Clerics**

(**Mullas**) were still struggling to redeem their anti-capitalistic edge to maintain public approval. Some **Muslim** student activists, who called themselves the Followers of **Imam's** doctrine (**Payro Khat-e-Imam**), took 55 hostages from the **American** embassy in Tehran. This sudden action bought **clerics** more time in the eyes of the wary public. Images of the **hostages** were in the western media; a lot of propaganda followed and about a year later they were released after 444 days with no positive outcome or demand during the first day of presidency of **Ronald Reagan**.[7]

Meanwhile, the suicidal hostage rescue attempt by the U.S. in April 1980 had failed, and this had caused a set back in negotiations for the release of the **hostages**. The **Party of God (Hezb-u-Lah)** grew to become the dominant political party inside Iran with the absolute right to nominate future presidents. This imposition had not come about amicably. Still an anti - American mood in Iran was kept alive, and the U.S. obscure foreign policies did not help this image.

Presidency in Iran

Because a nation has a president and free elections these facts alone do not guarantee even a slight degree of a Democracy, unless the public is literate enough to understand the issues — pro and con — that are being voted on. In 1923, **Kemal Ataturk** was elected as the first president of Turkey. His improvements began but did not continue long because a majority in Turkey does not understand the true meaning of freedom and value of human rights. Iranians paid dearly for the Revolution, but unfortunately it takes more than that to make a revolution truly successful. History repeats itself. Also, the **Afghans** recently experienced their first presidency elections. It happened in October of 2004 under the supervision of foreign delegates. Yet the realization of fundamental values underlying such system was not truly grasped by the men and women of any age group in Afghanistan. The question is this: which one can be the best remedy for social ills — a Presidency or Democracy?

The same issue applies to Iran. However, the presidency in Iran happened fifty-seven years after Turkey and twenty-four years before Afghanistan. Early in 1980 in Iran, **Abol Hasan Bani Sadr** was elected president with 75 percent of the vote. The majority of his parliament was occupied with the Islamic Republican Party that started its escalating feud with this **Muslim President** who had come from a long exile in France. **Bani Sadr** and most of his educated men were labeled liberals who would return Iran to dependence on the U.S. Even the **President** was denied his most basic rights as a citizen.[8]

By now the **United States** had already lost its friendly position in the eyes of the public. This hatred was a direct result of the previous U.S. support given to the tyrannical regime of **Muhammad Reza Shah**. The people of Iran had not and cannot ever forget the atrocities of **Savak**. Neither can the images of the unspeakable poverty be erased. The world has seen the grieving men and women who never had a clue what happened to their loved ones. It was at this period that the U.S. was busy fighting in several campaigns; it had allied itself with **China** and **Khemer Rouge**, which were killing the civilian **Vietnamese** in 1980s. This wrongful foreign policy cost the U.S. three billion dollars and the loss of the Far Easterners' trust. The **United States** violations against Geneva Convention were never discussed until several years later. In Korean War about 3000 **American** soldiers were killed, and the **U.S.** faulted continuously the treatment of the **Korean** POWs. These trends unfortunately are repeating themselves. Even right now, after the September 11 incident in New York City, many suspects are held at Guantanamo. These civilians are labeled POWs and are kept without their legal rights to have attorneys and under coercive tactics of interrogation. On top of these injustices, continuous covert support of the U.S. for the tyrants in the Middle East has been catastrophic.

In addition to these fresh images, **Iranians**, once again in 1979, asked where the friendly and strong **U.S.** was when **Saddam Hussein** raged a brutal attack against the civilians inside **Iran**. On the other hand, **Mullas** used this war as an excuse to suppress any internal opposing voice in the name of patriotism.[9] Not unsimilar to what **George Bush** did in 2004 to suffocate any criticism of the **U.S.** occupation of **Iraq**.

About a year into Iran-Iraq war, the death of the **Ex Shah** of Iran (**Muhammad Reza Shah Pahlavi**) happened in Cairo in 1980. The promised reforms inside Iran were delayed and the war was to be blamed for it. Unemployment was more than twenty-five percent. Wealthy people pulled their capital out of Iran and invested abroad. The **Social Activists** were printing a list of these withdrawals. Some were close to half a billion dollars.

On the other hand, **Iraqis** started using chemical weapons against tens of thousands of **Iranian Kurds** in northwest Iran. This brought the fighting to an unacceptable stage. The U.S. had ordered an economical sanction against Iran because of the hostage crisis, but **Iraqis** enjoyed a **Russian** supply of ammunition. The use of any chemical weapons was against the Geneva Convention, but because of the position of the U.S. against Iran, this case did not receive much attention in the U.N. The genocide of the **Turks** by **Saddam Hussein** was not fairly exposed to the world and secrecy about its detail resulted in eight years of war and devastation for both Iran and Iraq.

In 1981 **President Bani Sadr** finds no safety inside Iran. His life is in danger by the radicals. He resigns and flees the country. **Muhammad Ali Rajaie** replaces him, but soon he is assassinated along with his **Prime Minister** and seventy other officials in a meeting in Tehran. With no delay, **Ali Khameneie**, a radical **Mullah (Cleric)** was nominated by the **Hezb-u-Lah** party and elected as the third President. The fundamentalists among **Ruhanioon** were not serving the public: they were practically imposing control over it. Even **Pasdaran** (the religious Police) were dispatched to Lebanon in 1982 to resist the **Israeli** invasion in the area. This decision was never subject to a majority approval/disapproval by the **Iranian** people.

A lot of major decisions were being made without public awareness or approval. Even the universities and colleges were closed for "cleaning" around 1983—this meant cleaning away those (instructors, employees, and even students) who posed a threat to the main ideology of the regime.

Between 1983 and 1986, the direct control over the lifestyle of **Iranians** became a routine position of the **Islamic** authorities. Consequently, a sense of anticlerical feeling among **Iranians** was increasingly expressed. Many **Iranians** were imprisoned for their critical opinions. However, **President Khameneie** was reelected in 1985. He spoke bitterly against the accusations of the tortures in the jails in Iran. **Khameneie** did not like to be interviewed by the foreign press, and if he was given this chance he would chose to use a bitter and condemning tone towards all super powers. Because of internal social pressure and injustice, many students protested without results. Some were taken to jails. Jane Kokan is a reporter who visited Iran recently. She made a documentary about the tortures in the Iranian Jails of the political prisoners that was aired on PBS under "Frontline" in the Bay Area on July 12, 2004. The authorities in Iran still deny all of this. Because of the pressure from peace activists outside Iran, a committee has been assigned by the **Islamic** government to investigate the death of an **Iranian** woman reporter (a **Canadian** citizen) in the jail in Iran. However, none of these sessions, procedures, and documents is open to the public.

In 1986 **Oliver North** and other representatives of **President Reagan** (of The U.S.) tried to buy the freedom of some hostages in Lebanon by smuggling arms inside Iran. This was when Iran possessed a superior position in the war with Iraq around 1986, but the **Iranian** government refused the offer of a truce from Baghdad. The fanatic **clerics** greedily desired more time before attending to their true responsibilities in regard to the delayed internal reforms. This attitude cost the nation more lives in the war. In 1988 the **United States** army attacked an **Iranian** commercial airbus and 290 passengers, including 66 children, lost their lives. The U.S. offered condolences. Finally, in the same year, after loosing more strategic points to Iraq, Iran accepted the U.N peace resolution. **Ayat-u-Lah Khomeini**, over 90 years old, referred to this truce as drinking from the cup of poison. But he had no other choice.

Following the cease-fire, some superficial reforms took place immediately. Movies brought other subjects to their screens such as love and prosperity. Revolutionary guards, **Pasdaran** and other organizations, were removed so people could live a little easier without routine harassments. Chess was accepted again as a game rather than gambling or a symbol of the world monarchy. Women got a chance to relax their Islamic outfit and put on nail polish. People were given more freedom to travel in and out of Iran.

In 1989, when Iran was getting ready to celebrate its first decade of transformation, two direct orders from **Ayatollah Khomeini (Imam)** brought the old strict rules back. First, he ordered for the capturing of **Salman Roshdi,** dead or alive. This came as 'fatva' meaning a religious announcement from the leader. The Egyptian- English writer had used a humiliating and demeaning language against Koran and **the Prophet of Islam** in his satirical novel. Thus, his ordinary novel received a jolt of unjust international attention, while he hid in seclusion. Second, **Imam Khomeini** ordered for removal of **Ayatollah Montazeri** from the position of the future designated successor of **Imam**. **Montazeri** had referred to some unauthorized political assassinations in Iran and had expressed the view that **Islamic Republic** had failed in fulfilling some of its earlier promises to the public. These new orders from **Khomeini** shattered the hopes for a moderate rule during the second decade.

After the death of **Imam Khomeini** in 1989, **Khameneie** was elected as the successor of **Imam**; and **Rafsanjani** took the role of presidency. He was the fourth president after the revolution. The position of the Prime Minister is deleted from the amended constitution law. Up to 1993, **Rafsanjani** tried to bring more educated and experienced members to his cabinet and Congress. Coming from a wealthy family of landowners, he supported the idea of open markets and tried to get Iran into the world market.

It was during the first term of his presidency that **Rafsanjani** lessened the formal restrictions of importing **European** and **Asian** products for sale in **Iranian** markets. While this was ideal for wealthy landowners and merchants, the less wealthy and government employees were again left out. Some of the reforms actually backfired in 1992—without preparing the fundamental social attitude to absorb it, the radical change provokes resistance from the majority. Interestingly, **Shah** of Iran was accused of imposing same radical changes on the society. Again the wealthy were getting richer, and the poor continued in misery.

These new laws opened the Iranian market to foreign products which reflected foreign values. As a result, new questions as well as varied interpretations of the role of religion in society surfaced. **Abdul Karim Sorush** was another **Muslim** scholar who had scrutinized the strict limitations inside the realm of **Islamic** rule. In 1991 he urged his students in his first speech in Isfahan to look for answers to social problems without giving in to any pressure. He wanted **Ruhanioon (Mullas)** to get salary-earning jobs like anyone else rather than living off tax money. He criticized **Ruhanioon** for believing that force is the logic behind reforms and not liberty. **Abdul**

Karim Sorush wanted to draw a line between "faith" and what he called "perplexity" . For this speech, he became the target of fanatics in 1995: his office was rampaged by armed fanatic **Muslim** extremists who threatened him to death. **President Rafsanjani** refused to support **Sorush** when he wrote to him pleading for protection.

However, the public gradually lost hope and trust in **President Rafsanjani**. In 1993, only 57 percent of **Iranians** cared to vote. This was a sign of **Iranians'** lack of interest and trust in their government. **Rafsanjani** was re-elected, with much narrower results, for the second term from 1993 to 1997. The **Conservatives** grew wearier by **Rafsanjani's** rule. Again more strict and senseless laws refrained people from the simplest forms of pass time. Censorship heightened. Many were arrested because they were in possession of western videotapes and satellite dishes in their homes. The new government kept making the same mistake that the earlier ones did: oppression would control the people. The low GNP continued its downfall during **Rafsanjani's** second term. In 1996, the Department of Commerce announced that 40 percent of **Iranians** lived under the poverty line. The gap between the poor and the wealthy was widening and pillars of democracy were not strong enough to hold the weight. The U.S. put Iran under a complete economical sanction in 1995. (**U.S.** will neither buy nor sell to **Iran**—because of Iran's assistance to the **Palestinians** in their fight with the **Israelis**)

By the end of the second term of the presidency of **Rafsanjani** in 1997, the **Hezb-u-Lah Conservatives** had crossed over 200 names off the list of presidential nominees and pushed for their parliament leader **Nategh Nuri**. This caused more aggravation among people. **Muhammad Khatami**, the least promising clergy and a follower of **Rafsanjani** trend, won the elections in 1997 with 70 percent of the votes. Apparently, the disappointed public had found new hopes for 'changes' in **Khatami**. He had criticized some of the former authorities and promised a society with law and order. Upon election, **Khatami** opened doors to different political parties and urged more open debates and a free press. In 1999, he held the much needed elections for the decentralized town and state councils. The daily papers under this government gathered courage to criticize some of the suppressive authorities inside the government. Even the **President** took part in an **American** media interview in 1998 by

Christine Amanpour from CNN; she is an Iranian-descent citizen and reporter of the **U.S.** In this positive interview with wide exposure, **Khatami** chose to reflect on the beneficial ties between the two countries rather than old clichés and the stressful issues of the past. Of course, **Khatami** may not be credited for the establishment of this trend of thought, but his approach reflected the important reality that this direction within the administration is a result of the streets and neighborhoods of Iran and not from behind closed doors or mosques or specific political offices.[10]

Meanwhile, the peace-seeking speeches of **Khatami** in the U.N. meetings in December of 1998 showed a promising era in the relations of Iran and the western world. **Kofi Annan** endorsed **Khatami**'s suggestions to base the millennium's peace process on the beneficial common points between nations and ideologies rather than mere scrutiny of differences. This was a great change in attitude of Iran and had a profound resonance in the West. Ex-President **Khameneie** had the same chance of speech in 1987, but he had a bitter tone of condemnation towards western powers and the U.N role against the innocence of less-developed countries.

Regardless, the hardliners and extreme fanatical **Conservatives** in the regime started insurgencies by the assassination of five Iranian reporters. This increased the bounty for S. Roshdi. The efficient and popular mayor of Tehran, **Karbaschi**, was prosecuted by fabricated accusations simply because he had supported **Khatami** during elections.

The third decade after the revolution had forgotten the basic unsettling question about the performance of the government. Mosques were much emptier than in the last decades. The fire in voices had gone cold. **Islam**, in a way, was loosing its glory in the eyes of many who witnessed the flaws in the official **Muslim Cleric**. (This has been a bitter result of the totalitarian dominion of some corrupt **Mullas** who suffocated all protesting voices even from within the government). The poverty and lack of fair social laws to enhance economical reforms took its toll on the new generation's trust in religion and ethics. Pressure and corruption grew deeper; most of the working individuals in the bigger cities were forced to have more than one occupation to earn a living. Ironically, in this **Muslim** state many found refuge in drugs, alcohol, and even prostitution.

Under these circumstances, creating any reform seems extremely hard. But, **Khatami** held his stronghold against the accusations and intimidations of fanatic **Conservatives**. Although the wrath of militant **Hezb-u-Lah** would rise against him and his followers everywhere, he delivered major speeches. Regardless, he opened the 1999 Council members meetings in Tehran and called it a true step forward in foundation of the righteousness of citizens and their right to control the government. Two hundred thousand members for these councils were chosen to voice their side of the political and economic agendas. That is why **Khatami** was playing the role of a buffer between traditional hardliners and the young generation of reformists. Therefore, any radical or abrupt move could result in loss of his position as a leader and cause a revolutionary impasse.

This delicate situation is still hard for most of the **Iranians** to feel because of a continuous lack of open-and-free political debates for clearing old issues once and for all. **Dr. Ibrahim Yazdi** referred to the lack of organized and open political meetings inside Iran and called it a barrier against the president towards a direct contact with the people. **Amir Entezam**, the speaker for the ex-cabinet of **Bazargan** is still in prison for some unknown or unjustified accusations in regard to spying for the **U.S.** at the time of **hostages**. This lack of freedom of speech or open debates among political factions or organizations inside Iran is still a big constitutional problem. Under these circumstances, supremacy of one party over the rest cannot always stay democratic. In addition to the **Islamic Republic Party** (reflecting the sovereign power of **Hezb-u-Lah**) there are currently some other political parties inside Iran such as: **Nehzat –e-Azadi, Hezb-e-Mardom-e-Iran, Hezb-e-Mellat-e-Iran, Jebhe Melli Iran**, and **Hezb-e-Zahmat Keshan Melli Iran**.[11]

The pressure from **Hezb-u-Lah** party and other **Muslim extremists** still is unbearable. They determine what is legal and what is forbidden.

The lawmaking branch of the Iranian government (Legislative Branch) consists of two elected and two appointed bodies. The elected bodies are these: The Islamic Consultative Assembly (*Majlis*) and The Assembly of Experts (*Khobregan*). However, the appointed bodies of the lawmaking branch of the Iranian government (consisting of twelve members: The Council of Guardians and The Expediency Council) supervise new laws to ensure they comply with

Islamic principals and The Constitution. Many subjective points of views and fanatic approaches to social issues have been the outcome and have resulted in further disappointments among younger generations in Iran.

Unfortunately even still, criticizing the government is considered an unacceptable taboo in the social lives of **Iranians**. The punishment for this 'crime' is imprisonment and/or death. In the April of 2000, the conservative-controlled judiciary drew the line. Launching a wide-ranging crackdown, it closed nearly all of the reformist sanctuaries and jailed leading journalists. Over the night, these journalists became national heroes. Their names were on every **Iranians'** lips and their trials—a proof of severe censorship - were eagerly followed and buzzed about.[12]

In June 2001 elections, **Mohammad Khatami** proved the overwhelming popularity of his reforms by winning reelection with 77% of the vote. But his cabinet of 20 members was still too slow and many promises were not kept. There are many disappointed **Iranians**.

In January 2002, U.S. President **George Bush Jr.** referred to Iran as an "Axis of Evil" and accused it of illegal nuclear activities along with harboring suspected **Al-Qaeda** terrorists.

In March 2003 the U.S. President **George W. Bush** justified invasion of Iraq by saying **Saddam Hussein** posed a threat because Baghdad had stockpiles of chemical and biological weapons and was reviving its nuclear weapons program.

In August 2003, the International Atomic Energy Agency (IAEA) discovered traces of highly enriched uranium in a nuclear facility. Iran declared this substance was merely a futuristic source of energy. In December of the same year Iran suspended its uranium enrichment program as a sign of good faith in response to international pressure.

On December 26, 2003 a catastrophic earthquake devastated the historic city of Bam (southeast of Iran) killing an estimated 30,000 of its 80,000 residents. The **U.S.** and **Europe** extended a helping hand to cope with the devastation.

In January 2004, the elite **Clerics** (of the hard-liner **Guardian Council**) took the initiative to deny eligibility of 3,500 people who had registered to run for Parliament in February elections. Among these disqualified names, were more than 80 current members of the 290-seat Parliament. No explanation concerning the criteria of such evaluation was given to the public.

Participation in the Parliament elections of 2004 was still huge - partly because many side social benefits are tied in with such participation. If one is indifferent to voting he cannot obtain daily rations at a reduced price. The lack of a seal or evidence reflecting up-to-date participation in elections, however, will prove to be a burden for college students or travelers who seek passports.

On February 20, 2004 conservatism won back a landslide victory in spite of the loud protesting crowds on the streets. Today, **Iranians** are weary of set backs in reforms and also the pressure of the hard-liners in controlling the government.

In January 2005 preparations for elections in Iraq is underway. This election serves as a referendum on the current U.S. justification for deposing the infamous Baathist government. A national assembly will govern Iraq for a few months and will draw up a draft constitution by October 2005. It also chooses a president and two deputies. The Shiites hope to institutionalize "Shariat" in the constitution. There are secular communities, much smaller in number, who are anxious to exclude religion all together. This particular situation with the secular activists resembles the unfruitful struggle of the secularists inside Iran during the revolution of 1978.

Mercury News of February 02, 2005 reflects an article showing that a clear victory of **Ali Sistani** does not fit the White House neoconservatives' blueprint for creating a more pliable Middle East. He is a Tehran-backed Shiite religious and political leader, who has been very firm on wanting an accelerated time line for a U.S. withdrawal.

In an article by Reuters in Washington in February 07, 2005, David Kay, a U.S. official who led the search for banned weapons of mass destruction in postwar Iraq, said in a press conference: "What is in doubt is the ability (of) the U.S. Government to honestly assess Iran's nuclear status and to craft a set of measures that will cope with that threat short of military action by the United States or Israel ."

Gary Sick's congressional statement on U.S. policy towards Iran, which was given on February 16, 2005 in front of the Committee on international Relations, was a concern for human rights. He said:

"Despite all the efforts of the mullahs, Iran today has a vibrant civil society movement that is likely to make its influence felt in time. Although, perhaps more time than we would like. That movement and all that it represents in the way of internally-driven regime change would almost certainly be the first casualty of an American attack."

Many American writers and journalists are traveling to a more moderate Iran these days. A recent interview with Barbara Slavin who had just returned from her trip to Iran was aired on Q & A TV show on March 13, 2005.

Barbara Slavin, USA Today senior diplomatic correspondent, was very pleased with her most recent trip to Iran, which she called relaxing and enjoyable.

She believed that The U.S. had done Iran a great favor to get rid of its enemies among **Sunnis** of Iraq and Afghanistan. Yet calling Iran "The Axis of Evil," she confessed, was a sad and unfair accusation by **Bush** that unfortunately caused the moderate clerics to loose face between the strict leftist and extremists in side Iranian government. "This was a mistake," she said.

She referred to the 1950s CIA fabricated coup against the nationalist Prime Minister **Mosadegh**—portraying him falsely as a communist—as the root of hostilities between Iran and USA. This, she emphasized, had been implemented through helps from the corrupt clerics such as **Ayatollah Kashani**, a prominent pro-U.S. and pro Shah cleric among Muslims of the time.

Women in Iran are prominent in Parliament, social, and Governmental positions. They are much freer than other Muslim women in that part of the world.

Islam forbids intoxicants and imposes cover for women. Yet drugs like heroin are easier to purchase than alcohol! This shows the hypocrisy in the government.

Freedom is the most praised phenomena in the U.S. that **Iranians** admire. Seeking Democracy is afoot in Iran. Recent Iraq elections are a source of envy for **Iranians**. Next summer referendums for Presidency Elections is a hot debate.

Meanwhile, Iran is pressed by the U.S. to halt its nuclear enrichment program. In May of 2005, Iranian officials confirm that no weapons proliferation is being conducted and that a future nuclear energy is what Iran is seeking under its U.N. rights.

In June of 2005, **Mahmood Ahmadinejad**, a former fanatic hardliner, is elected new president of Iran.

In July of 2005, Iraq shows interest in close cooperation with its neighbor, Iran. Ousted **Saddam Hussein** was said to be the actual aggressor in 1980-88 wars against Iran.

In July of 2005, the U.S. President **George W. Bush** calls for the release of a jailed Iranian dissident who had been on food strike for over 33 days. Iranian authorities call the statement interventionist and refer to the U.S. foreign policy and its atrocities in trashing elected leaders in South Vietnam, Iran, Chile, Nicaragua, Guatemala, Venezuela, Haiti and other nations.

Iran is in pursuit of finalization of its first Russian assisted nuclear power station in Bushehr (near The Persian Gulf), which will be ready for test operation mid-2006.

The G8 summit in Scotland is interrupted with terrorist bombings of London underground. Many protestors blame the usual fanatic, religious terrorists of the Middle East, while some look at other European-based terrorist groups for this incident. Some in the Middle East assume 9/11 was the brainchild of the U.S. and U.K. spy agencies in a bid to prepare the pretexts for their governments to go inside Afghanistan and Iraq and perhaps Iran.

Amidst all these ups and downs, the majority in Iran has witnessed that social internal reforms do not come easily. They are learning, no matter how slowly, that programs upheld by their government must include foreign policy to ensure economic prosperity. This is a period of self-realization—a rude awakening. The role of the western nations in coping with revolutionary transitions in the countries of the third world should be that of patience based on humanitarian help rather than self-centered and opportunistic maneuvers. The U.S. Government took the policy of protecting its resources in the Middle East at any cost. This mentality backfired.

Edward Said refers to this issue; he believes that a very distinctive role of the Unites States in the Middle East and all oil-producing nations has been that of self interest in areas of oil and strategic power, which most **Americans** have been either shielded from or are simply unaware of. **Muslims** mostly see **America** as an unfair supporter of **Israel** against **Palestinians**: first, in its unilateral support of the establishment of the **Israeli State** in 1948, then in the occupation of 1967, and the **Intifades** of 1987. Finally in 2000, U.S. supplies Israel with enormous amounts of weapons that are used in regional wars. Same **Mujahidin** (and the **Taliban)** that are now labeled **Terrorists** (especially after the 9/11 incidents in New York) were actually invited to the U.S. and greeted by **President Reagan** in 1986. They were used, nourished, and supported by **U.S.** to rally **Islam** (in Afghanistan and Iraq) against godless **communists** of the **Soviet Union.**[13]

After September of 2001, the U.S. implemented a policy of direct confrontation with terrorism. This act was strongly criticized by almost half of its citizens as well as most of the **Europeans** and **Asians.** Many specialists did not approve of the retaliatory invasion of **Iraq,** which followed. The fact that terrorism cannot be stopped by bloodshed seems very hard to believe for those who are being targeted. Jessica Stern, a former Council to Foreign Relations and a former fellow at The Hoover Institution, interviewed several anti-America activists and religious militants in the Middle East. Her reflection is that **Americans** generally lack the true understanding of the causes and roots of terrorism. She insists that a different tactic to stop terrorism is necessary because terrorism is not susceptible to military solutions.[14]

The Italian playwright, Dario Fo, who won the Noble Prize for literature in 1997 said in his article in *Times of London* in September 15, 2001 that: "The great speculators wallow in an economy that every year kills tens of millions of people with poverty…Regardless of who carried the massacre of 9/11, this violence is the legitimate daughter of the culture of violence, hunger and inhuman exploitation."[15]

Shirin Ebadi the 2003 Nobel Prize Laureate delivered her speech, as an **Iranian** woman and a human rights activist, at Stanford University on May 22, 2004. She condemned the hypocritical policies of the U.S. in the Middle East regarding support of totalitarian regimes. Also, she expressed optimism for the imminent establishment of democracy by a new generation of younger **Iranians** inside the country. Ebadi explained that currently 63 percent of the students in Iran are women, and all college students possess a very high knowledge of global politics. She urged all the interested parties to look for world news from different sources to gain a correct image of what the reality may be.

Additionally, Fred R. Von der Mehden also refers to this problem in his *American Perspective of Islam*. He humbly confesses that **Americans** are poorly informed about Islam in general and misinformed about its resurgence in particular. This in part, he claims, is because of meager coverage of **The Middle East** events in the public schools and the media.[16]

Also, Bernard Lewis attacks the double standards of the West against the East. In his book *The Crisis of Islam*, he condemns the U.S. for taking advantage of tyrannies in the East while low productivity and high birth rate in the Middle East also makes for an unstable mix. As mentioned earlier, he believes that modernizing the countries of Middle East has been going on for some centuries. Yet, the military and economical reforms brought no success, but unhealthy dependence on super powers. But, worst of all was the political modernization or reform that ended with empowering of a string of shabby tyrannies, which only were modern in their manipulative and suppressive appearances. For these countries—like Iran—who once were leaders, there is the shocking question: "Who did this to us?" It is usually easier to blame others.[17]

With regard to such matters, in the Farsi periodical of *Rah Avard*, it is suggested that the solution for the internal problems of the countries of The Middle East may only be found by reflecting on the roots of the social inequalities inside these countries, rather than constant blaming of superpowers for every single thing that goes wrong.[18]

But before analyzing these social inequalities, some facts must be considered. It is understandable that for the western world, safekeeping of the Persian Gulf is highly valuable; and its uninterrupted flow of oil ensures peace and prosperity for all. **Iranian** politicians have always played an important role in this matter - although not very effectively at all times. **The United States of America** has repeatedly used its military force to secure its share of oil against the totalitarian regimes that failed to keep a peaceful production of oil in this region. Consequently, Iran is one of the most valuable nations for the West although it only has a population of about sixty-five million and a GNP of eighty-three billion dollars.[19]

Russia, on the other hand, lost its hope to reach the free waters of Persian Gulf, even though it had invaded **Afghanistan** in 1979. This occupation had increased its borderline with Iran—another 945 kilometers. By inhabiting Afghanistan, **Russians** would be at a dangerously short distance—only 500 kilometers—with this strategic oil-transporting region in Iran. (During the cold war period about 70 percent of the oil produced in the world was transported through the Persian Gulf). This data is referred to in the September/October issue of *Foreign Affairs* in 2001, emphasizing the fact that the universal supply of crude oil is 1028.1 billion barrels, and the Middle East supplies 71 percent of it.

Oil is not the only abundant resource in Iran. The potential of growth in GNP for Iran is very high because of its oil and other resources. Surveys indicate that Iran possesses extensive and widely varied mineral resources. Nearly 300 million tons of coal majorly deposited in Alburz mountain range in the north. Large deposits of copper are located near Kerman (central Iran). Nickel and silver mines exist around Anarak near Dasht-e-Kavir (desert). In 1973, Iran was the second largest producer of crude oil in the Middle East, behind Saudi Arabia with 7.4 million barrels a day.[20] Now it produces about 2.4 million barrels a day and is ranked 5th after Saudi, Iraq, UAE, and Kuwait.

Coming back to the analysis of the causes for the fall of Iran as a super power, many historians believe that Iran can grow out of its social and political miseries by its emphasis on education besides its resources. Illiteracy in Iran has almost disappeared. Based on figures in the Census 2000, **Iranians** inside the **U.S.** maintain the highest number of professionals with above-college degrees as a new minority (the **Chinese** and **Hindus** follow next). These **Iranians** have been extremely successful in helping the economy of the U.S. The new generation has learned that democracy and justice require hard work and respect for human rights. If representatives of the government are not answerable to the individuals in the society, the corruption may never be cured.

Darius Homayoon puts it this way: The people of Spain were able to rebuild their society on a moderately democratic basis after the departure of the tyrant **Franco**. They did it because they learned to forgive and to respect each other in order to survive. **Iranians** must do the same regardless of the injustice that goes on inside the country. Outside Iran, we must love ourselves even better and strive to improve our weaknesses, rather than submitting to pessimism. Not many nations can celebrate 3000 years of survival. Safekeeping of Iranian heritage and language is our duty abroad. We must learn from many internal disasters in the history that we caused and must understand that we cannot blame others for all of our miseries.[21]

Bernard Lewis wrote in his book: *What Went Wrong?*, in 1990, that after centuries of glory the Muslim world suddenly started to lose many battlegrounds since the defeat of **Kara Mustafa'**s military at the gates of Vienna in 1683. That setback was repeated in other spheres as Western (**Christian**) societies leaped ahead. When **Muslims** tried to adjust their position in the world, they confused Westernization (which they rejected) with Modernization (which they sought). He argues that the **Muslim** world needs to ask itself, "What went wrong?"—some may want to argue about who or what to blame?[22]

The question of whom to blame for the present shortcomings has been receiving some light during the last decade in Iran. Dr. Sadegh Ziba Kalam is currently a professor of Political Science in Iran. By looking deep into the question of how Iran became the way it is now, he searches for the causes within Iran in his interesting book: *Ma Cheguneh Ma Shodim?* (*How did we become the way we are?*)

Ziba Kalam argues that civilization started in the east because of the need for cooperative work on the lands and irrigation channels. Thus, Iran once became the center of the highest wisdom on earth. In analyzing its fall he contradicts the stereotype approaches of blaming **Marxism**, **Islam**, **Mongols**, or **superpowers**. Dr. Ziba Kalam argues that **Islamic Iran** enjoyed the zenith of scientific exploration between the mid 8th and 10th Century. Therefore, religion could not be the cause of the fall of Iran or as he puts it: "...the fading of the flame of knowledge."

He points out that many European nations were under religious dogmas, but they flourished out of their Dark Ages. Burning of books by the **Arabs** happened before the scientific climax in Iran. The massacres by the **Mongols** were shared by many nations. None of these are the cause for the fall of Iran. Dr. Ziba Kalam points out major causes for such diminishing glory inside of Iran. One is the infamous popularity of the school of **Scholasticism** (Ayeen-e-Modarresi regarding the restriction of text books and the subjects in all schools to those of the religious nature) in the 11th Century.

Furthermore, Dr. Mehdi Farshad studies this phenomenon in more detail in his book: *Tarikh-e-Elm dar Iran* (*History of Science in Iran*). This tight restriction resembles the restrictions imposed by **Bishop Cyril** in **Byzantine** Europe, pushing away many scholars out of the **Christian West** and into the **Islamic East**. Phillip Hitti writes about this in his book: *History of The Arabs*.[23]

On the other hand, another reason for the dimming light of science and social reforms in Iran is the **Abbasid Dynasty**. Their last rulers finally reverted the **clerics** to run their national affairs rather than the secular scholars in their courts. The **German** historian, Bertold Schpuler mentions the same opinion in his book about the history of the **Islamic Iran**.[24]

Ziba Kalam leads readers to ponder the actual reasons behind the gradual fading of science and social freedom in **Muslim** nations - especially Iran. He continues that this policy (restriction of subjects for scholars) gradually shifts the outlook of the nation; the **Islamic Scholasticism** slowly replaced the realm of the **Scientific Analysis** in the region. **Motevakel**, the ninth **Caliph** of Islam in 848 A.D., contrary to the founders of this dynasty, brought back the strict and traditional religious worldviews of " Sunnat" or "Traditions." This, in turn, caused a further deviation from the path of scientific explorations. **Ibn Khaldun**, the Islamic historian of the 14th Century, is a follower of such school of thought (*Sunnat*) and refers to the **Iranian scientists** of his era , **Abu Ali Sina** and **Abu Nasr Farabi**, as lost atheists. Finally, schools of "Nezamieh" under the supervision of **Khajeh Nezam-ul-Molk** abolished growth of any scientific or secular teachings in the country for the benefit of religious doctrines under the rule of the **Seljuk (Saljugh) Dynasty**.[25]

The direct outcome of such oppression is catastrophic. Iran has suffered deeply from the lack of freedom and democracy. Historical tradition of the centralized government has not permitted a free growth of public vision or thought among the occupants of the provinces and villages. For long, the tribal lifestyle of scattered communities did not help either. The lack of community meetings and coops has rendered the people without any organized civic gatherings to evaluate their needs and demands at any level. One cannot say for sure if an imported pro-human-rights government can be the answer. People eventually make or break their government.

Iranians must learn from their weaknesses and gradually start rebuilding their values based on equality and justice for all. It is extremely hard to cling to order and social ethics while being crushed under the burden of a lapsing economy.

Iranians abroad have accomplished great ventures and have helped the world economy with over 600 Billion Dollars of working capital by the year 2003. Only in the U.S., there are currently over ninety radio and television stations run by **Iranians**. They are socially and culturally active in their new lands and run over 400 cultural institutions all over the world. These **Iranians** have benefited from many social freedoms in the States and have tasted its sweetness. They must cherish freedom and carefully extend the recognition of its value to their new generation.[26]

While living outside Iran, **Iranians** have the opportunity to experience a relatively higher level of freedom. They have managed to show an aptitude for improvement in both civil and scientific areas. However, **Iranians** inside the country have learned that a sudden change in their government does not necessarily guarantee social improvement. New values must be reintroduced into Iran to ensure realization of the dignity of every individual in society. There are many changes needed internally that require time, planning, education and leadership. **Iranians** have seen it all, and they have outlived much harsher times...There is always a tomorrow for those who cherish it.

1.   *Negah Az Biroun*, by Dariush Homayoon, U.S., 1984, p. 108

2.   *Notes and Observations on The History of Iran*, Ali Mirfetros, 4th edition, p. 109

3.   *Kholaseh Tarikh Gozashteh*, p. 87

4.   *Jame Shenasi Nokhbeh Koshi*, Ali Rezagholi. 18th edition, 2001, Tehran, p. 180

5.   *Rah Avard*, Number 61, Winter of 2002, an article by Hasan Azin Far, p. 180

6.   *Jumhuriyat*, by Saeed Hajjariyan, 2nd edition, Tarh No publishers, 2001, Tehran, p. 251

7.   *Negah Az Biroun*, by Dariush Homayoon, U.S.A., 1984 p. 69

8.   *Roots of Revolution*, by Nikki R. Keddie, 1981, Yale University, p. 262

9.   *Negah Az Biroun*, pp. 71-80

10. *The Last Great Revolution*, by Robin Wright, translated by Ahmad Tadayon & Shaheen Ahmadi, 2004, Ghazal Printing, Tehran, pp. 1-64

11. *Guft va Guyha-yi Sarih*, Seyyed Ibrahim Nabavi, Tehran 1996, Rozaneh Pub. pp. 59, 132

12. *Persian Pilgrimages*, by Afshin Molavi, published by WW. Norton & Co., 2002, p. 5

13. *Culture and Resistance, A conversation with Edward Said*, by David Barsamian, Cambridge, 2003, pp. 103-114

14. *Terror in the Name of God*, by Jessica Stern, Harper Collins Publisher, 2004, New York

15. *Culture and Resistance*, p 116

16. *American Perspectives of Islam*, by Fred R. Von der Mehden, in The Spread of Islam, Greenhaven Press, 1999, San Diego, CA, p. 177

17. *What Went Wrong?*, by Bernard Lewis, Harper Collins Publishers, 2002, New York, p. 151

18. *Rah Avard*, No. 62, H. Shahbaz publisher, 'Iran In The Passage Of History' Winter edition 2002, L.A, CA. p. 118

19. *Bayad Haiye Siasat Khareji Iran*, Farhad Yazdi, Pars Printing, 2003, Reseda, CA. pp. 3-30

20. *Iran Past and Present*, Donald N. Wilbur. New Jersey, p. 263

21. *Gozaar az Tarikh*, by Darius Homayoon, Alborz printing, Frankfort, Germany, 2003, 2nd edition, p 92-181

22. *Time Magazine* , edition of 02/18/2002, an article by Johanna McGeary in *Books* section

23. *Ma Cheguneh Ma Shodim?*, by Dr. Sadegh Ziba Kalam, 4th edition, 2003, Tehran, pp. 223-226, in reference to 14th edition of *History of Arabs* by Philip Hitti, U.S.A., pp. 315-369

24. *Tarikh-e-Iran dar Ghorun-e-Nakhostin-e-Islami*, Volume1, by Bertold Schpuler, translated by Javad Falaturi, 3rd edition, 1990, Tehran, p. 280

25. *Ma Cheguneh Ma Shodim?* by Dr. Sadegh Ziba Kalam, 2003, Tehran, Chapter 5

26. *Jame-e-Shenasi Khodemani*, by Hasan Naraghi, Akhtaran Printing, 2003, Tehran, p. 152

Printed in the United States
48632LVS00003B/34

9 781413 767988